The words which are most used in religion are also those whose genuine meaning is almost completely lost and whose impact on the human mind is nearly negligible. Such words must be reborn, if possible; and thrown away if this is not possible, even if they are protected by a long tradition. But there is only one way to re-establish their original meaning and power; namely, to ask ourselves what these words mean for our lives; to ask whether or not they are able to communicate something infinitely important to us.

PAUL TILLICH, *The Eternal Now*, 1963, pp. 94-5.

It is an agonizing and unusual spectacle—a bishop groping for truth, admitting that he does not know all the answers.

DAILY HERALD, 19 March 1963.

*Some reactions to the book 'Honest to God'*
*edited by*

DAVID L. EDWARDS

*with a new chapter by its author*

JOHN A. T. ROBINSON
*Bishop of Woolwich*

Theodore Lownik Library
Illinois Benedictine College
Lisle, Illinois 60532

SCM PRESS LTD
BLOOMSBURY STREET LONDON

*The royalties on this book will be given to the*
*Church of England Children's Society*

242
.D830
R662h
Ye 26

FIRST PUBLISHED 1963
SECOND IMPRESSION 1963

© SCM PRESS LTD 1963
(OR AS STATED IN TEXT)

PRINTED IN GREAT BRITAIN BY
BILLING AND SONS LTD
GUILDFORD AND LONDON

considerable extent sympathetic with the Bishop's theological intention. As *Time* magazine observed from New York, this paperback had 'stirred up the Church of England's loudest row in years'. But Dr Robinson received much support from other bishops and from the Anglican rank and file, the *Church of England Newspaper* suggesting that a reading of *Honest to God* 'should be accompanied by a recollection of the conspicuous failure of the Church of England as a whole to make Christianity meaningful to this generation'. Something of the same interest and division of opinion could be seen in the other English churches and in religious circles in other countries. It is clear that the book aroused the interest of large numbers of laymen, whether or not they read it. An *Observer* columnist, 'Pendennis', wrote on 19 May: '*Honest to God* has taken theology right out of its old academic seclusion.' A friend of mine was questioned about it during a visit to a senior official in the Kremlin. Teased about listening to the BBC, the official replied no; he had read about it in a Swedish newspaper.

Part of the sensation was due to the fact that the public was unfamiliar with the intellectual and spiritual background of *Honest to God*. Although the SCM Press had published Paul Tillich's *The Shaking of the Foundations* in 1949, and Dietrich Bonhoeffer's *Letters and Papers from Prison* in 1953, Dr Robinson's approving quotations from those books astonished and mystified many. Although the Church of England has for a number of years been the scene of many new stirrings, so that many of the clergy felt sympathetic with *Honest to God* even if they did not agree with all its arguments, Dr Robinson was often thought to be an isolated figure. I therefore thought that it might be useful if I reprinted in this book an article which appeared (in a rather abbreviated and different version) in

... at points more
...... Dr Robinson's, as any curious reader
may learn from my books *This Church of England* and
*God's Cross in Our World*). Thus I write with a bias. Canon
Fenton Morley, Vicar of Leeds, is a more senior Churchman with a different bias. His review of *Honest to God*
in the *Yorkshire Post* was highly critical. I am therefore
grateful to him for permission to reprint from the *Sunday
Telegraph* his own assessment of reactions to the book in
the Church of England. At points it is different from the
assessment I should make. Of course, other commenta-
tors might disagree both with Canon Morley and with
myself.

The Bishop of Woolwich received over a thousand letters
from readers in the first three months of his book's life
(mainly from Britain, although later there was a substantial
correspondence from overseas). Fifty of these letters are
reproduced here, in whole or in part. It is not normal to
print this kind of correspondence, but in the few cases
where there seemed any danger of the writer's identity being
discovered the writer's willing permission has been obtained
for this use of the letter. The letters were chosen in order
to illustrate the religious situation in Britain. The Bishop
does not necessarily agree or disagree with any of the
opinions expressed. Since it is seldom easy to obtain good
evidence of public response to serious theological issues,
the letters were thought to be of interest, and to be of special

significance for those who wish to make a just assessment of the background and effect of *Honest to God*.

Next come 23 of the reviews, arranged in chronological order. Inevitably there is some repetition, even after the selection (with some abbreviations where indicated) which had to be made for this book; but it is hoped that the repetition is not excessive, in view of the importance of assessing the climate of opinion. A debt of gratitude is owing to the reviewers, and to the editors of the journals concerned, who have permitted this further use of their work. Only one review is included from the United States, but the American journal *Religion in Life* is to publish a symposium about *Honest to God* (Winter 1963). For other British treatments, the reader is referred to the booklets *Image Old and New* by the Archbishop of Canterbury (SPCK), *For Christ's Sake* by the Rev. O. Fielding Clarke (Religious Education Press), *Keep Yourselves from Idols* by the Rev. Dr J. I. Packer (Church Book Room Press) and *Four Anchors from the Stern* by the Rev. Dr Alan Richardson and others (SCM Press).

Three fresh contributions are printed here to supplement the reviews. The reader is to be warned that these require close attention. Earlier this year the Rev. Professor John Macquarrie sent me a copy of his Inaugural Lecture at Union Theological Seminary, New York. He has allowed me to reproduce part of it here because of its relevance to *Honest to God*, which had not been published at the time. As author of a history of *Twentieth-Century Religious Thought*, as a commentator on contemporary German theology (in *An Existentialist Theology* and *The Scope of Demythologizing*), and as translator of Heidegger's *Being and Time*, Dr Macquarrie has given evidence of his capacity as a philosophical theologian. Another Anglican philosopher

... ~~truth~~ and error in "religionless Christianity"'.
He took the chair in a long discussion of *Honest to God*
on the BBC Home Service.

In the next chapter another philosopher, Mr Alasdair
MacIntyre, finds a basic atheism in the theology reflected
in *Honest to God*, and considers the position of religion in
England today. This chapter is based on an article in the
British review *Encounter* (September 1963), and is accom-
panied by the Bishop of Woolwich's comment in the same
journal (October). I regret that by the time the article was
known to me space in this book was too short for a full
reproduction to be possible, but I am grateful to Mr
MacIntyre and to *Encounter* for their co-operation. Mr
MacIntyre is already known as a trenchant reviewer of
religious books, as the author of *Difficulties in Christian
Belief*, and for his share in two other SCM Press books,
*New Essays in Philosophical Theology* and *Metaphysical
Beliefs*. As a philosopher he would confirm the suspicions
voiced by two journalists, Mr T. E. Utley and Mr David
Boulton, among the reviewers printed here, but of course
most of the contributors to this book, including myself,
would disagree with much in his assessment. It is for that
reason specially valuable.

The Bishop of Woolwich then clarifies his position, and
I would ask readers to study with special care his explanation that this chapter is not intended as a comprehensive
reply to all his critics, or as an answer to all the relevant

questions. In an appendix, an article which the Bishop
wrote at the request of a mass circulation London newspaper, the *Sunday Mirror,* is reprinted to show how the
message of *Honest to God* may perhaps be communicated
to people unable to read the book. *The Honest to God
Debate* is itself not an effort at mass communication. A
more popular 'sequel' must await another time.

In a second appendix, an article which Ruth Robinson
wrote about 'religionless Christianity' for children is reprinted from the Anglican review *Prism* (with some
changes). Together with Sir Richard Acland's book about
religious education in schools, *We Teach Them Wrong,*
Mrs Robinson's article seems to be worth preserving among
the records of the 1963 theological ferment, for it begins to
tackle the day-to-day problems of Christian parents and
teachers. A number of the readers' letters here printed refer
to the question of religious practices in the modern family,
and it is perhaps not irrelevant to note that the baby mentioned on pp. 61-2 has now been baptized; but all concerned
know that much more thought and experiment need to come
in this practical field, as well as in more abstruse theology.

It should be evident that the debate about the problems
sketched in *Honest to God* is not closed by this new book.
Indeed, it is essential to see the debate as only one incident
in the task of Christian theology. The Bishop of Woolwich,
like the other authors whom it is my privilege to serve as
publisher, would never pretend to have the last word, and
would never think that theology's task will be over until
we all attain to the full vision of God. The debate continues, but it is hoped that this collection of documents will
serve some of the debaters in their common quest for truth.

DAVID L. EDWARDS

...rchbishop Fisher crowned Queen Elizabeth II, what hints were there in the ceremony that England is an industrial democracy in which organized religion is usually ignored? The historic pageant rolled on regardless. That may seem an extreme example, but conservatism is to be seen on any Sunday in most English acts of worship. Over 8,000 of the Church of England's 18,000 parish churches are medieval or earlier, and the Prayer Book used in them has not been revised officially since 1662. The Free Churches seem to echo with the energy of the Victorian Age. The Roman Catholic Church, with its Latin Mass, proudly continues a longer history. The preachers in these churches will make sincere efforts to make their message relevant, but many of their efforts are necessary because their message appears to belong to a vanished age. To an astonishing extent English religion has been like that for a long time. It has been the conservative religion of an island people, come Normans, come Protestants, come scientists. Through thirteen and a half centuries, many an English churchgoer has been suspicious of innovations and enthusiasms.

But as you look more closely at these parish churches with their lists of vicars from Chaucer's day to T. S. Eliot's, or at the Nonconformist or Roman Catholic chapels, you

[1] Reprinted with revisions and additions from *New Society* (30 May 1963).

see a fact no less remarkable. This is the fact of change
within the continuity. Conservative as many of the English
have been, others have been immensely fertile in producing
new religious bodies and trends. Essentially the great communions of the Anglicans, the Baptists, the Congregationalists and the Methodists, which encircle the globe today,
are English in origin. So are the Society of Friends and
the Salvation Army. Respectable as these organizations now
are, they all owe their present existence to the vision of a
few Englishmen who were once in revolt against convention. And the English churches have continued to nurse
rebels in their bosoms. The Church of England in particular
is indebted to its angrier and younger men, who generation
by generation have battled to keep it awake. Where would
the Church of England be without the Reformers, the
Puritans and the Evangelicals, without the Tractarians and
the Anglo-Catholics, without the Broad Churchmen, the
Christian Socialists and the Modernists? Similar records of
change within continuity may be found in the non-Anglican
churches. It is what you would expect. To speak socio-
logically: the continuity would have been impossible
without a substantial readiness for change. To speak
theologically: the essence of the continuity is the Gospel
of the One who sitting on the throne says, 'Behold, I am
making everything new' (Rev. 21.5), so that if true to
the Jesus of history mainstream Christianity will always
be fresh and revolutionary.

Today change is obviously desirable in English Christianity. Even more than the country's secular institutions,
the English churches need rejuvenating because they are
not doing their jobs efficiently in the modern world.
Although statistics are more than usually treacherous in
the field of religion, those which are available suggest that

*active* supp

ce

...ulation.)

...ually a secular

...ight not matter—and might

...their credit—if the churches possessed

...onfidence. It might then be suggested that people are offended by the churches' stern integrity, as people were offended by Jesus Christ himself. But as it is, we all know that, for all the devoted labour to be observed in them, the English churches need a revival. They are not aflame with faith or overflowing with purposeful activity. They offend England not because they are too lively but because most of them seem to have been decaying over the last half-century. This is why the stage is set in our time for a new Christian movement, to renew an ageing ecclesiastical tradition.

To succeed, it will have to be a movement which will change the ways in which people think and behave; and there is no way of avoiding the work involved. Television and the national newspapers play so important a part in contemporary England that Christians are sometimes tempted to hope that their job will be done by the projection through the mass media of a more favourable image. As a matter of fact the great attention given to religion by TV, sound radio and the press has been out of proportion to the vitality of the churches; and as a matter of fact it does not seem to have led to any great increase in churchgoing. And if the TV set cannot do the Church's job for it, neither can the school. It is not enough for Christianity to be taught in the nation's schools, as it is in England through daily acts of worship and through Religious Instruction in class. A fondness for certain hymns, and an acquaintance with the parables of Jesus or the journeys of St Paul, are evidently no substitute for participation in the life of the churches; and in the England we know it is the fact that religion in schools does not normally lead to active church membership. If the habits and attitudes of English adults are to be transformed, *Christianity has no real hope short of a renewal of the life and the teaching of its local churches.*

To some extent the renewal may be triggered off by economic necessities. Most of the English churches, being short of money and ordained men, are having to look at their methods. Here come the Christian Stewardship campaigns, to persuade the living English layman to pay for his local church. Since enough money and men cannot be raised for all the needs, the denominations have to try and be tough about closing or merging their dead churches. But this sort of administrative reorganization does not really satisfy most laymen. People can pay up, and still be critical of how the churches teach and behave.

When the churches try to modernize themselves inwardly, they may concentrate on experiments which bring the atmosphere of the secular world. Parish newspapers may look like the *Daily Mirror*. Religious drama may use slang. There are activities for teenagers—the coffee bar, the open club, liberty for dancing or talk as the young people want it themselves, 'epilogues' which will insert a few minutes of what might be called TV religion, perhaps pop music in special church services, perhaps even a Folk Mass. Or the feeling may be that the Church should meet the world on the world's own terms. Thus clergy go into factories, either as regular visitors or in a few cases as full-time workmen,

...ays are
...se experiments almost
...at so far they have done little more
...ratch the surface of the churches' problems in a
secularized world. For one thing, young people in clubs are
special, as are industrial workers in their work situations.
The local church, to be healthy, must appeal more deeply
to adults and to families. And problems go deep within
these experiments themselves. When you have got a teenager or a worker to listen, what are you going to say about
God? Or perhaps you should not say anything at all?

Beginning in the 1930s (with of course, considerable
antecedents), three trends have offered hope. They are
usually referred to as the biblical, liturgical and ecumenical
movements. Some of us in our more optimistic moments
have announced that they add up to the Reformation of
the twentieth century. These are certainly respectable and
sizeable movements. But the sobering fact of experience that
the deeper aims of these movements need to be explained
to most audiences suggests that so far the appeal has been
chiefly to the clergy and to the inner ring of the faithful.
Although the intention has been to renew the churches for
their work in the world, the solid results have been less.

The *biblical* movement springs from an interpretation of
the Bible which is both scholarly and religious in intention.
It avoids Fundamentalism's insistence on the literal truth
of everything; it recognizes that the Bible is a library, con-
taining a variety of ancient volumes each of which deserves

a carefully critical study against the background of its time. Books about the Bible—surveys, commentaries, atlases, dictionaries—proliferate. The German and Swiss universities produce the most distinguished contributions, and these are quickly translated, but Britain's own performance is not negligible. However, the biblical movement's main emphasis is not historical but hortatory. It stresses that in the Bible God reveals himself—through acts and personalities rather than propositions. The Bible contains the Word of God, or (as many would prefer to put it) the Bible witnesses to that living Word. This movement reads the Bible as the story of the People of God (Israel and the early Church). It learns here a thousand and one truths which connect with the experience of the People of God (Christians) today, and which purify and deepen their religious and moral life. The movement urges that all Christians should use the Bible as their daily strength and light, and to this end inspires many new translations (chief among them are the New English Bible and the Jerusalem Bible in France). Thus the Bible is treated as something authoritative and vital. People who want to know what Christianity is are asked to open its book.

The *liturgical* movement springs from an insistence on the corporate nature of Christian worship. This is not an obsession with the trivialities of the sanctuary, although it has been accompanied by keen interest among the more scholarly in the historic forms of worship. At its heart, this is a vision of the People of God assembled around the Word of God. The Word is proclaimed through sermon, scripture and sacrament. The book is opened, the Communion bread is broken, the wine is poured. The people respond by joyful praise and by a conscious dedication, as a fellowship, to their work of service and evangelism in the world. Just

...sequence of the feasts and fasts of the Christian year. These are all symptoms of the progress of the liturgical movement. In the Church of England, about a third of the parish churches have a Parish Communion at about 9.30 a.m. as the principal service of the Sunday. This is often followed by breakfast, as an expression of the wish for a parish community.

The *ecumenical* movement needs an even less full description, because its efforts towards the reunion of separated Christians have rightly attracted much sympathy. In England, the atmosphere between the denominations has been transformed within this century. The Roman Catholics and the rest are taking the first gingerly steps towards mutual understanding, and perhaps eventually towards co-operation. The Church of England, having temporarily failed to persuade the Presbyterians (led by the Church of Scotland) to have bishops, is now working towards reunion with the Methodists. The Baptists and Congregationalists, together with the left wing of Methodism, are traditionally more wedded to the dissidence of Dissent, but they also are speaking less of congregational democracy and more of the unity of Christ's people. At least in theory, all the denominations are willing to face change for the sake of reunion, which they accept as the will of God. Christian unity will, they believe, enrich them all with more of the treasures of Christ.

These, then, are substantial movements. But they all

share one defect: *they do not necessarily concern the truth of Christianity*. Theologians and preachers can wax enthusiastic about the 'acts of God' in the Bible without tackling the awkward questions whether God exists and whether, if so, he is credibly revealed to the twentieth century. In a parish of 10,000 the liturgical movement can confine itself to the outward (not the inner) lives of the 200 who will meet as the churchgoers of a particular denomination. The reunion of the churches as they are could be a marriage of the senile, and an 'ecumenical' agreement between Christians on the basis of their common tradition could be purchased at the price of excluding the awkward questions and needs of the irreligious moderns. For some time, therefore, thoughtful Christians have been coming to see that, if the biblical message is to be heard by the world through the churches in our time, a deeper renewal is needed, which may involve a costlier change.

My belief is that the required movement has now begun to appear. So far it is mainly Anglican in England, but the corresponding forces are Presbyterian in Scotland, Catholic in France and Lutheran in Germany. Under John XXIII we have had the great spectacle of the Vatican urging on its Church a 'renewal'—and no one can tell where the 'renewal' will stop. Essentially this deeper movement results from a desire to honour and to hear the secular modern world. The Church must *listen* to the world before it attempts to interpret the world's own spiritual experience—experience which the world already enjoys, but which it may not acknowledge as in any sense Christian. Here, the whole emphasis is on the Church as mankind's servant. At the centre is a vision of Christ as the man alongside his fellow-men, speaking to them of a God they are already beginning to know. In order that the Church may

...... to

..... Evangelicals or the
..... labelled in their days, I would call it
...... radicalism.

In 1962 the new Coventry Cathedral was consecrated.
The architecture which attracted the blaze of publicity may
be open to detailed criticism. What is impressive is the
courageous wish to find images of Christ and Christianity
in the contemporary idiom. Within a year of the consecration, three and a half million visitors have gone to see that
sight. And it is even more impressive that the cathedral, so
far from being solely an exhibition, has already come to
life as the base of a team of priests and laymen who are
ready for endless efforts and experiments in order that the
people of the city may express their faith through their
cathedral. The biblical, liturgical and ecumenical movements are present in strength, but they are subordinated to
the wider purpose of helping Coventry to find and adore
God in its own way. The new cathedral stands as a symbol
of Christian radicalism.

When the Bishop of Woolwich's *Honest to God* was published, some members of the staff of Coventry Cathedral
spoke up in its favour, one of them prophesying that it
would cause 'an explosion of truth'. For Christian radicalism has sometimes seemed a movement in search of a
message. That is the impression which might be gained
from reading (for example) the monthly Anglican magazine
*Prism*. To contribute to *Prism*—I do it myself—is to be

type-cast as an angry young man, although you may be a nun discussing the Atonement; and over the years this surprisingly successful journal has criticized almost every aspect of the Anglican establishment without being so clear about what should be sought in its place. However, in 1962-63 the fairly widespread radical spirit in English Christianity was given a sharp new focus with the publication of three semi-popular books by theologians associated with Cambridge University. In addition to *Honest to God* there were *Soundings* and *Objections to Christian Belief*, both edited by Dr Alec Vidler (editor of a more senior monthly, *Theology*, which also contains much radical writing). To some of the historically minded such books recalled the 1830s, when 'high church' *Tracts for the Times* issued from Oxford University, gradually changing the face of the Church of England. And the unconventional noises coming from modern Cambridge did indeed become an 'explosion', partly because of the publicity given to them by BBC television and by the *Observer*. The Bishop of Woolwich, a former Cambridge don, became in the eyes of the public the high priest of Christian radicalism. Many Churchmen denounced him. And many churchmen rejoiced, like this young man who wrote to the *Daily Telegraph*:

It appears that the Bishop of Woolwich is fated to undergo treatment similar to that suffered by Kierkegaard in the nineteenth century, a process which he aptly described as being 'trampled to death by geese'. Such, it seems, is the lot of those who attempt to bring some knowledge of the depths of human nature to the service of God.

As an Anglican theological student, I can vouch for the fact that numbers of men in training for the ministry are becoming increasingly dissatisfied with a theological preparation which consists largely of intellectual antiquarian-

... comfortable feeling of
... meaning and destiny, but has no value in itself.

The importance of Dr Robinson's book is not so much
that the author is 'honest to God' but the basic fact that he
is intellectually honest with *himself*. Regrettably, this particular *fundamental* honesty is virtually absent among
Christians. Piety still draws a silken veil over crucial and
difficult questions.

That letter may be thought rather shrill in tone. This
controversy has not always displayed either the radicals or
their critics at their calmest and most persuasive. A bishop
(Pontefract) who by no means occupies Dr Robinson's
theological position has observed that many of the reactions
to *Honest to God* were hysterical and savage, but I am
afraid that there have also been radical remarks which more
conventional Christians inevitably interpreted as insults. In
such an atmosphere truth does not get heard. Let me therefore quote a calmer letter. Published by *The Times* in July,
it came from Miss Violet Wilkinson, Lecturer in the Teaching of Religion at Oxford University.

It is important to realize that many people cannot distinguish
between truth and the words in which truth has been traditionally expressed, and that many others, maybe rightly,
consider it their duty to protect the consciences of such
people. But some of us, who do recognize such a distinction,
have found it for many years increasingly difficult to accept
the way in which the faith by which we live is stated and
explained to us by many of its recognized exponents.

The Bishop of Woolwich's attempt to find terms in which

the basic truths of Christianity can speak to this century has earned our lasting gratitude and admiration. Of course, there must be further thought and discussion and, of course, we all need to be much more open than we are 'to the absolute, unconditional will of God' as we feel our way to a new understanding and expression of the truth; but let us at all costs go ahead in fellowship, so that our criticisms may be positive rather than negative, 'to the building up of the body of Christ'.

Where will Christian radicalism go now? It cannot stand still without degenerating. It would be quite disastrous if every parish church modelled itself on Coventry Cathedral, or if every preacher aped the Bishop of Woolwich. What has been achieved so far has been little more than a series of gestures to show that some Christians are anxious to enter into a real conversation with more typical citizens of our secular society. What is needed is not a premature theological synthesis, and even more certainly not the organization of a new religious party, but a host of other experiments in thought and life. It is of the nature of experiments that some turn out to have been mistaken. It is simply impossible to be both creative and infallible. (Were not Paul and John, Augustine and Aquinas, Luther and Calvin, mistaken in some of their experiments?) Fortunately Christian radicals have so far shown little tendency to treat each other as infallible. Making their theological soundings in the age of science, or dropping their depth charges, they have shown themselves to be a happily disunited crew. The appearance of a skipper would mean a quick mutiny.

Many observers would say that this new kind of thinking cannot be honest until it has cut itself off from the historic churches. Quite a few people in the churches would like the radicals to go into outer darkness. All sorts of people

to ask for their own explanations of possible ambiguities in their positions. And already uncountable numbers of laymen with 'unorthodox' convictions have refused to put up with the 'orthodox'. They have made silent protests by refusing to be ordained or to attend what they regard as antiquated forms of worship and preaching; they have voted with their feet. Perhaps one day the patience of the radical theologians, or of their theological disciples, will also crack.

However, no one who knows these Christian radicals will talk lightly about the possibility—which clearly exists—that some of them (or their successors) and their churches will eventually part company. It is significant that the new Coventry Cathedral was inspired by the architecture and life of many of the great churches of the past, and that the Bishop of Woolwich has told us that from his boyhood in the Precincts of Canterbury Cathedral he has never seriously thought of any profession other than a parson's, and has never really doubted the fundamental truth of the Christian faith. Of course some laymen among the Christian radicals are not so deeply involved in the institutional Church, but the group as a whole has its roots firmly within historic Christianity. However bold may be its protests against 'religion' (protests which are usually milder than those made by the Old Testament prophets and by Jesus Christ), the group has itself been nurtured by the Bible and the Church's worship. (Indeed, the group includes outstanding pastors of the Church and theologians who have made distinguished contributions to biblical and liturgical studies, the Bishop of Woolwich among them.) These are Christian men who have willingly gone to school under the saints, and above all they have found truth in the essence of Christian orthodoxy: the adoration of God in the crucified and victorious Christ. No one can foresee what might

...ishment, any institutionalism, any orthodoxy: and it is an attitude that is relevant to far more than politics. Indeed, the essence of the radical protest could be summed up in the statement of Jesus that 'the Sabbath is made for man, and not man for the Sabbath'. Persons are more important than any principles. He illustrated this by his shocking approbation of David's action in placing concern for human need, even his own, above all institutions however sacred. 'Have you not read what David did, when he was hungry, and those who were with him: how he entered the house of God and ate bread of the Presence, which it was not lawful for him to eat nor for those who were with him, but only for the priests?'

Yet radicalism is not anarchy. It is not just being 'bolshy' or individualistic. It knows well enough that persons can matter, and freedom can flourish, only in a context of order. But, dissatisfied as it is simply with 'freedom from', it will always be asking: order *for* what? When the structures of order take over and persons become subservient to them, when the movement of the Spirit hardens into the institutional Church, then the radical voice will begin to be heard.

What the radical stands for can perhaps be more clearly seen by comparing him with the reformist on the one hand and the revolutionary on the other. The reformist—corresponding in political categories to the Tory reformer—continues to accept the basic proposition, that man is made for the Sabbath. But, he says, the Sabbath regulations have become too rigid; we must modify them and bring them up to date. So he steals the Whig's clothes while he is bathing and lifts planks here and there from the Liberal platform. He overhauls the institution and titivates the orthodoxy;

[1] See the *Listener* (21 February 1963).

and in this way everything is enabled to go on smoothly, and the revolution is averted. The revolutionary, on the other hand—in political terms the Robespierres and Lenins of this world—will have nothing of the Sabbath at all. The institution is rotten, the orthodoxy stinks and enslaves. The entire structure must be changed if man is to be free.

The radical will often be found siding with the revolutionary in regarding the reformist as the real enemy. For the reformist would lull people into supposing no revolution is necessary, whereas the radical knows that for man to be made for the Sabbath is ultimately death. But equally he sees that if man is to live—rather than be subjected to a different, and perhaps deadlier, Sabbath—another revolution is required. The radical's response is to go to the roots —hence his name. It is to ask what the Sabbath is for, what human values it exists to frame, and then to try to see, at whatever cost to the institution or the orthodoxy, that it does so. Unlike the reformist, the radical is concerned constantly to subject the Sabbath to man. Yet, unlike the revolutionary, he *believes* in the Sabbath—for man.

This introduces another important characteristic of the radical viewpoint. Being a radical means being an 'insider', an insider to the Sabbath—as Jesus was. The revolutionary can be an 'outsider' to the structure he would see collapse: indeed, he must set himself outside it. But the radical goes to the roots of *his own* tradition. He must love it: he must weep over Jerusalem, even if he has to pronounce its doom. He must believe that the Sabbath really is made for man.

This means that the radical must be a man of roots. The revolutionary may be *déraciné*, but not the radical. And that is partly why in our rootless world there are so few genuine radicals . . .

But it would not be fair to equate the Christian outlook with the radical, to suggest that all Christians should be radicals any more than all radicals should be Christians. For radicalism is simply an attitude of mind and its relevance is to some extent a matter of degree. The radical cannot claim to have the whole truth. To remember that should help to keep him humble, for the besetting sin of the radical is self-righteousness, as complacency is of the re-

... the English churches
...uch sense to join in a clamour for the
expulsion of these radicals. Perhaps they remember what
a debt the Church of England owes to Archbishop Randall
Davidson for making William Temple a priest and Hensley
Henson a bishop when, earlier in this century, both men
were suspected of heresy. Perhaps they remember another
Archbishop, Frederick Temple: 'If the conclusions are
prescribed, the study is precluded.' Any conscientious
church leader would have to take note of a genuine heretic
(i.e. a Christian who deliberately chooses to deny the
Church's essential faith)—but it would seem that history has
taught the present generation in church leadership to hesi-
tate long. Although rightly they may warn that in their
view certain opinions tend in the direction of heresy, they
have no zeal to brand as a heretic any Christian scholar
who humbly seeks to restate what is essential in the old
faith, and to relate it to new knowledge, or any Christian
minister who struggles to reach the common people, as his
Master reached them.

This caution is wise, because there can be little doubt
that a premature heresy hunt directed against the radicals
would lead to a voluntary exodus from the English churches
of some of their finest members. It would paralyse the freedom of theology, and wreck many evangelistic and pastoral
experiments. And in the long run the Church's rejection of
contemporary, experimental thought would also do a

deeper damage, touching the very heart of the spiritual life. Religion can, and does, express itself in systems and formulae in which it honestly believes. But its inner spirit slows down and dies if, for the sake of conformity with 'orthodoxy', it has to accept—either in pretence or with only part of its mind—systems and formulae which, however venerable, now lack the fundamental authority of truth and realism. At present many in the churches would protest that they can honestly accept the time-honoured traditions, but it is probable that, as time goes on, the slow influence of contemporary ways of thinking will diminish the number of those who can be completely 'orthodox' in the old style with complete happiness. If the churches rid themselves tomorrow of all those whose views the 'orthodox' would regard as heretical, they would end up as deserted museums.

Of course there are dangers in permitting radicals to have their say within the churches. There is a danger of radical views hurting the faithful deeply. More important still is the danger that the faithful will be misled by their own accredited teachers, because these teachers, without being honest enough to say so explicitly, will by implication abandon the essential faith in God through Christ. And of course the churches need to guard against such dangers. Fortunately there is little possibility that in the English churches the conservatives will be silent or powerless. The causes of pastoral tenderness and of doctrinal caution are not likely to be starved of expression. But there is also a danger in silencing or excluding the radicals—a danger which is less frequently noticed. This is the danger of forcing those who seek an honest religion to seek it outside the religion of the churches.

If Christian radicalism can remain in its present creative

ten...

... It is
..., these questionings,
...tinue to be contained within the
...ions of Christian orthodoxy, for no sect, no
splinter group, has the resources for the tensions, freedom
and faith required.' But it is also true that the churches will
gain, for, as Mrs. Blackie pointed out, the new radicalism
puts the world's questions to the churches. 'Such a theology
does not need to be made relevant to us; it speaks to us
exactly as we are.' In his pamphlet *Image Old and New* the
Archbishop of Canterbury wrote movingly to welcome
challenges: 'As a Church we need to be grappling with the
questions and trials of belief in the modern world. Since
the war our Church has been too inclined to be concerned
with the organizing of its own life, perhaps assuming too
easily that the faith may be taken for granted and needs
only to be stated and commended. But we state and commend the faith only in so far as we go out and put ourselves with loving sympathy inside the doubts of the doubting, the questions of the questioners, and the loneliness of
those who have lost their way.'

What, then, will the English churches discover if under
radical pressure they can be persuaded to put themselves
inside the modern situation?

They will discover afresh the freedom with which Christ
has made his followers free. This is freedom from anxiety,
and it includes freedom from compulsive rituals. It includes
also freedom from that basic insecurity which is expressed

in the hysterical defence of beloved religious phrases. It is a freedom born of a personal trust: a trust in God through Christ which is as strong (although also as elastic) as a good marriage. Where is such freedom to be seen in English Christianity today? In the Free Churches, certainly; I note the opinion of the news editor of the *British Weekly* (8 August) that of the Congregational and Presbyterian church magazines which he had read 'about eighty per cent have welcomed the publication of *Honest to God*, even though they may not have agreed with its conclusions'. And the Roman Catholic Church was not nearly so hostile as might have been expected (there were calm reviews in the *Tablet,* etc.). This contrasts with a comment by the Provost of Derby Cathedral (*Derby Evening Telegraph,* 12 August): 'Of the indignation and bewilderment roused by the publication of *Honest to God* there can be no doubt. It must be a long time since the ranks of so many Christians, owning to such widely differing images of God, closed in condemnatory agreement.' (The Provost continued: 'But this is only one side of the story. . . .') Although the more hostile reaction in the Church of England may be attributed partly to the fact that Dr Robinson is one of its own bishops, it may be relevant to recall the verdict of Dr F. R. Barry, Bishop of Southwell 1941-63, that in the Church of England in recent years 'what has been squeezed out is liberalism'.[1] But the odd fact is that the Established Church is in some ways more adventurous than the Free Churches.

For fear of compromising dear friends, I will do no more than mention the central London church of St Martin-in-the-Fields, which I serve as an assistant curate. This is, I believe, a place of Christian freedom. Other local churches have much the same ideals. Anglicans can point

[1] See his *Asking the Right Questions* (1960), p. 33.

...the
...ss with their details.
...nest *to God* controversy the Bishop
...wark wrote in the *Evening Standard* (9 April):

The men who try to break new ground are pilloried by the reactionaries and the fearful, but they usually live long enough to be accepted as pillars of orthodoxy. Maurice, Gore, Henson and Inge, like Temple, were among the more famous who received their measure of abuse as heretics, but today are honoured for their theological perception. My guess is, the Bishop of Woolwich will go the same way.

I have known John Robinson for twenty years. He has proved himself a faithful pastor, a fearless thinker and a dynamic Christian. Although I cannot pretend to keep abreast of his thinking, there is no man in the Church for whose mind I have a greater admiration or for whose integrity and singleminded devotion I have more respect.

I have read *Honest to God* three times, and it has taught me much. Although I might be described as a liberal in my theological views I am basically orthodox: by which I mean that the traditional language of the Church presents few difficulties and I can recite the creeds with a clear and glad conscience. It never occurs to me that in making these statements I am placing God 'up above', 'out there' or 'down here'. But when I address audiences in factories, technical colleges or universities I am forced to admit that the language I use often fails to register and gives rise to misconceptions. My hearers insist that I am localizing God and committed to a view of the universe that is incompatible with modern science. It is untrue, but because of my traditional upbringing I am unable to express the truth in an idiom meaningful to them.

B

The Bishop of Woolwich is trying to break through this barrier. Time and time again he says in his book that he has no wish to hinder people like myself who can use without embarrassment the traditional language of the Church. In fact he uses it himself. . . . Whether he will succeed in making sense of the Christian faith to a generation that has fallen away from the Church, time alone will show. . . . I shall continue to proclaim the Gospel in the language with which I am familiar, even though it may appeal to a minority. Meanwhile, I am glad that I have in my diocese a suffragan bishop who has the intellect and competence to do what I cannot do and who, like Archbishop William Temple, believes that 'although it is difficult to avoid blunders, it is better, with whatever friction, to bring forth things "new and old" than to keep exclusively to the old'.

That, I suggest, is a statement which is an example of courageous and constructive liberalism. But what is the freedom likely to produce? Can we see any emerging truth or achievement by which the new Christian radicalism will be remembered, any positive contribution which the movement will make if allowed freedom?

Of course, the safest answer would be that Christian radicalism covers too many subjects for any summary to be worthwhile. (The volume *Soundings* touched on many themes—and still critics complained about what it left out.) But I shall now be brave, and hint at a possible pattern of the Christianity which is to come.

*Honest to God*, although it is original in the sense that the author's personality is injected into everything he writes ('Dr Robinson', the *Baptist Times* once wrote, 'cannot touch anything without making it throb with life'), was inspired by three German theologians who have been passionately concerned to put themselves inside our age. These are Rudolf Bultmann, with his programme for 'demythologizing' the Gospel; Dietrich Bonhoeffer, with his vision of

...challenge the *biblical* ...questions which perhaps recent ...ologians have been tempted to avoid: 'Did it really happen? Did Jesus really say it? Anyway, is it truth for us today? What in the Bible is kernel, and what is husk?' That encounter between Bultmann and the biblicists could renew English preaching (already Bultmann's questions have shaken much in theology).

Bonhoeffer's challenge must be allowed into the *liturgical* movement, asking: 'In your church services do you seek to escape into a world of fantasy? Do you use the Bible uncritically? Do you pray superstitiously? Is your Holy Communion part of a retreat from the modern world, or is it the climax of a strengthening for life in the world?' Bonhoeffer's shocking prophecy that real Christianity might be 'religionless' (perhaps he meant unpietistic, or perhaps he meant more) could rescue our worship—and some worship we must have—from an escapist, archaic pietism.

And Tillich can show us that the unity which we seek as Christians must involve our denominations in changes even greater than those which many of us now expect. His insistence on taking seriously the gropings of all men for the truth about their lives must be allowed to remind the *ecumenical* movement that the word *oikoumene* is Greek not for 'the Church' but for 'the whole inhabited world'. The ecumenical movement is more than Christian patriarchs kissing. Christian unity means the unity of mankind

in finding and obeying God. Tillich can teach us that the
Church must not shut its door to celebrate a family reunion
while a single child of God remains outside.

Christian radicalism should drive many now in the
churches, and many now outside, to take a fresh look at
the reality which is clothed, and in part concealed, in
traditional religious language. What is the nature of the
experience, past or contemporary, which this language reflects? That is a question which is now being asked by the
philosophers who analyse traditional religious expressions.
It is also a question which concerns the man in the street
or the woman in the pew. Too often both believers and
sceptics, repeating traditional phrases, have trivialized the
religious experience which they assumed or rejected. 'Your
God is too small' (the title of a book by J. B. Phillips).[1]
Today, when every creed is being questioned, our ways of
knowing God are being related afresh to our ways of knowing people or knowing things, and the result of the painful
process of thought may be a fresh sense of the mystery
which has always lain at the heart of all true religion : the
mystery which speaks of the purpose of the universe, yet is
encountered in daily life, which will always baffle our little
minds, yet fascinates and grasps.

Although the radical theologians have been criticized
for bewildering the public by airing their doubts, in fact
the English public has not recently been in a state of inno-
cent contentment with orthodox Christianity. Not the
public, but some churchmen are those to whom 'doubts'
are evidently novel—a condition which could not last. Some
who are themselves agnostics say that they like it when

[1] Fascinating light on the ideas which young people have about
God, Christ and the Church is thrown by *Teenage Religion* by
Harold Loukes (SCM Press, 1961).

when
doubt—that their faith
the fires of doubt. Such theologians can teach
the duty of each individual and each generation to make
that personal response which, when its integrity leads to
full commitment for life and death to God in Christ, is
properly dignified with the name of Christian faith. Christian teachers who acknowledge the mystery at the heart
of religion may, unless meanwhile suppressed by their
churches, in the end win a hearing from a public unper-
suaded by dogmatism.

One of the discouraging features of the 1962-63 con-
troversies has been the readiness of some to jump to the
conclusion that Christians who are 'honest' in the Bishop
of Woolwich's sense have abandoned, or will before long
abandon, what is essential in the belief in the personal God
described in the Bible and the creeds and encountered
in Christian prayer. Paul Tillich in particular has been
blamed for this. Tillich's theology is open to detailed criticism (as I can testify, having been the editor responsible
for the publication of two critical books about his
thought[1]), but it is demonstrably wrong to assume that
he is a prayerless atheist ('there is no God') or pantheist
('everything is God'). Tillich teaches that the descriptions
of God in the Bible—'Lord', 'Father', 'the Holy One',
'Love', etc.—are *symbols* of greater realities. All reflective

[1] Kenneth Hamilton, *The System and the Gospel*, and J. Heywood
Thomas, *Paul Tillich: An Appraisal* (both 1963).

Christians must agree, for no symbolic statement about God should be taken literally or by itself. He teaches also that God does not exist as a person separate from the world. That may sound shocking, and I am not sure that it should be said to people without any power of reflective thought. To them it may look like atheism. Tillich sympathizes with atheism's protest at the triviality of much of our 'theism', but he is not an atheist. Everyone who has begun to think about biblical religion philosophically must on reflection agree with Tillich that (1) the God of the Bible does not exist as you and I exist, but is greater; (2) the God of the Bible is not a person as you and I are people, but is greater; (3) the God of the Bible is not cut off from the world—which is fortunate since it means that you and I, who know only this world, can begin to know him.

Tillich says that 'the symbol "personal" God is absolutely fundamental', but it does not mean that God is *a* person. 'It means that God is the ground of everything personal and that he carries within himself the ontological power of personality. He is not a person, but he is not less than personal.' God is not a person, Tillich explains, because God transcends individuality by participating in the life of all individuals. On the other hand, God can be known and addressed in prayer, and in Tillich's words 'an existential relation is a person-to-person relation'; therefore Tillich, like every other Christian, uses the word 'personal' about God and speaks of God as 'thou' and 'he'.[1]

This deep theology reflects the nature of Christian prayer. Tillich prays in public, and presumably in private, to God as 'Lord' and 'Father'. His sermons should be read by anyone who thinks that he is not devout. But the Father Almighty who is known in Christian prayer is a God who is

[1] See his *Systematic Theology*, vol. i (1953), p. 271.

. subject and is
..to which theism has forced
.. aware that personalism with respect to God
.s balanced by a trans-personal presence of the divine. They are aware that forgiveness can be accepted only if the power of acceptance is effective in man—biblically speaking, if the power of grace is effective in man. They are aware of the paradoxical nature of every prayer, of speaking to somebody to whom you cannot speak because he is not 'somebody', of asking somebody of whom you cannot ask anything because he gives or gives not before you ask, of saying 'thou' to someone who is nearer to the I than the I is to itself. Each of these paradoxes drives the religious consciousness towards a God above the God of theism.[1]

That is probably not language which most laymen will readily understand. It is the language of a profound philosopher. But theologians can, and should, study it sympathetically, and my instinct is that it does connect with the experience of laymen. Laymen feel in their bones that God, although he can be prayed to and obeyed, and even loved, remains infinitely mysterious, so that many doctrines about him are too trivial to be true. Perhaps, therefore, it is good that some English laymen now know how theologians such as Tillich wrestle with the mystery of God. This thought leads me into a few simple reflections about Christian radicalism as a layman's religion.

So far most of the standard-bearers in Christian radi-

[1] *The Courage To Be* (Fontana Library paperback, 1962), pp. 180-1.

calism have been clergymen. But these theologians have themselves said that the theology which is most needed must come mainly from laymen. If it is true that Christian doctrine needs to be revitalized by immersion in experience and reality, then it is surely also true that a social worker, or a housewife, or a commercial traveller, is likely to be at least as useful as a parson in coming up with the right material. The call to be in some sense a theologian will alarm many a layman. (The layman has been more accustomed to think of himself as one sheep in a flock which consumes—or more often spits out without troubling to chew—food provided by the professional pastor.) But this call must be heard if the Christian message is ever to be restated in language understood by our secularized century. That is the chief reason why I am so delighted that in the 1960s theology is being popularized by television and by paperbacks.

It is easy to say that the TV and paperback public is attracted only by sensationalism, and in recent months many Christians have said it. And certainly people's curiosity about 'doubting parsons' or 'the atheist bishop' contributes to the attention which is paid to some Christian radicals. But my own view is that the public is not quite so low-minded as some Christians appear to reckon. The Foreign Secretary, the Earl of Home, addressing the General Assembly of the Church of Scotland, came closer to expressing the main motive in the layman's interest in these difficult matters. 'Too often the simple, basic teachings are overlaid by doctrine and dogma against which the intelligence revolts,' Lord Home said. 'Books like *Honest to God* show that there is a passionate desire that religion should appeal to the mind. Do not let us fear this search for the truth.'

... ... ООК-
... (Up and Down in Adria) and by Mr
Fielding Clarke in his more breezy reply to *Honest to God*
(*For Christ's Sake*). As I hope is shown by the fact that I
have edited *The Honest to God Debate*, I do not regard
*Honest to God* as beyond criticism; and I have reviewed
*Soundings* critically. Let other theologians now write better
books! But theologians who propose to improve on the
radicals' performances need to remember that a major
reason for the popularity of *Soundings* and *Honest to God*
in many quarters was precisely the element of incoherence
and inconclusiveness which was the necessary accompani-
ment of their authors' intention to think aloud honestly
about the most subtle and difficult matters which the mind
of man can tackle. Many laymen, and some clergymen too,
are unattracted by the 'clear teaching' which some Christians think they need. They prefer to have the difficulties in
the open, rather than concealed under what they regard
as superficial clarity. They feel that (to quote again the
Provost of Derby Cathedral) 'most traditional, conservative
theological writing of today is lucid, correct and dead'. They
do not care for pulpit rhetoric (to which I am personally
prone). They are moved and impressed when theologians
say those great words 'I do not know'. They prize above
everything else the virtue of honesty in the search for
truth.

A clergyman in a position to observe has given me this
description of the attitude of many hundreds of thousands

who listen to religious broadcasts. It is the *Honest to God* public.

> They are anti-authoritarian. Many of them are anti-clerical because they identify clerisy with authoritarianism. They are ready to accept the responsibility of their own search for meaning and truth. They suspect the motives of all modern persuaders, but are open to an honest examination of any moral situation, including an examination of their own motives and attitudes. In Jung's words, 'they have heard enough about guilt and sin . . . and want to learn to reconcile themselves with their own nature and to love the enemy in their own hearts'. They want to say 'yes' to life as a whole. They question all religious and moral absolutes, not in the name of a *laissez-faire* relativity, but in the name of the freedom of the human spirit. They accept the essential mystery of human existence, but most of the symbols in which the churches clothe this mystery have no longer any meaning or power for them.

How on earth are such people to meet God?

The Bishop of Woolwich quoted a text from the prophet Jeremiah: 'Did not your father eat and drink and do justice and righteousness? Then it was well with him. He judged the cause of the poor and needy: then it was well. *Is not this to know me?* says the Lord.' That, we may think, is a religion which can speak to the English layman—who all through history has respected sober ethics, rather than cultic ecstasies. It *is* sober ethics that Christian radicalism wants. I cannot see how anyone can read the Bishop of Woolwich's chapter on 'The New Morality' in *Honest to God* without being impressed by his great ethical seriousness. Some recent incautious utterances about sex relations by radical theologians—or by critics who misquote them— may have temporarily obscured this, but I am sure that in the end justice will be done to the Bishop and to the main radical concern. Ethical judgments—related to world

...al code.

... *Honest to God* said so—but is
more basic. Of course 'love' can be twisted to justify im-
morality, but then so can 'law'; through the centuries
plenty of wicked things have been done in the name of the
law. It remains true, as *Honest to God* declared: 'Love's
casuistry must cut deeper and must be more searching,
more demanding, than anything required by the law, precisely because it goes to the heart of the individual personal
situation.' And as the book of Jeremiah shouts from every
page, this ethical religion when it is true to itself is not a
shallow religion. Its insistence that true religious experience
equals true human living is accompanied by the knowledge
that human life includes exaltations and agonies, in which
God is also to be known. Whatever may be said about the
religion of Jeremiah, the prophet was not chatting about
a cosy God who is content to be met in a garden or on a
golf-course. For Jeremiah, God was to be met in the fall
of Jerusalem, and in its rebuilding. The God of the Old
Testament was to be met as Jacob met him in the Genesis
story, in wrestling; in and beyond tragedy.

The great task of Christian radicalism in this country
will be to take the Englishman's present liking for eating
and drinking and doing justice and righteousness, and interpret it all with adequate depth. Perhaps someone will

---

[1] It is curious when people with properly high, even rigid, attitudes to sexual morality do not believe that there are any rules for
Christians in war.

be able to persuade the Englishman that in what is most real to him—not in what is most remote—he may meet his God. If in due course that can be done, the English churches will find themselves renewed, and perhaps crowded, without concentrating on such incidental results of the communication to the people of the vision of God.

in the upper class and middle class strata. Here the proportion of those who have bought and read the book is small. Their acquaintance is mainly with the discussion of it in the Press and on television. These are some typical reactions: Of the copies of the book on the church bookstall, only one has been sold. An ordinand found the book stimulating but wondered why the author took such a poor view of the biblical evidence. A technical college student thought it was the work of a man trying to come to terms with science and to get away from old fashioned ideas. Grammar school sixth formers attending an Evangelical church could not understand how the author could claim to be a spiritual leader and still think like this. A rare attender at church summed the book up as 'God is unknowable. Love equals Jesus. All life is prayer—so why bother to come to church?'

The people who seem to be completely untouched by the whole controversy belong to the vast majority outside the collegiate world and the middle strata. One of the very few reports of any awareness came from a factory hand who is a committed Christian. 'What I get in the canteen,' he said, 'is that they always said there isn't a personal God, and now one of the bishops has said so too!' In spite of the publicity *Honest to God* seems to have failed to get through to the man in the cloth cap. Clergy who try to establish contact with him suggest that he has not only rejected any idea of God as out there, up there, or in here. He has also rejected any view of his own life as having a meaning beyond that of self-interest, the satisfaction of temporal needs, and happiness in immediate relationships.

The reactions of the parish clergy have been varied and vocal. Many have valued this book for its expression of their own uncertainty about the effectiveness of the Church's communication with the student, the inquirer and the out-study of the book, are critical of what they regard as the Aunt Sally descriptions which Dr Robinson gives of traditional Christian teaching—in respect, for example, of anthropomorphic ideas of God and images of Him as One who is 'up there' or 'out there'.

From their pastoral experience of human nature many clergy question whether mankind has so come of age as to be able to do without religion, and is so mature intellectually as to be in no need of signs or symbols. Others feel that Dr Robinson's description of the purpose of worship is too one-sided in its stress on the manward aspect and its virtual omission of the Godward. Again, they would say they have found value in withdrawal and renunciation as well as in involvement in the world. They believe revelation and grace to be facts. They accept as valid and meaningful Christ's description of God as Father.

In general the clergy have readily acknowledged the effect of the book and the controversy as a challenge and a stimulant. They agree that the questions which the Bishop poses are real and important. But many of them doubt whether the answers he gives are adequate, and whether there are not other questions of equal significance which they find themselves facing in their contact with people within the Church, on the fringe and beyond it—such questions as 'What is the purpose of my life?', 'What's wrong with me?', 'What lies beyond death?' Strangely enough, none of these comes to the fore in *Honest to God*.

# III

## SOME READERS' LETTERS

### edited by DAVID L. EDWARDS

THE thousand readers who took the trouble to write to the Bishop of Woolwich about his book in the first three months of its life, or about the accompanying articles and broadcasts, in many cases said that they had never written to an author before. Most of them were sympathetic. This does not necessarily correspond with the state of public opinion. Many printed comments, and reports of sermons and addresses, emphasized the distress of many Christian believers. Care has been taken to include in the next section of this book a representative sample of hostile *reviews* (and in any case reviews tend to be critical). Hostile *letters* are not printed extensively here. Many of those which the Bishop received came from unrestrainedly emotional, uneducated people, and although that background by no means discredits them it might be thought that the Bishop and his publisher were seeking to hold them up to ridicule by printing such protests. Even reprinting hostile letters from newspapers might not entirely remove the danger of leaving that impression. All that needs to be said is that all the reactions, whether in the newspaper cuttings supplied by a Press Agency or in letters, were examined and preserved, and that neither the Bishop nor his publisher was unmoved. Indeed, *Honest to God* more than once shows that the Bishop expected hostility, and expected it without pleasure.

Here is one l...

... in the
... or a God up
...ntradicting everything
...e working man has started
... parsons say everything they have
...ong, how can they be right as to what they
...ow?'

If the whole image of God we have been taught in the past is a myth, it is a myth well worth it, as it has meant decent lives and has softened hearts and nations, for centuries. These new beliefs will smash Christians in believing there is a God and it could be the Church in general will break up. The words of the creed will mean nothing. It is suddenly like telling a youngster who believes whole-heartedly in Father Xmas, 'There isn't a Father Xmas, it's your Dad'. The whole world would collapse beneath them.

One rural dean in the Church of England wrote: 'I have read your book. There is only one course open to you, honest to God, and that is to resign your bishopric and get out of the Church of England. So long as you remain, you are a stumbling block and an offence to all who have not your intellectual pride.'

A colonel wrote:

Groping as so many of us, including yourself, obviously are for enlightenment to cure our lack of Faith and moral fibre, it seems to me incomprehensible that anyone who has attained to your high clerical office should go out of his way to offend so many by such objectionable publications as your latest effort *Honest to God*. This book does little more than to quote from the heretical outpourings of Bonhoeffer, Tillich and other alien agnostics. What little more it contains serves only to express in arrogant and often incomprehensible language your own pitiful lack of Faith and to undermine the Christian Ethics and beliefs of those who are unfortunate enough to read it and ignorant enough to be impressed by it.

Some of the protests concerned Dr Robinson's summary of his book in the *Observer*, rather than the book itself. A priest wrote:

In this parish, which I suppose could be called an average country town parish, I doubt if 1 per cent of the population would read or could understand your book; but I expect 20 per cent or so read the article in the *Observer*. Have you thought or considered what a somewhat sceptically-minded person (not a scholar) who had briefly glanced through this article, would say? 'Well, I've always said it's difficult to believe in a God who allows all this suffering and misery that goes on in the world—and now, see—a bishop tells us we needn't believe in God at all—nor go to church. He says religion isn't necessary—it's all phoney; all we need do is to lead decent lives and be kind to others.'

Now I know you did *not* say that, but it is what some have imagined you said in your article. If there are any Christians who really picture God as 'the old man up in the sky', or who imagine that the astronaut is nearer to God than the humble person kneeling at prayer in his own room, they would hardly be of the intelligence required to understand one page of your book. It would not do this if people were to read it very carefully, but I deplore that newspaper article most deeply. You do not make the task of your clergy easier, and I, as a much older man than you, would beg you not to publish these sensational advanced ideas in the public press; for you are not there speaking to trained minds, but to people who need—not the strong meat of the advanced theologian, but the simple milk of the Gospel. We must blend discretion with honesty.

Other protests concerned Dr Robinson's status as a

bishop. It was thou?
university tea?

                                               you
                                      arly the
                            p. I fully allow
                    to the expression of
               justified in taking advan-
            e way you have. I could wish
         ent to remain as a don at Cambridge,
      you would have been in good company. At
    you would have been less of an embarrassment
ose who have more first-hand experience of ordinary
pastoral work in the Church at home and overseas.

The validity of such criticisms obviously depends on
one's estimate of the religious situation. Some correspondents thought that 'simple' faith needed to be shaken,
rather than preserved. A woman wrote from Devon:

> One tries to understand and to say to oneself that they
> are simple people who must be left with their simple faith.
> But I had two shocks recently.
> In the recent Arctic spell a woman fell over on the ice
> and chipped a bit off her elbow. This meant going into
> hospital for a small operation and not unnaturally she had
> some pain. On her return (she runs a shop) I met her and
> sympathized since I realized with one arm in a sling she
> was handicapped in business, but she grumbled and com-
> plained about everything. Having never had any illness
> before she resented the pain, with no thought for the
> terrible pain others suffer without hope of recovery, and
> said, 'I am bitter. I have always said my prayers and had
> faith. Now this has happened. God is cruel. . . .'
> Another woman I met coming away from a funeral. It
> was a tragic case of a young married woman dying just
> after childbirth. To my surprise this woman said, 'I have
> always gone to church and believed in God but I must

admit this has shaken my faith'. The reason for this was that her friend, a young married mother, had died, whereas a girl who had had an illegitimate baby about the same time, had lived!

What does one say to anyone in the street on such an occasion? And what has a lifetime Church membership taught either woman? It is not a simple faith but frightening ignorance and what I can only call witchcraft! And because we cannot fit into such an atmosphere we are called Outsiders.

A civil engineer wrote:

This great argument which you have started is going to bring the Church back into the market place, and involve the spiritual interest of millions who have chosen for a variety of reasons to consider themselves as not 'religiously minded'.

One of the best of London's recent Lord Mayors said to me 'I don't consider myself a deeply religious man', but during the same conversation he told me that he had considered it his duty as chief citizen during his year of office 'not to refuse to meet at the Mansion House anybody who had asked to see him'.

That is my conception of a religious man, and I have long since ceased to take any notice of the labels which people choose to attach to themselves.

But note how that correspondent wanted a 'spiritual' interest! It is evident that if Christian morality (or an attempt at it) is going to be supported by Christian belief (or a new form of it) in this England, there is first going to be much spiritual travail. At present the respect for Christian morality often appears to rest on a spiritual vacuum.

A schoolteacher wrote:

May I quote to you from one of Dannie Abse's poems which seems so well to express this need and inability to accept the popular image?

Dear God :
Dis_

..s are writing this way
_ource of their creative power;
_ and pull at the umbilical cord it
_ck again, until like T. S. Eliot and Thomas
_.u they 'break through' the veil of reasoned dis-
_usion and the outworn creeds of man's convenience.

A cry from this waste land:

I have a deep inner desire to return to church, which I
find I can satisfy by attending church services abroad where
I can understand nothing of the message, yet can be reminded by the environment and by the deeply reverent
attitudes of the worshippers, as well as by the magnificent
music and the religious pictures, of the intention behind the
ritual, and of the deep religious experiences I used to feel as
a boy.

So often I find myself wishing I had never grown up. As
a child during the first war, and in the knowledge that my
family were utterly impoverished by the untimely death of
my father—a tireless Christian worker, and much loved—
I was none the less happy in the knowledge that we would
see him again, and that Jesus was in His Heaven, all must
go well with the world. I loved the Christmas story.

Now that has largely diminished or departed. I *wish* that
I could once again believe what as a little child I believed
implicitly and unquestionably. Instead I find that Christ-
mastime is sullied partly by commercialism, and partly by
the insistence that Christ's birth was magical. Once upon a
time the Virgin Birth would have been a reason for belief.
To me, and I must say, to my infinite regret, it is a
stumbling block, a reason for UNBELIEF.

But one correspondent told how some faith had come:

During the war I felt unable to believe in anything, despite a deeply religious upbringing, but eventually emerged from this spiritual limbo to the belief that God was an ultimate reality which we could not hope to comprehend with our finite and three-dimensional understanding, and that the part of us which would eventually lose itself, and merge with that ultimate perfection, would find its way there through Christ.

And another:

I am 77 and a widow and I taught science in London and South Africa earlier in the century. Although I was confirmed in the Church of England and tried very hard to be 'religious' at that time, none of it was real to me and I have had to work out my own philosophy.

I think that the ultimate reality is consciousness in every stage of evolution in a living universe and harmony which is Love between all the parts of that universe, and that as we are conscious we must be *eternal*—the outward form renewing itself somewhat as the leaves of a tree—and in process of *evolution*. It is only when we can lose our own identity and become not only part of the universe but immersed in it as a drop in the sea—that everything we do becomes spontaneous and intuitive, almost without thought, and *right*, and the stresses and strains resolve themselves. It is at such times that everything in life becomes exciting and wonderful, even ecstatic.

Some women look at the Church from the world, as in these letters.

I wonder where you feel people like me belong? Perhaps if I were inside the Church I could stay there, but I cannot make the step in to the Church as I find it here. I find myself more immediately at home with humanists and yet I know that I have a conviction about love, which is faith and won't do in a purely humanistic setting.

Perhaps for myself I could accept the position of outsider, but I have four young children and I wish somehow we could shelter under the Christian umbrella.

And from an old la[...]

I as a chi[...]
At six[...]
[...]

[...] in-
[...]ieved in
[...]umanist. I am
[...] and beauty with a
[...], for in spite of the misery
[...]n goodness. Perhaps this faith is
[...]rom progressive teaching within the

[...]oman wrote from Canterbury:

I personally found the chapters on prayers and church-going in particular removed a vast load of guilt and misery. So many of one's repeated efforts merely ended in failure and a despairing effort to do better next time, and then more failure and guilt.

Unlike the medievals we are now educated to think for ourselves, and cannot help thinking about, questioning, and reading about all aspects of our belief, and finding things which strike with an inner certainty of truth. It is just so marvellous to have all this coming from a bishop of the Church, and having one's thoughts and hopes confirmed, not rejected, from inside the Church. I am certain this must help a great many thinking people to remain in the Church, and to bring back others who have felt increasingly alienated from it.

A voice from the pews:

I am simply an ordinary housewife with an ordinary history, but probably representative of many others, who like me have been inspired and encouraged by your book and who, like me, have not really got the time to write and tell you so.

I started as a Roman Catholic but left the Church and nearly all belief, as I thought then, forever at the age of

20 (1934). I came back into the Church of England five
years ago when my children decided they wanted to be
Christians and wanted me to be their witness. I had come
back to a belief in God and prayer and the Resurrection. I
have continued to 'support' the Church to the best of my
ability although passionately dissatisfied and conscious that
its symbolism at present is useless to my husband, friends,
relatives, although they are all people who love truth and
love and do not label themselves as anything, but are cut
off from Christianity in England today.

What is perhaps worse is that the younger generation, the
ones who care most to reach the truth, cannot recognize it
in the present 'mould'. I would not say that the Church has
'nothing to lose but its chains' but it is peculiarly near to
that, and I hope you have started a revolution.

And a woman's voice from a vicarage:

There are many causes for this indebtedness to your
book, the greatest being your reconciliation of the divine
and the human in Christ. The orthodox teaching has always
maddened me; so many other humans have sacrificed themselves for us, endured more sustained and prolonged tor-
ture, without the comfort of being the 'favourite son'. If,
however, as I have understood from your book, Christ's
divinity lies in his struggle, as a mortal, and his success in
emptying himself of self, so that God might shine through,
this truly is of God. Any of us knows the impossibility of
the struggle; what you have helped to remove is my constant annoyance that Christ always had an unfair advantage.

Perhaps one of the greatest blessings is that you—and the
men who have inspired you—have made the Church seem
alive again, when for years it has seemed so unbearably
dead! My children, with the gap of one generation, are
directly descended from parsons back to 1513. This is a
heritage which has been of great support to me and I should
like to pass it on as a living thing. I am much more hopeful
now of being able to do so.

Another 'ordinary vicar's wife' wrote:

Before reading it, I was full of fear and trepidation, ex-

pecting the found———
reverse ha———
late———

———nker, and a
———ery necessary jolt—
———who are intimately in-
———the Church. All the rather irksome
———a vicar's wife (plus, of course, the joyful
———the disappointments, etc., suddenly seem so much
——ore worthwhile.

I used to wonder so often if it was worth the effort, when Christianity seemed so far away from 'religion' (as you define it). From the help given in your book, I can see a 'breakthrough'. I just hope that we on the Church side of the fence have the courage and initiative to make it.

A less faithful churchgoer wrote:

As a husband, three daughters, an elderly aunt, three cats and a large old house take up rather a lot of my time, I have had to do most of my reading on top of a double decker bus on my way into town to do the shopping. Not the best places for trying to study a book of such depth, especially as not being a classical scholar I found some parts rather difficult and quite a number of words which needed looking up in the dictionary!

I can't tell you how much better I feel for having read it.

Ever since I can remember I have had doubts—I have never been able to go to a church service without having a wild desire in the middle of the sermon and sometimes the lessons to stand up and start asking questions which I felt sure to the average churchgoer, priest or layman, would sound utterly blasphemous. Yet to me these questions seemed to be begging for an answer, and as the years passed I just became more and more frustrated in my efforts to find God in church. It seemed to be the one and only place where I just couldn't get near to him at all. There seemed

to be so many things which I was expected to believe and
accept unquestioningly if I was to be a true member of the
church and I found so many of them utterly illogical and
to my way of thinking, unnecessary. The church seemed to
make Christianity so terribly complicated when to me it
seemed so simple.

About eight years ago I just gave up the struggle—I told
my vicar that after much heart searching I had reached the
conclusion that the only part of the service I could repeat
and honestly believe was the first four words of the Apostles'
Creed and in the circumstances I felt any further attempts
to take part in church services would be extremely hypo-
critical. He was duly sympathetic and hoped I should continue to attend church as an example to my children (an
example of what?!).

For some days after this decision I suffered pangs of
guilt and secretly wondered if perhaps I was wrong after
all and if the vengeful god of the Old Testament might perhaps strike me down any minute with some terrible afflic-
tion for my sins, but as the days passed I became aware of
something stealing quietly into my life which I can only
describe as 'that peace which the world cannot give'. It has
remained with me constantly ever since.

Like you, I firmly believe that nothing can separate us
from the love of God. It is with us, and around us and in
the very depth of our being, and closing our eyes or ears to
it can never send it away.

I suppose I am really a heretic in the eyes of the Church, I
don't really know. I certainly don't do all the things which
my vicar considers essential for my salvation. I go to church
periodically because my husband is in the choir, and I encourage my daughters to think and never stop searching for
the Truth, and to see the love of God in all life.

I think what I have really been trying to say is that I
believe there must be many ordinary people like myself
who have just the same doubts and who long for the
Church to give them a helping hand, but who have become
bogged down by the mixture of man-made dogma and
ancient mythology which seems to be the present basis of
Christianity. If only you would write another *Honest to*

*God* in really simple
mind could rea
amazed at
the

a way
ny. I should
eprooted habit of
atter to me most; and
be deluged with such letters.
passed at Convocation, I think that
received a good many letters and com-
other sort, and that my reticence should this
overcome.

I've been married for over 25 years to an engineer. He has just retired from the Overseas Civil Service after 30 years in Africa. We have two children now at university and their education has meant that for ten years we were separated quite a lot. One of these long periods of separation coincided with the Hungarian Revolution. I was in England: I speak German and French, and I had a car. So I went to Austria to see what I could do; the children were at boarding-school. First I floundered about in the mud on the border and in a big reception camp, and after the Christmas holidays in England I went back to take charge of a camp for refugee students, men and girls from 16 to 25 —about 50 of them. Ninety per cent had been fighting, all were in a highly nervous state. They quarrelled, they drank too much, they engaged in violent love affairs, they fell ill.

I would have thought that I would be no good at all at the job of looking after them—no self-confidence, rather nervous, easily hurt, not very brave. But I couldn't put a foot wrong. All the time I had the feeling I was being helped to do and say the right thing. I loved them all so much I hadn't time to be 'hurt in my feelings', or to wonder if they loved me, or to be afraid of driving on icy roads, giving them hell if they misbehaved, arguing their cases with Austrian officials. All the time it seemed that God was there, and in a way this bothered me, because I have never

believed in a god who can, so to speak, tell me, from
'without' or 'beyond' what to do—I should have said, too,
that I didn't believe in prayer as I understood it. But I
prayed for those young people; that is, I thought about
them, pitied them, and hoped for them until it hurt—
physically.

This was the first of such experiences: it gave me
confidence and courage, and increased my capacity to love.
It also put me in a dilemma: whether or not to accept a
nine-months' job helping in the resettlement of refugees,
and to delay by that period rejoining my husband. It didn't
'feel' right to take the job, but perhaps it would be shirking
to refuse. In the end I spoke to a priest about it, a priest
who preached often about service to the unfortunate and
involvement with one's neighbour. He said I should go to
my husband, that wherever I was I should find work to
do if I looked for it. He was perfectly right. I was asked
to take charge of the adult literacy programme in a 700-
bed government hospital in Africa. I had to learn the language properly, find helpers, organize a rota and transport,
and spend every afternoon from 1.30-4 at the hospital.
Most helpers could give only one afternoon a week, some
only one a fortnight: whatever they couldn't do I tried to
do. We worked mostly in the surgical wards and during
the hottest time of the day. It was extremely tiring, and
often the wards smelled awful. But I found myself going as
though to a party and coming away as exhilarated as if I'd
had a good stiff drink. I've never met such wonderful
people: patient, enduring, cheerful, eager to learn, and incredibly brave. Their love was an honour and a benediction,
and again I felt I walked with God, even though I rejected
the image of somebody 'up there' putting out a hand to
me. When I had time to think about it I used to wonder if
I were becoming what one might call a love-addict, the kind
of person who will do anything to win love, and who goes
about the place behaving as though she thought she was a
mixture of the Lady with the Lamp and Napoleon! You
know the sort? But nobody around me seemed to think so:
my husband and children would never have let me get away
with it if *they* had noticed. So I gave up fussing and just

worked on till w...
I had don...
t...

...ow
...in if all goes
...im he'll go into an
...ny children enthusiastically
...se he loves me. Often I'm terrified
...iat I'm taking on, and if it hadn't been for
... and Africa I shouldn't be grown up enough to have
considered it. Fundamentally, however, I'm not afraid. I
know I can bring him up, love him, and keep him out of
my husband's hair! It is a job to last me till I die. I think
it must be right, or I wouldn't be so happy. In prospect, at
any rate, it isn't narrowing: all sorts of people seem nicer
and more lovable because of this small coffee-coloured
child!

I have told you these things because your book—which I
might not have read if I hadn't heard what you said about
radicalism on the BBC—has made clearer to me *why*
I think and act as I do, why the last few years have been
years of growth and change and happiness. It has made
many things fall into place in my mind and helped me to
understand myself as I used to be and am now. I used, I
think, to look for God when I was miserable, or felt inadequate and unloved. ('Nobody loves me and my hands are
cold'—'God loves you and you can sit on your hands!'). I
didn't find him because he wasn't there, and I had the
brains to recognize this and to learn to do without him.
And then, when I was too busy to think and worry about
myself, there he seemed to be. But I was too conditioned by
an agnostic background—'agnostic', be it said, in the true
Greek sense of the word—to turn round and believe in
'that gentleman who's always there' (as the small boy complained!). So I just shelved the problem, because I was
too ignorant to know that better and cleverer people had
spent and were spending their time and thought on it. That

is why I thank you most earnestly for your book, for explaining what you and they have made of it, have pondered and written about the nature of God.

There are parts of the Creeds I can't say. I don't see how I could honestly be confirmed. I don't know of any church where communion is celebrated in the spirit you describe. I am sure that Jesus is the son of God but am obscurely comforted by the N.E.B.'s 'beloved' instead of 'only'. I don't know whether I have the right to have my little foster child baptized. '*Wherein* I was made, etc.', sticks in my gullet. Are the Tibetan children and the Moslems I love not children of God and inheritors of the Kingdom of Heaven? I don't understand the Resurrection as any churchman I know seems to. But Matt. 22.37-40 [our Lord's summary of the Law as love of God and neighbour] has meant increasingly much to me for a long time, and I think you have shown me why. Is it because those words are the core of the matter and so enough?

If this is a gross oversimplification of what you have written, I'm sorry: misdirected thanks are worse than none, and yet I wouldn't dare to ask you to argue with me or try to correct me. So this letter must stand, as the best explanation and expression of my gratitude that I can give.

## A woman of 20, an undergraduate at Oxford, wrote:

Many prominent men in the Church of England have allowed their unmeditated reaction to your ideas to appear in print. Such men are unaware of the urgency of the need for a new image, and of the harmful contempt for the Christian religion which the old mythological image arouses amongst the younger generation, both at university and in the ordinary grammar school.

The C. S. Lewis type argument, which is so popular amongst teachers and progressive Bible study group leaders, only alienates this youth further. They turn to Eastern religions, but practice is difficult and soon interest fades. Eventually they enter the rat race after 'O' or 'A' levels, diplomas or degree, without committing themselves positively to a particular way of living their lives.

Large numbers
tian herit...

..., and

... interested in more than 'the
..., wrote: 'Although a fairly regular
...er I have for many years been full of inward
...s and questionings. Your book has answered them
and for my short remaining time on this earth I shall be
more at peace and more ready to cope with life and its
many contacts. Thank you, and again thank you.' A number of other old people wrote in similar terms.

Now for some men. One correspondent wrote: 'I have
been an actor for twelve years, and this is the first time I
have seen another actor reading a religious book in a
dressing room.'

All the more fortunate that your book has been attacked
and you yourself reproached by the hierarchy! The one
way in which what you have had to say could have been
killed would have been for the 'official Church' to have
taken it to its already overcrowded bosom and pronounced
it blessed. If that had happened all the people I know,
who are religious but not ecclesiastically inclined, could
only have turned yet again to the Church to find a theoretical welcome, but a fundamental rejection by defunct
forms expressing dead thoughts.

But it is not only for the outsider that you have in part
spoken. I regularly take Communion and am a lay reader
of our church. But it is absurd for archbishops or bishops
or clergymen to assume that regularity means that I, and
many other people, am content or that we get refreshment
from attending the tired motions of a minority cult. I am

tortured by churchgoing. Each Sunday I make intellectual reservations behind what I am saying and singing. I wonder whether in fact I am doing something that is wrong in being in church, by helping to perpetuate something in all but its essentials I know to be dead. Each Sunday I wonder whether I am aiding and indeed being contaminated by the paternalistic hypocrisy which preaches 'Go forward', 'Live by the Spirit' and which itself never budges from the tired patterns of yesterday's pieties, the prayer wheel of Evensong and the ambiguities of the Eucharist.

The theatre suffers within the same paradox. But at least the theatre doesn't do just Shakespeare and make the pretence of modernity by having a tract stall in the foyer with pamphlets on 'The Inner Meaning of the Drama' written by Samuel Beckett and Harold Pinter.

A professor of mathematics wrote:

I do understand from personal experience the almost pathological fear of 'orthodox' Christians that any relaxation of their beliefs will lead to the extinction of their faith. But I do know, also from personal experience, and with ever increasing conviction over the years, that this is simply not true. One simply finds oneself standing at last on the solid rock of truth about God and Christianity—the ultimate truth which has been the living heart of every form of Christian 'religion' and which is the meaning of its survival. It is this, I think, which you have expressed so well in your book; and if this in time is got across, as it certainly will be, there will be no problem of church unity.

In the meantime you would be surprised to know how much we have learnt from your book, and how deeply it has been discussed and appreciated on all sides, even by those who cannot as yet adopt all you say. We had never heard of the names Tillich and Bonhoeffer and Bultmann: but in the last weeks they have almost become household words.

A medical professor wrote:

I had been becoming increasingly out of feeling with church activities; and indeed was only continuing to go to

church on [...]
[...]

[...]p by
[...] was that as
[...]usly envisaging not com-
[...] time since confirmation. Why?
[...] feeling increasingly dishonest in attaching
[...] to a church of which I was so critical and which
often made one angry. Since I don't think one can ever
detach oneself from Christianity, once exposed, the prospect
of keeping one's Bible-reading going in sanctimonious isolation was all that offered!

However—to find you voicing so many of my feelings,
in the same mood, and from a position firmly within the
Church, made me feel that I could and ought to tag along
(I can't dignify it by any better name), because there was at
last hope that there would be room for 'unreligious' people.
Also one of your main themes, of God as ground substance,
rang a terrific bell. 'Ground of being' has I suppose been a
phrase in use for decades or centuries: but you unpacked
its meanings and implications in a way which converted it
from one of the phrases one used to resort to to translate
a church archaism into something meaningful; out of this
to an expression carrying, for me now at any rate, more
meaning than the whole of Christology put together. Again,
I suspect, because of a scientific background.

There seem to be some problems—the significance of
petitionary prayer—is it necessary for Christ to be unique
(I don't care for the latter-day saints, but is there any
logical reason why a man should not, again, become trans-
parent to God?). But no matter; as on a good line in one's
research, there will be a way through, over or round. One
can intuit such things, and I trust such intuitions.

I don't find I have expressed myself accurately: and the
egocentricity of all this is unpleasant. But I hope it helps
to get across a very deep gratitude.

C

Some correspondents felt that theology of the kind expressed in *Honest to God* might be used to help the man in the street:

> I believe that all you have written has real practical implications and should help the clergy to understand better the problems that face the so-called unchurched masses. Again and again with monotonous repetition one hears the remark—'I don't go to church, I'm not a religious man, but . . .'. It is that word 'but' that is so significant. And always those people, when pressed, say that they feel something 'deeper' than self.

A businessman wrote from New York: 'We've all been reading *Honest to God*, and it is the first book I have ever read that seems to understand exactly what my problems are with regard to Christianity and to provide almost a viable interpretation of what it is all about if one is alive today.'

An English doctor wrote:

> It is quite extraordinary how many people I see complain of their difficulties in praying in the orthodox way and feel very guilty about it. Quite a number of them have understood your expressions of prayer in relationships and have felt an immediate relief. One said, 'I've felt this all along, but I've never tried it properly because I thought it wrong'.

A doctor who might have been a priest wrote:

> Had such thinking as has led to *Honest to God* been the case in my Cambridge days (some thirty years ago now) I might well have found my way into the Church (in fact this may even happen now although probably I am called to continue in my present job as a GP with a large country practice). But at Cambridge I just couldn't face the dreariness and apparent impracticability of this Church image at that time. In different ways I think this was also true for many of my contemporaries.

How dif

yo

-ome-
use the good
implication of being
than anyone else's mode of
avelengths suit different purposes in
...ications, and differing modes of thought suit
...ing purposes in human communications. If ours is
best for our purpose, we are not being 'uppish' in using it.

You mention in your book that you have not experienced 'being born again'. May I suggest that you are undergoing that very process at the moment? It is my belief that it happens to those of us who were brought up as Christians, and have remained such; and that perhaps it is a more traumatic experience for us than it is for non-believers.

If my assessment is right, and you are undergoing something akin to what I have undergone in the last two years, then you have a hard but wonderful road ahead of you; and God *will* be with you in a new way, and you will find yourself being 'as a little child'—wondering, questioning, enjoying, learning and growing.

A well-known politician wrote:

Reading it, and hearing you speak of it, has done more to make the basic validity of the Christian message seem relevant to me than all the sermons and services I have ever heard or attended.

The mythology *is* a real barrier even when it is only used symbolically. For it leads us to look upwards and outwards when we should be looking inwards and downwards. From the very depths of human experience comes an understanding of what we are and may be, and the mystery that is there is quite enough without contemplating the possibility of man-made mysteries that are outside our experience and hence often ridiculous rather than mysterious.

One letter came from a modern university in England:

This is *just* the kind of thing which we have needed in this University certainly, and I believe elsewhere in the student world in this country, to stir up the discussion, not only with Christians, but also among self-styled atheists and agnostics. Many people in this University who have seen the book are deeply grateful to you for this courageous piece of writing.

Another told of a ferment in Edinburgh: 'For many, reading this has been a conversion experience, with all the emotional clarity and mental confusion that they have ridiculed in fundamentalists since they clambered maturely out of the pram.'

An English country vicar wrote: 'With all my heart I know you are right, and that somehow Christ is struggling free from the grave clothes of our binding, and that a revolution, or resurrection, of Christian thinking is most marvellously in the making.'

Such a revolution would have to affect schools. Several correspondents said that the schools needed a revolution.

Where our folly starts is trying to perpetuate this old religion in an age when school children begin to laugh at the fairy-tales their scripture teachers try to impose on them in all seriousness. One lesson later, their science teacher— not in so many words, but nevertheless with deadly efficiency and unwittingly—gives the lie to everything their religious teacher has said.

This is where the death of the Church starts, this is where you find the cause of empty churches. The boy or girl, once escaped from school, shies away from this bewildering conundrum and wants to have nothing more to do with it. It's too much for them to sort out. Pop music and the 'Beat' is less problematic. . . . Can you blame them?

A young Englishman, now working in Africa, wrote of

his reli...

...on t
...would like to
...have always found that
...known have been the best listeners.
...ined at the age of 14 or 15, at a time when
...was beginning to lose interest in the forms of Christianity, primarily, I must admit, because of the practical inconvenience and apparent shallowness of feeling in the school's services and teaching, rather than any particularly deep theological argument.

The three main things which disenchanted me initially were the 15-minute daily morning chapel, a hasty and insincere ritual which was little more than a roll-call; the extreme dullness of the greater part of church music, and what seemed to me the remoteness of our present forms of worship; and finally a book by the former Bishop of Bradford, Dr Blunt, called, I think, *The Way, the Truth and the Life*, which made me feel completely and hopelessly lost. It seemed so impracticable and remote from my own life that I had the same sort of feeling of exasperation that most people have when they try to understand contemporary power politics.

A little later, I started linking this disillusionment with the idea of God which I had been taught, the idea which you reject. I wondered what relation a remote universe-creating Being could have to *my* life, to my work and games, my small crimes which seemed amply punished on the spot. Above all, I found, and still find, it difficult to grasp the idea of punishment for sins, atonement and reconciliation, a whole concept which seemed so out of reach of any practical context, so utterly above my head. I went to chapel, not to pray, because I felt in no way able to talk to a person whom I could not begin to understand or imagine, but because I loved to sing in the choir. I stopped going to Communion after a year because, to use your own phrase, I couldn't with integrity continue, for the sake of appearances, to attend and take part in this central act of faith, when my heart was not in it, when I was not entirely convinced of what it meant. I thought it was dishonest. I have never been an atheist; but I have never found an idea of God which I could accept and understand (as far as one can understand God). As far as the exterior forms are concerned, I have always admired the idea of Quaker meetings, although their beliefs do not attract me. This has been perhaps a reaction to the Anglican High Church which I attended with my mother: I have always liked simplicity in a church.

If I have understood your article, you have described a far more practical idea of God, as the love, the good, that must be in the depth of our nature. This, it seems to me, would account for the morality of human society, and for the good which can be found everywhere among the evil of many people's superficial actions. It means that there is something more underneath the superficiality of everyday life, rather than outside—a very great difference, to my mind.

If I have understood, it seems to me to be something like what I have been thinking of during the past few years. But do you feel that the idea of worship and prayer can be linked to this conception? This has been the problem which has puzzled me most: how to equate prayer and worship to a God who one does not believe to be personal in the traditional sense. It is for this reason that I have felt unable to take a proper part in church services, and I am sure that this problem, and more often the apparent remoteness of the present forms of worship, is the reason why less young people of my generation are active churchgoers.

Perhaps such young men would be helped more at other schools. One public school headmaster wrote:

Our experience in conversations with boys about (say) 15½ bears out all you say. We can have fruitful discussions about 'Christ-in-our-personal-relations', provided we *begin*

with the pres...
Revel...

...ٹٹ be
... Church. This
...ence than Luther's and
... consequence as Constantine's.
... we must now go into a period of
... the worrying thing is that while intelligent and
...oughtful people can clearly accept the *sturm und drang*
which is about to descend on the Church, or well up from
in it, what is going to happen to the admiring believer?
What happens to our school chapel and our teaching in
what may easily be 50 years of redefinition? For as yet the
*positive* side of the post-Bonhoeffer redefinition is the
vaguest and least explored part.

We must still commit ourselves to a person, as ever, but
what we must present to the young will look to them like
a form of agnosticism. They want *answers*. We have to
teach them not to expect that sort of answer at all. We have
to teach them, I suppose, to think existentially—and one day
they will—just as the seventeenth-century philosophers had
to teach people to think in terms of scientific explanations
—and it took many years before most people did. All this
will happen, I'm sure; but we live in the exciting but disturbing interim, as disturbing as the Reformation must
have been to the faithful Catholic population of England;
and a lot of thought is needed about this interim.

From another headmaster:

I always find what you write exciting, though our tem-
peraments are poles apart; and *Honest to God*, whether it's
breaking new ground or mediating the incomprehensible
Tillich, is very exciting. I've been busy recommending it
to boys (especially unbelievers!).

Yet I understand the doubts about its effects, and to
some extent share them. Consumer research and a desire to

be 'with it' dominate so much shallow thinking that I am
uneasy at any trace in deep thinking of 'What will Jones
swallow?'

Isn't it rather as if somebody said 'This old habit of
using the word "heart" to denote emotion and will is quite
out of place in this scientific age, when we know that the
heart performs no such function'? He would be right, of
course; and yet the determinists would interpret this as
being, underneath his new language, an acknowledgment
that glands and inhibitions were sole king, and that free-
will and genuine, disinterested choice of good did not exist.
An inadequate comparison, but it may show what I mean.

When Ronald Knox taunted William Temple with paying
undue attention to modern scepticism ('What will Jones
swallow?'), Temple replied: 'I am Jones, asking what there
is to eat.' And so it turns out that some schoolteachers are
worried not only about communicating but also about
believing the traditional expressions of Christianity.

A woman 'firmly within the Anglican tradition' experiences difficulty as she trains other teachers. Her letter is
quoted by permission.

May I say first that I am grateful to you for *Honest to
God*, primarily because here is a book that speaks very
clearly to my condition? My own thinking and reading in
combination with my work in the past ten years have led me
to the conviction (of which you speak on p. 123) that,
revolution apart, Christian faith and practice must ultimately be abandoned. Certainly this is true for me and it
is, I think, equally true for many of the present student
generation. So it is that I am both refreshed and stimu-
lated to read what you have to say.

I am concerned with the training of teachers, and particularly with religious education. Increasingly I find a
problem. With those students who select Divinity as a main
field of study, the problem is there, but not quite so
prominent. The more able, at any rate, can read and discuss, and ultimately either accept or reject ideas which con-

flict

learn-
portion become
them there is a danger
may be disturbed and not re-estab-
majority are fed back into the schools, often
enough to perpetuate the kind of teaching which disposes
young people to turn against Christianity.

Now maybe the fault lies with the requirement of the
1944 Education Act in the matter of 'religious instruction'.
I am still not altogether certain about this—although I am
certain that, as interpreted in many schools, it is harmful
rather than helpful. Even so, I am required to work under
that Act, and to try to help students with the giving of
religious instruction to young children in school. Can this,
should this, be done? That is my practical problem.

You say, for example, '*If I had the courage*, I would start
the other end in teaching the discipline of prayer'. What is
the answer here? There is, I find, a constant tension between
my own approach, however tentative, and the traditional
theology in which I have been trained and which I am
expected to teach. I might, perhaps, say something comparable to your words in relation to my specialist work (i.e.
with 'Divinity' students), but not in what we call 'basic' or
'curriculum' courses. I feel increasingly that many teachers,
and often those of good will, do ultimately more harm
than good in their 'religious instruction', and I do not myself
see the beginnings of a satisfactory answer at the training
level.

Theology is my subject, but I am tempted to wonder,
again and again, what place there is for it in the general
educational system of our time. One possibility that occurs
to me personally is to seek to become a lecturer in Education. Over these years, and perhaps alongside the development of my own thought, I have been aware of a shift of

emphasis. At the outset of my teaching career I was a
college-trained teacher. Then I myself studied theology at
a university because I wanted to see teachers with a sound
theology. I want this still, but now perhaps I look first for
sound teachers—in a much wider sense.

Confronting these great questions, even preachers may
be more worried than they seem. This letter is typical of a
number which came from young priests of the Church of
England:

I had come to the same conclusions as you have described in *Honest to God* some time ago and I was beginning to feel that I couldn't stay within the Church any
longer as I felt that I was the one out of step. Recently I
have read Bonhoeffer and Tillich and realized that I wasn't
alone by any manner of means, and now your book which
draws the strands together and beds them in the New Testament has filled me with a joy that comes from being liber-
ated from a sense of guilt about not being able to believe
what I felt I ought to believe.

Your book has given me the last bit of courage I needed
to go looking for the truth with no reservations of *any*
kind: to follow where love leads, to trust to life, to glory
in the depth and mystery and not be afraid of what may
be found in the depth or through the mystery.

From a 'high church' vicar:

It seems to give coherence to a whole lot of ideas that
have been bubbling under the surface for several years. I
didn't at first dare tell my curate how much I liked the
book (I thought he was too Mirfield and wouldn't understand) but I was delighted when he too got the message.
Perhaps we who are the hangers-on of a tired Anglo-
Catholicism need it most.

It links too with a lot of deeper pastoral work we are
doing for Telephone Samaritan cases; this is the kind of
way of thinking about God that alone can help them.

From another parish priest, at work on a housing estate:

For

...at matter.

...at Christianity was

... something entirely new in your book, ...ade large areas of my experience most wonder-...ly meaningful. It fills me with deep sadness and fore-boding that the *Church Times* should interpret the most deeply Christian book I have ever read as an attack on the Faith.

Thank you so much. You can have no idea with what a sense of relief and liberation your book has come! A relief from the unending strain of trying to reach up to God—and having all my religion and morality composed from out-side. Indeed so far from 'pouring God out', for me you have brought him right into the centre of life, to be found in my deepest relationships, and to be confronted in every truly honest situation of life. I still want to shout with joy at parts of it!

From a professor of theology:

Before mail of a possibly rather different sort begins to arrive, may I say, that after re-reading your book this week-end, I'm definitely with you? Without necessarily agreeing with absolutely everything you say, I think the contents, and—what is just as important—the tone, are excellent, and I greatly admire your courage in saying what you do as a bishop.

From another theological professor, two months later:

As one would expect, it has had a wonderful effect in opening up serious conversations with non-Christian aca-demic colleagues. I think in particular of a young research fellow in physics in my college with whom I have had a good many rather futile exchanges in the past, but who now tells me that he begins to see what it is all about and wants to discuss it at a different level than before. What really has moved me is not that sort of thing, which would naturally happen, but the experience of having a pretty simple and toughly materialistic farmer buttonhole me at a cocktail party and ask to come and discuss Christianity in the light of your book, which, he says, has made him aware for the first time that it might make sense and be important. I have no doubt that he is only one of a very large number who are grateful to you.

A priest in another English university wrote (and is quoted by permission):

I live, I suppose, mostly in theological circles where *prima facie* you would not expect the book to be well received. But I find wherever I go that it has already had results which are surprisingly positive. I believe that practising Christians and parish clergy are often not so unaware of all these problems as you fear that they are, and as the *Church Times* seems anxious to ensure that they stay! It seems unnecessary to speak of the reaction from agnostic circles, or from those on the fringe of the Church. I have experienced, and I suppose many have, how the possibility of conversation on the deepest questions has been opened up there. The sales figures are eloquent of the way in which the book has reached a large public who never normally touch this sort of thing.

But inside the Church, what?

(*a*). A theological college principal: 'It's like living in a volcano, here at present. We are all asking ourselves whether we believe in God or not.' And teaching and conducting a seminary there, I have found the same thing: a new willingness to get down to first principles, to ask fundamental questions about the nature of theology and faith.

(*b*). A group of theologians coming out of their academic specialization in order to discuss together, and possibly to write something together on the Christian doctrine of man in the light of modern psychological knowledge. A meeting not *caused* by H. to G., but certainly sparked off by it.

... Anglican religious com-
......ges trom it to her nuns. Very positive
......s among some of the — Fathers.

(e). Younger clergy almost unanimously *feeling* with it,
if not always agreeing with it. It expresses what we all *feel*.
I think probably only among the Conservative Evangelicals
could one find a blank wall of resistance.

(f). A conference of Roman Catholic clergy last month;
many of course had not read the book, and were not concerned. Among those who had read it, *great* appreciation
of its spiritual and pastoral concern and power. 'Much my
best reading in Lent' coupled with a feeling that the book
was maladroit at the level of what they call fundamental
theology. (See Michael de la Bedoyère in *Search*.)

Your book has a closer and more dynamic relationship
to certain perennial themes in Christian thought and life
than perhaps you recognize. Its negative attitude towards
conventional images (even when they are Biblical in origin)
takes up the Old Testament protest against idolatry, which
it seems to me has been maintained in the Church by the
great masters of the spiritual life. God is infinitely greater
than our images of him; and the images always tend to
become idols. God is not only beyond—he is within us, and
he is at work in all things. Hence there is no gap, no division
between sacred and secular. I know it is customary to contrast 'mystics' with 'prophets'. Personally I think there is
*much* more in common between them than is commonly
allowed. I was reminded all the way through of a saying
of Eckhart (I think it was). 'He who thinks to get more of
God in church than he does at his own fire-side, does but
wrap God up in a blanket and put him under the table.'

From a chaplain in the Royal Navy:

I wish our religion wasn't called Christianity so much, as it places too much (I think) emphasis on Christ and doesn't direct us enough to God the Creator Father and God the Holy Ghost. I see God the Holy Ghost in the surgeon's *hands* as I see the love of Jesus in the physician's *care*. I see God the Holy Ghost down a microbiological microscope as I see God the Creator in our navigator's sextant. It seems to me that the three are one and indivisible in this constant activity and that we are suffused with this activity whether we like it (know it) or not.

Another parson echoed that chaplain:

Thank heavens there will now be at least one book one will be able to put in the hands of the intelligent and inquiring late teenager and others without feeling one is just giving him ammunition simply asking to be used against Christianity. My own thoughts had been turning of late to the impossibility (and probably folly) of trying to present more than a third of our conception of God under the personal category, and your book has brought relief and delight.

From a veteran in the Anglican ministry:

I do not know what some of the theological colleges have been teaching, but there is an extraordinary amount of babymindedness, sheep talk and blindly dogmatic party spirit abroad today. Perhaps you will provide the needed focus and rallying point for a rational approach to doctrinal matters so that it will become respectable to want to make the dogma fit the facts, in the face of the prevailing tendency to follow the reverse order.

Perhaps not all the theological colleges should be blamed. One college principal wrote:

It can certainly do nothing but good in theological colleges such as this. I would hope that most of our men are already conversant with the line of thought that you present, but the publication of this book as a popular paperback will have the effect of making its challenge quite inescapable,

... I stopped saying my prayers—and felt terribly guilty about it, especially when training young folk for Church Membership! (You will know what I mean if I anticipate by saying that I still don't say my prayers, but that for nearly twelve months now I haven't stopped praying during my waking life.) The real breakthrough began when I realized that I had far more in common with the honest agnostic than with the average Christian. It continued to a crucial point during a period of six months two years ago when my secretary's husband was dying of cancer. For once I could not avoid the problem by popping in to see the patient occasionally and saying a few godly words. Every morning I had to face his wife (who turned out to be highly intelligent theologically) and questions about death, the hereafter, and prayer. By the time he died we were both agnostic about a personal consciousness outside this life, and our understanding of the nature of prayer had begun to mature.

The process of re-orientation and building up has been a tremendous time of release and joy and this side of the experience has given me a deep understanding of 'hot gospel' religion. There are some chorus hymns that by a process of demythologizing I can now sing with fervour!

This is one of the most happy things—a sense of identification with absolutely everybody. I can understand the 'trad' Christians because I was one, the agnostic and atheist because in a real sense I am one, and the perfervid evangelical because I have in common with him a quite unavoidable sense of being 'in God', 'in Christ', or however you choose to describe it.

A Roman Catholic priest wrote:

It is being said that Roman Catholics can only be horri-

fied by the book, and that reunion is made more remote,
and so on.

In fairness to myself, as well as to you, I should like to
say that *Honest to God* impressed me very favourably. I
think the hostility expressed mostly arises from the un-
familiarity of the ideas. I have spent seven years teaching
Scripture and Doctrine to grammar school boys and it
seems to me that Biblical studies and missionary concern
do make necessary in our thinking some such adjustment
as you suggest.

A writer on religious subjects in 'great excitement' welcomed the stir caused, and added:

Of your own contribution in *Honest to God* I fear I am
somewhat critical. I lunched with — when I was in London
recently and we spent most of the time talking about your
book and article. We both agreed that *Honest to God* was
'woolly', not likely to convince the intelligent, while the
simple would not know what it was all about, except that
it seemed to be taking their God from them. I hope you do
not mind my saying this; but, if it is to have any value,
discussion must be frank. *Honest to God* is the thinking
aloud—and interesting thinking it is—of a sincere mind
facing boldly fundamental issues as he sees them and trying
to suggest answers. And it has done something that is going
to be of great value; it has started 'the great discussion'. I
hope that you will continue to be part of it; for it is of
supreme importance.

I wonder if you will agree with me when I say that
Christianity is facing a crisis similar to that which it had
to face in its beginning when, in order to become a universal
religion for the Mediterranean world, it had to make its
peace with and take into itself the thought patterns, spiritual
and conceptual, of that world, and that without losing its
essential revelation. Now it is not the limited world of the
Mediterranean area, but the whole world, with its other
higher religions, some of them more spiritually aware and
more redolent of the divine compassion than conventional
Christianity is. Not only that, it has to face up to these new

... secularism is part of the essential work of reaching the new pattern of spiritual awareness. Side by side with it, or perhaps within it, is a vast resurgence of the Spirit. It is very evident in the more intelligent of the younger generation. But is the Church giving them the food they are crying out for, or speaking a language they can understand?

# IV

## SOME REVIEWS

### 1 · ERIK ROUTLEY

*Congregational minister and historian*[1]

I CANNOT write objectively or dispassionately about this. I can only record that the reading of it gave me more comfort, more encouragement, and more sense that life is worth living, and the ministry worth exercising, than any book I have read for years and years.

I was brought up in the days when a new orthodoxy seemed to be the only way of defending the faith. This orthodoxy was well stated, and soundly lived, by our teachers. It was perhaps a little dry and hot; but then there was a great deal of water to be evaporated out of the doctrine in which, before we met those teachers, we believed. We were taught to pay new respect to the ancient disciplines of prayer and liturgy and dogma. We would not have missed a word of that.

But we are now moving out of the age of neo-orthodoxy. We are ready now for a real restatement of our belief, having spent a generation reminding ourselves what the historic content of that belief was. I speak, of course, as a Dissenter. We were more vulnerable to the temptations, and receptive to the benefits, of neo-orthodoxy, perhaps, than were the Bishop of Woolwich's co-religionists. Well, we were at the time, anyhow. The things we had to repent of in English Dissent (and in the Church of Scotland, too, to a less extent) were very different from those which the Anglicans had to

[1] Reprinted from the *British Weekly* (21 March).

.........., John Mac-

... course Dietrich Bonhoeffer. We have in this great question a dogmatic meeting point in ecumenical Christianity which is established for the first time as such. On that ground alone we have reason to judge this an historic book.

What is the question we are all asking? Why, it is the question Bonhoeffer asked—and hardly answered (so that he has, by his untimely death, sowed what others must be privileged to reap)—'What is religion?' Honestly, what do we believe? Superstition apart, convention apart, custom and tradition and 'Hark, hark, my soul' apart, what is this thing which has been delivered to the saints?

Dr Robinson's task, then, is to expound this new idea of 'religionless Christianity'. He does it better than anybody has so far done it—and it has already been ably dealt with by Alec Vidler and Daniel Jenkins. But Dr Robinson goes further, and is more ruthlessly practical. His point of departure is our belief in God. In criticizing superstition here he shows a closer understanding of Wren-Lewis than has yet appeared in print. He goes on to argue in terms of what he calls 'A Depth at the Centre of Life'. This conception he substitutes for that transcendence which has led to so much anthropomorphism, and so much pantheistic vagueness. He here expounds Bonhoeffer's 'God is the beyond in the midst'. A Christological chapter follows which in itself is a classic; but this will have to be taken much further, and soon.

Then we come to 'Worldly Holiness'—and the section on prayer here (pp. 99-104) is one that I had to read walking up and down the room—such was its compelling sense of liberation. 'Prayer is the responsibility to meet others with all I have. . . . The matter of prayer is supplied by the world—that is why too rarefied an atmosphere may be harder to pray in as it is to breathe in.' Prayer and the Bible (another field of argument in this book) are two centres of religious hatred, superstition and wickedness. None of us has been brave enough to say so, but now that Dr Robinson has provided a reasoned diagnosis and a wise cure, we can. It is true. It will continue to be true: but we shall have less excuse now for accepting that state of things.

The consequences of all this are radical and revolutionary, of course. The Bishop says so. A *Bishop*! Well, Dr Robinson says that he may be thought heretical. I can see no point at which he comes within ten miles of heresy. But there is no paragraph here which does not demand revolution—the revolution of clear thinking, of shameless honesty, of what I have called before in these pages mental chastity. I hope a hundred thousand copies of this are bought, read and acted on. I am so partisan about it that I cannot write in any other terms.[1]

[1] In the *British Weekly* of 16 May, Dr Routley wrote: 'I still stand by what I said.' But when he wrote his review, five weeks before publication, he was 'firmly convinced that the sale would be the usual two or three thousand'. The Bishop's *Observer* article was 'unwise, presumptuous and liable to provoke endless misunderstanding', and 'I am pretty sure that a reading of the article first would have coloured my review of the book and made it considerably more cautious'. 'The Bishop of Woolwich may come to blush for the newspaper article; but if he has to repent about the book, I think that it is the technique rather than the doctrine which will be the ground of repentance.'

‑gn

... that the

... given in the art

... ᴗpecial hours and forms of

...ar use to him: he prayed best in

... ordinary occupations.

...verse reaction to times and seasons has come to
...colour much of his thought. No one could feel more keenly
the 'scandal of the particular'. All precise definitions, rules
and regulations with which we have hedged about our
spiritual life he clubs together under the disparaging name
'religion', and he dislikes religion as the enemy of true
spirituality. He does not say that these elements of precision
can never have been necessary. Indeed he thinks that the
Chalcedonian Definition, for instance, may have been
admirably suited to its age. But, now that we have arrived
at the period of 'adult man', we should be prepared to put
away childish things.

If we ask what has marked man's coming of age, it
is a little difficult to say. Unfortunately the Bishop's three
heroes are Bonhoeffer, Bultmann and Tillich, the three
theologians of the modern galaxy who are admittedly the
most difficult to understand. Indeed a good proportion of
the theological world is engaged in a wordy battle as to
what they do mean. However, if we may rush in where
angels fear to tread, the point of departure seems to be that
man no longer believes in a three-storeyed universe. When
Bishop Barnes used to insist that this demanded a revolu-

[1] Reprinted from the *Church Times* (22 March). See p. 127 below.

tion in theology, we used to laugh and say it did not matter. But to the present generation Dr Robinson thinks it matters a great deal.

His argument is as follows: The spacemen have searched the skies and have failed to find either the Christian heaven or the God who was supposed to dwell there. The result has been to make our traditional way of thinking of God as someone 'out there' quite outmoded. If we wish to keep in line with modern scientific thought we must think of God as someone 'in here' at the root of our being, or, better still, not as a being at all but as the ground of all being. It is believed that this will involve a radical re-thinking not only of Christian doctrine but also of worship and ethics. Worship will belong not to some special department of life, but to all life: to work is to pray as to pray is to work. Conduct will be regulated not by a set of rules given from outside, but by the need of love as the very spring of all our actions. However, just as it is necessary to retain the name God in spite of the erosion of the personal element in describing the divine existence, so the rules and regulations are maintained in spite of the blunting of their fine edges by emphasis on the exceptions.

To the Bishop all this comes home with the force of a new revelation. He will hardly expect the rest of us to be quite so moved. The few top-ranking scientists one has met would probably prefer the precision of traditional belief. Such theologians as do not yield to the general disparagement of mysticism would say that they already have the ground of being as well as the starry heavens within their purview. Historians faced with what purports to be an unusually liberal attitude on sex would remember that St Augustine in a particular set of circumstances argued for a charitable judgment many centuries ago. The man in the

of God. There is much still to be learnt, and a humble agnosticism is the mark of the greatest Christian thinkers. It will help us also to exercise greater charity in our application of conventional rules.

One hopes, however, that the Bishop will not find it necessary to continue girding at religion. On his own showing, to be honest to God means to be honest to our fellowmen. For the man in the street, as well as for the man in the pew, the word 'religion' stands for the best that he knows. Is it really honest to let him feel that he has got to get rid of it before he can come into vital contact with God? After all, Jesus, in spite of his revolutionary teaching, claimed that he came not to destroy the law but to fulfil it.

## 3 · BRYAN GREEN
### *Rector of Birmingham*[1]

THE wind of change has been blowing within the theological circles of all the Christian Churches. I am not referring so much to the mild restatements of Christian belief or to the new translations of the Bible in modern speech. Something much more radical and far more disconcerting has been blowing up, though very few ordinary Christian people have been aware of it.

[1] Reprinted from the *Birmingham Post* (21 March).

The new book by the Bishop of Woolwich seems likely sharply to focus attention upon what has been happening, and maybe will help to stimulate a much more radical and open examination of the Christian faith than has happened since the Reformation. It is an important book for two main reasons. First of all, it is written with humility. Secondly, Dr Robinson writes plainly and fearlessly. [A summary followed.]

I find this book stimulating and most challenging. As a theologian the writer is expressing some of the things which I as an ordinary parson who tries to be an evangelist have both thought in my own mind from time to time and have experienced very often in dialogues with fine and splendid people who are quite outside the Christian faith. Many people never discover what Christianity has to offer through apathy and sin; but there are others—and many more than we suspect—who are intelligent, sincere and moderately well-informed people who are hungry for a faith concerning the meaning of life and yet who simply cannot stomach or even begin to stomach the words and phrases we use when we try to express the Gospel. The Church still uses the terms of a pre-Copernican, pre-space and pre-psychological age.

The book will raise a hornet's nest about the author's head. He will undoubtedly be called a heretic and be attacked from within and without the Church, all the more because he is a bishop. I admire his courage and integrity and am glad he has written the book.

One point, however, disturbs me. The Bishop has written a dangerous tract published in a paperback edition. Anyone, whether equipped or not to understand it, can easily buy it and read it and they probably will in great numbers because of all the publicity and outcry resulting

from its publication. This ████████ ██████████ ████████
is not intended for everyone. ████████████████████████
and all well-educated laymen who are ████████████████
tianity. Other people may well be more ██████████████
helped by the tentative, exploratory, question-raising ████
of the book. Before a new restatement of the Christian faith
can be offered to ordinary men and women who are seeking
faith for daily living, a long theological task lies before the
scholars of the Christian Churches. Until then ordinary
Christians must use the old categories in their prayers and
in their preaching, allowing their lives to bear witness to
the truth.

## 4 · MAX WARREN

*Canon of Westminster, formerly General Secretary
of the Church Missionary Society*[1]

Do you know somebody who thinks quite hard, finds life
extremely difficult to understand, but who can make no
sense whatever of the Christian religion?—the nice man
next door who catches the same bus as you do each morning, the fellow at the office you sometimes have lunch with,
that chap at the works, a pal you meet at the pub—and, of
course, the feminine equivalent of all these?

With the best will in the world these folk just do not
understand what the Christian means when he talks about
God. Jesus is something of a mystery man, very wonderful,
but he lived a long time ago. The Holy Spirit—that just
does not register. The Bible—Sunday School stuff. Religion

[1] Reprinted from *The Bridge* (the magazine of the diocese of
Southwark) and from *Outlook*, a national supplement for parish
magazines.

—all right for those that like it, but it doesn't seem to fit into Telstar, automation or even *Emergency Ward 10*, though perhaps . . .

We all know people like this. And most of us feel a bit hopeless about doing anything about them from a Christian point of view, except being good neighbours, though that is an indispensable first step.

But the Bishop of Woolwich's new book will perhaps help some of us to meet some of these people. First, let it be said, this is an *honest* book. Dr Robinson, as we have learnt to expect, looks fearlessly at the real problems which the thoughtful man has about all religion, and about the Christian religion in particular. He also looks quite fearlessly at our Christian vocabulary, and he asks whether that vocabulary is good enough. It may be all right as a sort of religious shorthand for use among those who accept the Christian Faith. But can it be used to commend Jesus Christ to those who don't know our shorthand? That is an honest question. It calls for an honest answer by the reader. Dr Robinson burkes none of the difficulties.

Then, let it be said, this is a *gentle* book. That may seem a curious adjective to use about one of the hardest hitting books the reader is likely to have met.

Yet Dr Robinson remains all the time very gentle, very sensitive not only to those whom he is trying to reach but also to those Christians who will find his approach very disconcerting and puzzling, and who will not be able to follow him. For all that it is very powerful writing this is not a dogmatic book. All through it the reader will recognize that Dr Robinson is asking himself questions. He is an explorer.

Finally, let this be added, the book is fairly tough going. If you take it to bed with you it will either send you off

THE Bishop of Woolwich will disturb most of us Christian
laymen less than he anticipates. We have long abandoned
belief in a God who sits on a throne in a localized heaven.
We call that belief anthropomorphism, and it was officially
condemned before our time. There is something about this
in Gibbon. I have never met any adult who replaced 'God
up there' by 'God out there' in the sense 'spatially external
to the universe'. If I said God is 'outside' or 'beyond' space-
time, I should mean 'as Shakespeare is outside *The Tem-
pest*'; i.e. its scenes and persons do not exhaust his being.
We have always thought of God as being not only 'in' and
'above', but also 'below' us: as the depth of ground. We
can imaginatively speak of Father 'in heaven' yet also of
the everlasting arms that are 'beneath'. We do not understand why the Bishop is so anxious to canonize the one
image and forbid the other. We admit his freedom to use
which he prefers. We claim our freedom to use both.

His view of Jesus as a 'window' seems wholly orthodox
('he that hath seen me hath seen the Father'). Perhaps the

[1] Reprinted from the *Observer* (24 March). This article, like Dr
Mascall's which follows, referred to Dr Robinson's article of the
previous Sunday. The *Observer* also printed articles by Prof.
A. G. N. Flew and Sir Julian Huxley (referred to on pp. 131 and
154 below), and statements welcoming Dr Robinson's aim by two
distinguished London preachers, Edward Carpenter and T. R.
Milford.

real novelty is in the Bishop's doctrine about God. But we can't be certain, for here he is very obscure. He draws a sharp distinction between asking 'Does God exist as a person?' and asking whether ultimate reality is personal. But surely he who says yes to the second question has said yes to the first? Any entity describable without gross abuse of language as God must be ultimate reality, and if ultimate reality is personal, then God is personal. Does the Bishop mean that something which is not 'a person' could yet be 'personal'? Even this could be managed if 'not a person' were taken to mean 'a person and more'—as is provided for by the doctrine of the Trinity. But the Bishop does not mention this.

Thus, though sometimes puzzled, I am not shocked by his article. His heart, though perhaps in some danger of bigotry, is in the right place. If he has failed to communicate why the things he is saying move him so deeply as they obviously do, this may be primarily a literary failure. If I were briefed to defend his position I should say 'The image of the Earth-Mother gets in something which that of the Sky-Father leaves out. Religions of the Earth-Mother have hitherto been spiritually inferior to those of the Sky-Father, but, perhaps, it is now time to readmit some of their elements.' I shouldn't believe it very strongly, but some sort of case could be made out.

## 6 · E. L. MASCALL

*Professor of Historical Theology in the University of London*[1]

I AGREE with Dr Robinson that Christianity must show that it is 'relevant to modern secular man', but this means

[1] Reprinted from the *Observer*. See note on p. 91 above.

persuading se□
sec□

□, and
□ is not just a
□ but unending life of
□ happiness in and with God him-
□ other hand, Dr Robinson is right in saying
□ God is teaching us that we must live as men who can get on very well without him', then the Church has no need to say anything whatever to secularized man, for that is precisely what secularized man already believes.

Consistency is not Dr Robinson's strong point, for having quoted from Bonhoeffer that 'Christianity has been based on the premise that man is naturally religious', he goes on 'The corollary has been that to the non-religious it has nothing to say. A person had to become religious first . . . then Christ could come to him as the answer.' But if man was naturally religious, he would not have to become religious; he would be religious already. This is, however, merely one of Dr Robinson's odd pieces of reasoning.

'Our image of God must go,' Dr Robinson proclaims. 'Our whole mental image of God must undergo a revolution.' But what is this image? As he describes it, it is a mere caricature of anything that any intelligent Christian has ever taken literally. For the Biblical image of God 'up there', he tells us, modern Christians, under the influence of science, have substituted the image of God 'out there', though he admits that this was understood 'metaphysically' and not 'literally'. But what is he asking us now to abandon as 'more of a hindrance than a help?' Not just this crude image, but the belief that 'somewhere beyond this universe (is) a Being, a centre of personal will and purpose, who created it and who sustains it, who loves it and who "visited" it in Jesus Christ'. In its place he offers us the assertion, based apparently on no rational argument whatever, that 'the world, incredible as it may seem, is built in such a way that in the end personal values will out'. What is meant by asserting that God is personal is simply that ultimate reality is personal, and this is what the life of Jesus means. But whether this ultimate reality is anything more than the world itself Dr Robinson does not tell us, though his rejection of the images 'up there' and 'out there' suggests that it is the world itself, and nothing more.

Having rejected these two images, Dr Robinson shows a quite naive predilection for the equally spatial image of 'depth', which he thinks will appeal to modern man with his interest in depth psychology. Now every orthodox Christian writer from St Paul onwards has recognized that God is 'depth' as well as 'height', though with a less crude interpretation of depth than Dr Robinson's. He really ought not to ascribe this shattering discovery to Dr Tillich; he could have found it equally in St Augustine. And his demand for radical reformulations of doctrine, worship, ethics and evangelism may, as he says, be 'welling up from within', but I think it is not from within the Church but from within Dr Robinson's own psyche.

Much of what he says a theologian will recognize as platitude in the form of paradox; some of what he says, if taken literally, would make Christianity, in any sense that the word has ever held, altogether superfluous. Some readers will no doubt think that he has abandoned the Christian religion, but I do not think he is guilty of anything more than considerable confusion of thought. But when I

see at the head of h··
must go', I a··
presum··

··· (24 March)

··· to an Anglican bishop who does
···od? This, I hold, is the condition of the
··· Woolwich, as revealed in his paperback, *Honest
God*, and it raises, I maintain, a question of Church
discipline which cannot be shirked without the gravest
repercussions on the whole Anglican Communion.

The Bishop, of course, says that he is not trying to de-
throne God but to redefine him in a manner acceptable to
those who will not adopt the premises of the Christian
religion. He sets about the task in the familiar manner of
liberal theology: there is a great deal of ruthless analysis
appearing to lead to atheism but always stopped short at
the last minute by the invocation of that dependable *deus
ex machina*, the inscrutable mystery of the Christian faith.
In the end God pops up again—as a principle of harmony
at work in the universe, as 'Love', or as 'What we take
seriously without reservation'. As a person, however, he is
simply abolished.

Now, whatever this religion, it is not the Christianity of
the Nicene Creed, which consists of a number of crude and
precise historical statements about the respective activities
of the three members of the Holy Trinity. What the Bishop
requires of a Christian is not that he should believe that
Jesus was born of a virgin, crucified under Pontius Pilate

and rose again from the dead, but simply that he should believe that there is something 'sacred' at the bottom of human existence, that he should love his neighbour and that he should be indisposed to make absolute moral judgments such as are implied in the orthodox view that fornication is always wrong though often difficult to avoid.

The avowed object of the exercise is to make religion acceptable to the irreligious, to prove that it is possible to be in reality a Christian without believing in the teachings of the Church, and to accept God without using the word.

The Bishop writes with the authority not only of the Apostolic Succession but also with that of a witness for Penguin Publications in the case of *Lady Chatterley's Lover*. To that extent, what he says is liable to cause a degree of scandal which must raise the question of whether he can properly retain his office . . . [A comparison with Bishop Barnes and Dr Hewlett Johnson followed.]

Where, one must ask, will the ravages of liberal theology end? The Devil and Hell went long ago; the position of the Blessed Virgin has been seriously undermined; God, who until last week was invulnerable, is now distinctly on the defensive. What will ultimately be left except a belief in the need for bishops, if only to give evidence in trials about obscenity and to talk to pop singers on television?

The Church of England has always had a horror of heresy-hunting, stoutly holding that conformity in morals and worship is more important than the acceptance of agreed definitions of doctrine. Added to this is a new obsession, which appears to afflict the entire Episcopal Bench, with the importance of not appearing to be old-fashioned. Furthermore, there is really no way of getting rid of the Bishop of Woolwich except by prosecuting him for heresy, with an ultimate appeal to the Judicial Committee of the

Privy Council w̶

ment o̶

... of

... surely be

...om no deanery or

... is rendered more difficult

...ishop of Woolwich.

... the simple lessons that they were created

... sonal God to whom they will ultimately be account-

able, that they are commanded by him to do their best to live in chastity and charity, that by diligently seeking his aid in prayer and faithfully receiving His Sacrament they can find the power to obey His Will and eventually earn His Eternal Companionship—these traditionally are the Church's practical tasks. The aim of this teaching is to induce men to follow a particular discipline of life which clearly depends on the acceptance of certain historical assumptions about the truth of the Scriptures: these assumptions are now either denied or treated as irrelevant by the Bishop of Woolwich.

It is one thing to restate the eternal truths of religion in contemporary language and quite another expressly to repudiate fundamental doctrines which were believed by those who learnt Christianity from the lips of Christ. It is not always clear, indeed, whether the Bishop's aim is to convince agnostics that they can conscientiously go to church or to persuade Christians that there is no real need to do so. At the lowest, he seems to me to be violating the principles of honest commerce by trying to sell as Christian a commodity that bears no relation to the historical and accepted meaning of that word.

D

Can the Church of England, in the name of intellectual liberty, be content to allow its bishops to use the authority of their office, and by implication that of the Gospel, to support any trend of the opinion they happen to favour? I cannot see how, on this occasion, the Church can avoid the duty of facing the question squarely—yes, even at the cost of being thought 'square'.

## 8 · THE TIMES

### an anonymous review (4 April)[1]

'IN the English Church a man succeeds not through his capacity for belief but through his capacity for disbelief. Ours is the only Church where the sceptic stands at the altar, and where St Thomas is regarded as the ideal apostle.' If it seems a little unkind to quote Oscar Wilde against a bishop who is obviously well meaning, the justification must be the disturbance he seeks to cause sophisticated as well as simple Christian minds.

Dr Robinson maintains that scientific man has 'come of age' and can no longer believe in the mythological and supernatural framework in which Christianity is traditionally presented; its essentials must be salvaged and preached in a way acceptable to modern reason. The doubt is whether what he retains amounts to Christianity.

The trouble begins with his idea of God. Instead of a supernatural Being or Person with whom men can nevertheless be in relationship, God becomes for the bishop, as for Spinoza, 'ultimate reality'. Some of the classical Christian definitions of God sound little different, it is true, and

[1] © Copyright *The Times* Publishing Co. Reprinted by permission.

the Bishop's is at lea...
other mystical ex...
is this 'reali...
Bishop...
l...                                                                    ...es—
                                                          ...raditional
                                              ... space-trip and
                                           ... man'. All the same,
                                   ...rs', we see the true 'ground
                            ...Love, which is God, which is
                       ...us the central message of Christianity
                  ...e move on to its application in everyday life.
             ...here much which is common ground with many
      ...istians today. Personal relationships are the stuff of our
existence—'all real life is meeting' as Martin Buber said—
'we are rooted and grounded wholly in Love'.

Having disposed of God as a separate Being or Person,
Dr Robinson is in difficulties over many Christian activities,
including prayer. How does one pray to 'ultimate reality'?
There is a chapter on the matter, but it would take a wise
man to understand what the Bishop means. Traditional
Christian morality goes much the same way home. 'Nothing prescribed', says the Bishop, 'except love.' So to a young
man wanting to take a girl to bed, you do not say 'it's
wrong' or 'it's a sin', but 'do you love her?'. One gathers
that if he replies 'Yes', he still ought not to because he will
then 'respect her far too much to use her'. It is rather con-
soling to see how this most latitudinarian of bishops still
retains the old Protestant suspicion of fornication.

*Honest to God* is an odd title for a book assuming that the
Church of England may continue with a liturgy and creeds
which, if they mean anything, certainly do not mean what
they say. The old myths and imagery, Dr Robinson urges,

need to be discarded for they retain their 'numinous power'.
Bishops from their thrones may still look down on congregations saying 'Our Father, which art in heaven', hear the
priest intoning 'Therefore with angels and archangels', and
the words read out 'Thus saith the high and lofty one that
inhabiteth eternity . . .'. But they will know that in fact we
have no Father and that there is no heaven, no angels and
no archangels, while eternity is empty of inhabitants and
will not receive us. The picture is so bizarre that perhaps
the comment may be made of Dr Robinson that was made
of Auguste Comte: *Une religion sans Dieu! Mon Dieu,
quelle religion!*

## 9 · A. LEONARD GRIFFITH

*Minister of the City Temple, London,
in a sermon preached on Sunday 7 April*

I THINK it is a brilliant piece of work.[1] I admire him for
his outstanding work in the New Testament field of study.
I also admire him for the frank and fearless statement of
his own doubts and convictions. It takes courage for a
bishop of the Church of England to publish views which
he knows will draw fire from all sides, even within his own
Communion.

He will not expect unanimous approval when he dares to
concede the possibility that there may be times when the
way of love must end in marital divorce. He has returned
the most persuasive answer to Professor Carstairs who set
up the false dichotomy between chastity and charity; and

[1] The first half of the sermon, printed in full in the *City Temple
Tidings* (May), described the book, which 'can hardly be called
heretical'.

he does this by remind:
of charity becaus
exploit the
to th

...chani-
...kly examines
...s a re-awakening of
...evived churchiness but in
...ew initiatives of the Holy Spirit.
..., however, my main reaction to *Honest*
...ot so much that of criticism as that of concern.
...ot wish to be classed among the Bishop's 'critics'.
After all, he and I are fighting on the same side in this war.
At least, I think we are, and I hope the Bishop thinks so
too. I am concerned, however, that in recovering one important Biblical truth about God, it may have done so at
the expense of another important Biblical truth about God.
To be sure, Tillich, Bultmann and Bonhoeffer might replace the God 'out there' with a God 'in here', but they are
not the only prophets of Christianity in our age. Alongside
them stand other theological giants, men like Karl Barth,
Reinhold Niebuhr and Emil Brunner, who hold very firmly
to the traditional image of a God separate and distinct from
the world which he has made. These other theologians do
not deny that the ultimate reality and ground of all being is
God; to do so would be to deny some of the deepest insights of the Bible. They do believe, however, that this does
not exhaust the *whole* truth about God. They believe that
the nature of Deity is too sublime and mysterious to be
packaged in neat little definitions; and they insist that when
everything has been said about Jesus as the perfect revelation of the ground of our being, he still represents the in-

vasion of time by eternity. This has nothing to do with the dimensions of outer space; it is simply a means of saying what the Bible repeatedly says and what human experience proves, namely, that *God is not man*, that he stands over against man, creating him, providing for him, judging him and redeeming him. What really matters in this view is not what the Bishop thinks about God, but what God thinks of the Bishop.

It concerns me also that *Honest to God* may diminish rather than enlarge the Gospel. The author would deny this; he claims that his radically new interpretation of the Person and Work of Christ in no way impairs the fundamental beliefs and practices of Christianity. He has to work hard to prove his point, however, and in the end he leaves us with the impression that he has tried, not always successfully, to eat his theological cake and have it. This becomes strikingly apparent in his treatment of the Holy Communion. As a loyal Anglican he preserves the centrality of the Sacrament in the public worship and finds its meaning in a penetration of the secular by the sacred. But how can the Holy Communion be a means of grace to Christians apart from the meaning which Christ himself gave it—'My body and my blood'? Unless Christ did, in fact, accomplish something for our salvation on Calvary and unless the Communion be a re-enactment of the Cross, then why celebrate it at all; or why not serve cakes and caviar in place of bread and wine?

I think the Bishop takes too much for granted. Repeatedly he uses Bonhoeffer's phrase about 'man come of age', and though he explains in a footnote that Bonhoeffer did not equate intellectual maturity with emotional and moral maturity, especially in the Nazis who imprisoned him, yet the Bishop himself does not always make the

distinction. He leads us t...
grown up and there...
himself. Wou'...
situatio...
'r...

...ysical
...his attitude
...oy. A civilization
...on the moon and simul-
...king 'Freedom from Hunger
...zation come of age, capable of find-
...the means of its own salvation.

...I am concerned that while *Honest to God* may
...peal to a few intellectuals outside the Church, it may
prove a stumbling-block to many humble Christians inside
the Church. Whether it will actually impress the intellectuals remains to be seen. I find that atheists and agnostics
rarely respond to a 'recasting' of religious truth; and they
resent nothing more than being treated as unconscious believers. It is interesting that the author should refer to the
one sermon that Paul preached in Athens. It was the only
occasion when the Apostle tried to meet intellectuals on
their own ground, the only time when he started with their
presuppositions and moved on to a statement of the Gospel. Normally he began with the Gospel itself and preached
so persuasively that his listeners had to alter their presuppositions. Paul did not succeed in Athens; it was the
one major city in the ancient world where he failed to
sow the seeds of a Christian Church.

Any book must be evaluated not only for what it says
but for what people infer from it; and although the author
gives no grounds, there will be readers who infer that man
is his own God and that morally he has no higher authority

than himself. Unwittingly, this book plays into the hands of the French philosophers who declare that a thing is right because we make it right, or wrong because we make it wrong; but this is not consistent with the teachings of Jesus. To be sure, Jesus pointed to love as the fulfilment of the Law, but he also made it very clear that love does not abrogate a Divinely-ordained Law. In the New Testament love is a plus-factor, a higher order of morality to which his disciples move when they have obeyed the commandments of God—'Thou shalt not kill . . . thou shalt not steal . . . thou shalt not commit adultery'; and if obedience to God be the pre-requisite of love, then the world is no more ready to practise love now than it was in the pre-Christian era.

I am thinking about those people with whom we began, the ordinary citizens who appeared on the television screen. It is a serious thing to take away their image of God 'out there', a God who created us and cares for us, who sent his Son to redeem us, a God who answers prayer and to whom we go when we die. While Dr Robinson has served the Church as a scholar and more recently as a bishop, I have been a garden-variety preacher and pastor counselling people in their troubles, comforting them in their sorrows and helping them to face death unafraid. What new language must I now employ? 'The eternal God is thy refuge, and underneath are the everlasting arms'—symbolic language, to be sure, but how else mediate the comfort and strength of God to a patient about to undergo surgery? Many years ago, in a poor district of Aberdeen, a Unitarian minister preached to an open-air congregation a message that left out the saving Gospel of the Cross. A prostitute standing near by said to him, 'Your rope is not long enough for me'. At this season of the year, as we approach the

Cross and the Empty To⸻'
there' has let dow⸻
heaven to th⸻
wha† ⸻

⸻ᴅ BOULTON

⸻*.alist review* Tribune (*12 April*)

⸻ᴏɴ south of the Thames has become the Red Belt
of the Church of England. Mervyn Stockwood, Bishop of
Southwark, is mild enough himself but he enjoys the company of turbulent priests, and behind every other dog collar
in the pulpits under his charge you will as like as not find
a secret Aldermaston marcher, a furtive abortion-law reformer, or a militant campaigner for the Socialist Kingdom
of God. That is the environment in which Dr John Robinson, Suffragan Bishop of Woolwich (a division of Southwark), has written *Honest to God*.

The argument of the book has been muddied by the head-
line writers and satirists and it is necessary to state it
clearly. [A summary followed.]

Traditionally the bed-rock distinction between the Christian and the humanist position has been that the Christian's
system of thinking has centred on and drawn its authority
from a personal God, while the humanist's frame of reference has centred on what Tillich called 'the infinite and
inexhaustible depth and ground of all being', but conceived
of solely in human terms without recourse to the word God.
The crux of *Honest to God* is its attempt to show that this

traditional distinction is unreal. Having disposed of it, Dr Robinson has to find a new distinction. Humanism, he suggests, says 'love *ought to be* the last word about life', while Christianity says that 'despite all appearances it *is*', Jesus being the 'window' through which we see it in action.

The Bishop has burnt his boats. If this distinction cannot be made to stand up, then we have the spectacle of a humanist holding a bishop's office in the Church of England. And I am afraid it doesn't stand up. For to say with the humanist that love *ought to be* the last word about life is to imply that if we lived out the brotherhood of man everything would be all right. It is to say that love is the right relationship, the practical relationship between human beings, the only relationship which can overrule chaos.

Having rationalized and redefined God himself, the Bishop has to follow that process where it takes him. The prayers he reads each Sunday, traditionally thought of as communication with a personal God, have to be redefined as 'openness to the ground of our being' and 'unconditional love of the neighbour'. We are here perilously close to the sentimental meaninglessness into which Victorian modernism led, 'Each smile a hymn, each kindly deed a prayer', where words which once had well-defined meanings are stretched and redefined to such a point that they cease to mean anything because they have been made to mean almost everything. And that brings me to a final personal note.

Reading *Honest to God* was for me a moving experience because it describes a path I have walked myself—which is my only qualification for writing this review. I was brought up to accept orthodox Christianity. Prayer and worship were for a long time not only real but the most real things in my life. From my belief in a personal God stemmed the conviction which shaped my political atti-

tudes: that love, fellowsh...
will—was written i...
love *ought to* '...
I found ...
th...

............................................... ...ᴄn
............................................. ᵧ ɪs what

.......................... ...ᴎether it was useful
.............................. ...ᴎg of words as to change
....................... ..ɪnally render them unservice-
..................... ...ᴜt something clear and definite. So
..................... ..ᴜ 'prayer' and 'worship'. Was there any
................. ..ᵧ continuing to use the same words but giving
....... ..ᴏf them a special, private meaning? Was this not to
ɪnvite misunderstanding? To say 'God' instead of talking
about 'the depth and ground of history' was certainly to
save breath, but did not the word 'God' have so many
unwelcome associations that the longer term was actually
preferable?

To put the questions is to imply my answers. That is why
I am no longer concerned to inject new meaning into the
word 'God'. That is why I found my own attempt to be
honest-to-God made me cease to apply to myself the label
'Christian'.

## 11 · R. P. C. HANSON

*Lightfoot Professor of Divinity in the University of Durham
and Canon of Durham Cathedral*[1]

HONEST this book certainly is. It is not a stunt, nor the
attempt of a Bright Young Bishop to gain publicity, nor

[1] Reprinted from the *Irish Times* (16 April).

the diversion of a theologian who is anxious (as theologians sometimes are) *épater les bourgeois*. It is the transcription into pamphlet form of the doubts, conjectures, aspirations and half-formed prophecies of one who is deeply concerned for the Christian faith and entirely in earnest about his search for the right terms in which to commend it to men and women of the twentieth century.

Dr Robinson's manner of writing suggests that he knows what he is writing about, and there can be no doubt that his point of view chimes in with many notes struck in contemporary thought. He is deeply influenced by Bonhoeffer, Tillich and Bultmann and by the current flight from metaphysics in philosophy. At first sight he appears to be ready at the bidding of these authorities to abandon everything traditional in Christianity, dogma, prayer, Christian morals and even the belief in a personal God. But nobody who has read the book attentively to the end can continue to think this. In the course of a tentative exposition of a 'religionless Christianity' he puts all these things back again. It would be quite easy by selection of passages to represent the book as more atheistic than the work of Voltaire, but another selection could depict it as full of warm piety and strong faith. An honest book like this demands honesty in assessing it. Let the reader wrestle with the questions which it compels him to ask himself before he either condemns or approves it. [A summary followed.]

I suspect that at the critical point of his philosophical argument there lurks a confusion. This God is not 'outside' the world and is not a divine Being separate from it, yet he must be a Person, for how can love (which is his very essence) be anything but personal or experienced by persons? Dr Robinson never faces this dilemma. Again, a transcendence which is not 'outside' or 'above' our world, but part of it, withou

sophically *ersat*

Christian

tra

...n (pp.

...ommand the

... races the fact that

... and self-abandonment of

... and irresistible attraction is that

... of the sovereign God of the Old Testa-

...s in command of the world which he is redeem-

... We cannot apprehend the depth of the divine love displayed in the self-emptying until we apprehend the mightiness of the God who empties himself. Or is this mightiness merely 'primitive philosophically' (p. 33), and part of an obsolete myth, a 'superworld of divine objects'? Again, our Lord did not claim to reveal to us the love of the 'transcendental, the unconditional in all our experience' (p. 131), but of our heavenly Father. There is something slightly ludicrous in the Bishop's attempt to reduce God to 'the ground of existence' after the manner of Tillich, and then to insist that he is nothing but love. Dr Robinson will have to consider much more carefully what he means by 'love'.

The Bishop appears to be almost intoxicated with the thought of Bonhoeffer. We must honour Bonhoeffer as a martyr, but we must also remember that the Arians in the fourth century appealed for support in their heresy to the words of the martyr Lucian of Antioch. Bonhoeffer's theory, much admired by the Bishop of Woolwich, that man has now 'come of age' seems to me a silly and unprofitable one. How can we know whether the human race has come of age till we know for how long it is going to exist? Dr

Robinson appears to use this concept in order to maintain the autonomy of modern man, his non-dependence upon God. Has man, having come of age, ceased to be a sinner? Has he ceased to be limited and mortal? But if we admit the concept of sin (and presumably the Bishop would not abandon this) it is impossible logically to exclude from ethics the concept of law (and apparently the Bishop wants to do this). Once again, he ought to think more carefully about the meaning of the words which he uses.

Finally, will the Bishop succeed in commending the Christian faith by his new ideas? He may commend it effectively to intellectuals. But will this new approach appeal to the housewife in the housing estate, the trade-unionist in the factory, the railwayman on the footplate? Are people like these really concerned about images of God, or is their lapse from religion derived from a much deeper, more complex movement of society dating from the beginning of the last century and concerned with authority and freedom? This does not mean that the Bishop's re-appraisal should not be made, for the sake of honesty, but it is hard to envisage the book resulting in an upsurge of Christianity. It will, however, certainly result in a number of people asking themselves searching questions, and this alone should justify the publication of the work.

## 12 · CHRISTOPHER EVANS

*Professor of New Testament Studies in the University of London in a BBC broadcast on 18 April*

THERE is no need to introduce this book. It has introduced itself in a way no religious book has done for years. After all the talk about it—some of it, especially in the

Church newspapers
thing left to
basica<sup></sup>

...on.

...is, where

...nk I would say

...s of devotion. For all

...ings it says, this is where it

...sionately concerned with God, and

... of a book of devotion. When it says that

...t any longer think of God as 'transcendent' in the

...se of 'beyond' or 'out there', and that we must substitute for this what we can think—God as 'depth' and as 'the ground of our being'; when it says that we cannot think of Christ any longer as a divine visitor to earth from a supernatural realm, but that we must think of his divinity as consisting in this—that he was the man completely for others, that he was completely united to the ground of being, which is Love; when it says that the so-called 'religious' activities—prayer, worship, the pursuit of holiness—must not be ways of retiring from the world to seek God at the point where our own capacities give out, but should mean seeking God in the world in the total commitment of ourselves to others in love, and that Christian morality is this total commitment and not a number of laws laid down from outside by a divine law-giver; when it says all these things, it gathers together a number of protests of different origin and fashions them into a single passionate concern for God. The book is a *cri de coeur* against any tying up of our talk about God with outmoded views of the universe which the modern man cannot, with the best will in the world, adopt. And surely there is ample evidence that this cry finds an echo in the hearts and minds of many not only outside the Church but inside it.

But I would also put *Honest to God* among the books of devotion for another reason. Such books tend to be lop-sided. They are bound to be, because their authors feel so intensely what they have to say. Such books have to be put alongside one another so that they may rub off some of their lopsidednesses. Take, for example, one of the central points in the book, the point that we must now think of God in terms of depth and as the ground of our being. A reader could deduce from the book that this is a new idea, first thought of by the American philosopher Paul Tillich. It is, in fact, as old as the hills. If I take down from my devotional shelves another book—Professor Demant's book *A Two-Way Religion*— I find him writing as follows: 'Re-ligion has always been at its strongest when the usual ways of seeking God have been reinforced by another, namely the way of looking downward and inward through the depths of our own being. This way has a long history in the great religions, and Christians have adopted it.' Note that Demant says that religion is reinforced by this way, not identified with it. After all, phrases like 'depth' and 'the ground of being' are just as much symbols as words like 'transcendent', or 'beyond', or 'out there'. Now it seems to me that one set of symbols is strong where another is weak, and is weak where another is strong. Some are good for one thing, others for another. What the Church has always refused to do is to say—as this book tends to say—that this way is the only possible way for intelligent men. The Bible, I believe, uses a whole riot of symbols, and allows them to clash against each other, so that no single one of them shall dominate and capture us. If any one of them does capture the field queer things can happen. The

Bishop is so sure t¹
separate fr
wo¹

ρⱱⁿ,
...cans—and
...ueepest level per-
...ₜ ultimate significance in
...ₙverse'. Now it is odd, to say the
...ₙₒ have to assert the personal nature of
...guage as impersonal and abstract as that, rather
...ₙ by saying 'I believe in one God, the Father, Almighty,
Maker of heaven and earth'.

This is perhaps why I find the chapter on Prayer and
Worship—for all the good things that it has to say—somewhat disappointing. For prayer is the touchstone of thought
and language. We then have to open our mouths and
say something about God and to him. What on earth do we
suppose that we are doing, and what on earth is our language good for—any language, whether of height or depth?
This is an urgent question which we think about far too
little. This book may well help us to do it, provided that we
do not simply use it as an instrument for criticizing what is
traditional or even for criticizing ourselves, but that we also
exercise the same criticism on the book itself.

## 13 · GLYN SIMON
### Bishop of Llandaff[1]

I T is unfortunate that the majority of early comments on
this book must have been made without its having been

[1] Reprinted from the *Church of England Newspaper* (26 April).

read by their authors, for the modest first edition of some six thousand was sold out almost immediately. Now that the book is more generally available, it is apparent that much of the early comment was misdirected, and that it is the work of a scholar deeply concerned about the gulf that exists between Christianity as traditionally expressed, and the large numbers of men of goodwill who are accustomed to think. It does little to bridge the gulf between Christians and the larger numbers who do not think much but have difficulties of their own about it.

When the book first appeared, notices of it in the Press were accompanied by little quotations out of their context and obviously open to misunderstanding; it was also accompanied by a kind of summary by the Bishop himself in a Sunday newspaper which seemed to do his thinking rather less than justice. It can now be seen, however, that some of the confusion apparent in the summary is a reflection of that in the book itself.

For example, it remains far from clear in what sense the Bishop understands the word transcendent, nor do we know, despite more than one moving profession of his faith in Christ as 'the revelation . . . of the very heart and being of ultimate reality' what he really means by the phrase 'the Ground of our being', or why he prefers it to the term 'God'. He sees the pantheism which can result from his phrase; many of his readers will not be so clear-sighted. Again, the Bishop owes much to Lutheran theologians, particularly to Bonhoeffer and Tillich, with Bultmann in the background. The same query must stand against him as against them. Does he accept the events described in the New Testament as events which happened in history? What does he understand by the Resurrection? When one has finished 'demythologizing', what is left?

The Bishop is lavish
he uses them th
'the dog
of

was a

m of spiritual

ialistic stories from

this kind has always haunted the
men; is there not a danger when the
ts are treated as 'mythological', of our being
only with a theosophy? The Bishop is aware of this danger, and can combat it, but part of our trouble today is that the same words are used by different people to mean different things. To the ordinary man 'myth' does not mean what it means to Robinson, Tillich and Niebuhr, and here lies a real danger, for the 'ordinary man' in this context can mean almost everyone who is not a professional theologian.

Another word used in a special sense is the word 're-ligion'. Following Bonhoeffer, Dr Robinson uses it to mean something in which an individual is primarily concerned with himself, something in which 'God' is a 'Being coming in from outside to help'. It is something which is really a kind of separate department of life, pushed back more and more into insignificance by scientific discovery, and so forth. It includes 'all those activities which go on within the circle of the sanctuary, whether literal or metaphorical'.

Having developed in growing isolation, Christianity uses ways of thought and expression which make it more and more unintelligible to those not brought up in its increas-ingly narrow circle. The Bishop is rightly concerned about this. Christian images and ways of talking with non-believers need constantly to be re-examined. But there is nothing new about this concern. Five centuries ago an English mystic told us that 'Time and Place and Body should be forgotten in all spiritual working. For heaven ghostly is as near up as down, and down as up, behind as before, before as behind.' A thousand years earlier still St Jerome wrote roundly: 'Nonsense is often talked in the Church: for example, if anyone says that a throne is placed in heaven and that God really sits in it like an emperor and judge; and that the angels stand round to obey his word of command and to be sent on different missions, he is talking nonsense.'

The Bishop, then, is simply trying to discharge in our century a constantly recurring task of the Church. In doing so he has written a book which will be easily misunderstood and rouse great hostility. But in it is much to provoke thought and to challenge us to examine our attitude to the Gospel. Many of his phrases and paragraphs are provocative, some needlessly so, but they serve to arouse us to the detached triviality of much that passes for Christian faith and practice.

We find ourselves obliged to ask questions about things which we have thought and said and accepted for years, and when we try to answer them we find the Bishop's answers often ring more true than our own. This is particularly the case when he faces the question of the significance and meaning of Jesus. He sees the 'Incarnation' as meaning that 'The Life of God, the ultimate Word of Love in which all things cohere, is bodied forth completely, unconditionally and without reserve in the life of a man. . . . He is perfect man and perfect God . . . as the embodiment through obedience of "the beyond in our midst", of the transcendence of love'.

It is in terms of

prayer an

'

... p is . . .

...se to the world

...oint of ultimate concern;

...oves in the light of Christ's love;

...d the grace and power to be the reconciled

...nciling community.'

It will be seen, I hope, that I think this to be a book that ought to have been written. There is much in it, however, in addition to what I have suggested, which one is bound to disagree with. The chapter on 'The New Morality', for example, is particularly disquieting. One feels that a careful study of the troubles that befell St Paul in Corinth, as a result of misunderstanding of his teaching that the following of Christ meant freedom from the Law, would be profitable to the Bishop. It is likely that the Apostle would prove a better guide than D. H. Lawrence, that devotee of a religion far older than Christianity and still one of its principal rivals.

The book is one that will help many who find the language of the practising and devoted Christian unhelpful. But for all its sincerity and pastoral concern, I doubt if it will help the great 'unchurched' majority. For them, it is not so much the intellectual difficulties that matter as the spectacle presented by that 'organized religion' in which both Dr Robinson and I are involved. Bonhoeffer saw this clearly. 'The Church is her true self only when she exists for humanity. As a fresh start she should give away all her endowments to the poor and needy. The clergy should live solely on the free will offerings of their congregations, or possibly engage in some secular calling.' I believe this aspect of the Church's *practice* counts in the end for more estrangement from her than the theological and intellectual difficulties which this book is concerned with, and it is one harder to face. Dr Robinson does not face it. Instead he confronts it with a debunking quotation from Dr Vidler: 'It is consistent with accepting Bonhoeffer as a prophet for our times to acknowledge that, like other prophets, he saw things too much in black and white.' Here speaks to the prophet the age-old voice of establishment. It is possible that this is how the rich young man saw the challenge of Jesus to forsake all and follow him. It is possible that it is here, more than anywhere else, that we may see the challenge to the Church which Dr Robinson serves today.


## 14 · JAMES ROSS

*in* Shire and Spire, *the newspaper of Coventry Diocese* (May)

WHEN I was a child I suffered from the distressing complaint of overhastiness, and although the increasing pile-up of the years has brought a mollifying influence to bear on this disease, I still have to acknowledge the mortifying fact that I am not yet free of it. For it is both annoying and a blow to one's precious ego to realize that one has been overhasty in an initial appraisal of one of the most controversial books of this decade . . . *Honest to God.*

In that initial appraisal, having read the critics, the correspondence columns and numerous articles, and having heard dozens of forcible—and mainly highly indignant—views propounded on the book, I came to the conclusion

that here was another of
by equally objecti
to the Bish
SCM

 as

 on why he

 e Church of Eng-

 found myself forced to swallow

 ceived notions. When I first opened

 a, my anger at de-bunking bishops rattled on

 ine thirty or forty pages. Then it wilted, and before
I was half way through the book it gave its death rattle!
For whatever else he has done, Dr Robinson, with deep
conviction and sincerity, has tried to put into terms which
modern, non-religious man can understand precisely what
St John records of Christ's teaching in Chapters 14 and 15
of his Gospel.

In a recent television broadcast the Archbishop of Canterbury said that Dr Robinson was building his theses on a
'caricature of Christianity'. That, I think, is true, and it is
such a presentation of the Church and Faith today which
seems to have upset people most. And not just those stalwart
churchgoers who do tend to cling to a somewhat remote
image of God, but a great many intelligent, straight thinking
Christians, who have worshipped a very real conception of
God, as the ground and root and depth of their whole being,
from childhood onwards. But, while acknowledging that it is
a pity to upset people, especially in the things they hold most
sacred, surely the point to be remembered is that millions
of other non-churchgoing, non-'religious', ordinary, decent
people, who are neither very good nor very bad, see in the

outward life of the Church only that caricature, and have no conception of what real Christianity is. For although the message of Jesus Christ—the Gospel of Love; the Kingdom of Right Relationships, as I have so aptly heard it called—has always been the root of the teaching of the Church, it has so often been overlaid by frills and furbelows (both Catholic and Protestant varieties!) that that message has simply failed to come through. As a convert to Christianity of only eight years' standing, I can state quite simply that it was the 'religiousness' of the Church which not only kept me clear of it for the major part of my life, but made me unwilling and unable to learn what it was really all about. And that is what Dr Robinson is trying to do in this generation.

No matter how repugnant or revolutionary some of his ideas may seem (and when examined thoroughly they are not very much of either), he is trying to help the indifferent and the seeker alike to see beyond the conventions and traditions, beyond the beauty of words and music; beyond the loveliness of services and buildings, to the pure, all-pervading, ever-present love of God in whom and with whom we have our being. [A summary followed.]

Whether it is the chapter dealing with the Christmas story, or the one on The New Morality, there is much to upset, and which seems very like the tearing down of precious . . . even holy things. But, for all that, I think the honest reader will see that Bishop Robinson is a very far cry from trying to tear down our Christian Faith. He is merely trying to undergird that faith, to sweep through the mass of externals—a few of them quite useless ones—with which we have surrounded our Lord and our God, and to spotlight the truths which are very far from modern. I believe that a book and controversy like this current one

can only be produ
are alive. I

···g. For
··· truths of the
···se truths can be de-
···images of God many people
···their minds, nor by the scrutiny of such
···kers as Dr Robinson.

## 15 · ALEC GRAHAM

*Fellow and Chaplain of Worcester College, Oxford*[1]

HONEST TO GOD is an attempt to help us discover the one thing needful. We may disregard some of the Bishop's Aunt Sallies; it is hard to believe, for instance, that many Christians really do think of divine transcendence in spatial terms: we recognize that hymns which speak of Jesus 'far above yon azure height' or as a 'a Friend for little children above the bright blue sky' express in terms of spatial distance what we should prefer to put in terms of spiritual otherness. Furthermore, few, if any, communicants really do think of God as 'out there' beyond the east end of the church rather than as powerfully active in the Eucharistic action. But it would be foolish for us to let ourselves be irritated by these Aunt Sallies, for if we sit at the Bishop's

[1] Reprinted from the *Cowley Evangelist*, the journal of an Anglican religious order, the Society of St John the Evangelist (May).

feet, we may hear him reminding us of disturbing truths which it is comfortable for us to forget. We sometimes hear complaints that there is no open vision in our day, but perhaps at last we are witnessing a rebirth of prophecy, and we should be careful not to quench it before its disquieting message can make us once again aware of the one thing needful.

The Bishop reminds us that we should not think of God as a Person or a Being. We might go one step further and remind ourselves that when we talk about 'Three Persons in One God', we certainly do not use the word Person in the way in which we use it in everyday speech. Again, the Bishop reminds us that the Chalcedonian Definition does not exhaust or explain the mystery of the person of the incarnate Lord. It is unlikely that the fathers of Chalcedon themselves ever thought that it did, but it is just as well for us to be reminded that we cannot explain the mystery of his person in fifth-century terminology, or, for that matter, in twentieth-century terminology. There was at least a generally accepted philosophical terminology in the fifth century, which is more than can be said for the twentieth century, but no human terminology can ever adequately do justice to the mystery of the Lord's person or to the mystery of the threefold being of God. Those who have met and known the living God on their knees and in their lives have always recognized this. In Isaiah we read 'My thoughts are not your thoughts, neither are your ways my ways, saith the Lord. For as the heavens are higher than the earth, so are my ways higher than your ways, and my thoughts than your thoughts.' Augustine tells us that 'the supereminence of the Godhead surpasses the power of customary speech': therefore we say something only lest we say nothing. Some of the Eastern fathers were even apprehensive about saying

that God is one, for ...
about him ...
must ...

... e . . .'

...es of love and
... its difficulties, for if
...u say what is the exact point
...y particular analogy, we find that we
...ifficulties and that we can do no more than
... that God may be said to be like us in such and such
respects, but that his ways and thoughts are so far removed
from ours that we cannot be any more precise. Of course
we possess and have to use the commonly accepted Trinitarian and Christological formulae, but the Bishop has
caused us to look at them again and to think about them.
He has made us ask ourselves whether orthodoxy in the
generally accepted sense of the term is the one thing needful which it is so often supposed to be, or whether it may
well in fact be for some of us a convenient line of least
resistance which saves us from coming face to face with all
sorts of difficulties concerning the nature and grounds of
faith.

Again, the Bishop reminds us (and we can never be reminded of this too frequently) that prayer and worship are
not activities separate from real life and that living and
praying are not two activities which should be carefully
prevented from meeting. It is true that some people nowadays treat the church and its worship as an escape from
the hard demands of life, and no doubt some people have
done this in every age; so it is important for us to be
reminded that the one thing needful is not the mere ob-

servance of religious duties. The classic example of the man who thought that the outward performance of his religious duties was the one thing needful is the Pharisee in the parable of the Pharisee and the Publican, but if we find ourselves saying, 'Of course, I'm not like the Pharisee', then the time has come for us to realize that we are. Most of us probably need to hear again and again the Bishop's message that we must not compartmentalize the sacred and the secular, religion and life, worship and work. Probably many of us need to take seriously to heart the prophetic message which is now being ever more loudly proclaimed that worship so far from being the one thing needful can be an activity which prevents us from meeting and responding to the active, living God, who all the time stands over against us and seeks to elicit from us the response of self-giving trust.

But it is not only the one thing needful in belief and worship which the Bishop tries to lay bare for us: he also recalls us to the message of the Summary of the Law as the basis of all Christian conduct. Just as he would not let us take refuge in credal definitions or in formal worship, so here he will not let us be content with rules for Christian conduct: a Christian's behaviour cannot be adequately prescribed by rules any more than God can be adequately described in words. All along the line, in matters of belief and worship and conduct, the Bishop reminds us that the rules of thumb are no more than rules of thumb, and we must be careful not to place our reliance on these rules instead of on him who stands behind them and above them.

One feels that the Bishop might well have gone further and reminded us how many other familiar landmarks give the Christian only a rough indication of what he should be believing or doing. He might well have drawn our attention

...unou
...uch suffer, what do we
... of original sin, then we have to realize
...at in the long run we cannot be content with any of the answers which are conventionally given, for at long last Christians are learning a little humility and they are not quite so ready with all sorts of speculative answers. It is only when we see or experience suffering that we can find any answer to some of these questions, but we do not find it in terms of a neat formula which we can hand on to other people and which they can correctly pass on to others. For some people it is only beside the cross that any answer at all is possible to the insoluble problems of life, and even then the answer will not be capable of proper expression in conceptual terms.

Perhaps we are reminded of Bishop Lightfoot's statement, 'I find that my faith suffers nothing by leaving a thousand questions open, so long as I am convinced on two or three main lines'. One of these main lines must be that in the New Testament we read of One who calls us to be his followers and seeks from us the response of self-giving trust, that this trust admits us to a close relationship with him (which, like all relationships between people, cannot be adequately described in words and in which there must be many questions left open) and that this trust needs to be constantly renewed and kept supple by repeated acts of self-giving in prayer, sacrament and action. Of this self-giving the action of the lad in St John's account of the feeding of the 5,000 is perhaps typical: his gifts seemed insignificant by comparison with the crowd's need, but he surrendered them to Jesus, who used them in a totally unexpected way. Is not this the one thing needful? Not merely to sit at Jesus' feet and hear his word, but surrender oneself wholly to him, to be completely devoted to him as no doubt was Mary, the sister of Martha. But the act of devotion at Jesus' feet is not all there is in this act of self-surrender, for in it is included the surrender of our time and money and ability to meeting human need, to obeying the imperative of the parable of the Good Samaritan. And if we prefer, as the Bishop of Woolwich does, to act first and to withdraw in prayer afterwards, who can say we are wrong? Our devotion in prayer and our devotion in action are equally components of our worship and self-surrender: properly speaking, they should be indistinguishable from one another: *laborare est orare*, and *vice versa*. Perhaps the one thing needful is as simple as that, and the Bishop of Woolwich has done us all the service of reminding us of it.

## 16 · F. GERALD DOWNING
*Lecturer at Lincoln Theological College*[1]

NORMALLY in this country, theological currents pass through many transformer stations before they reach 'lay' homes; and in many places, such stations have never been built, or if built, they have fallen into disrepair. And there are many Luddites who applaud this state of affairs, for

[1] Reprinted from *Prism* (May). The same issue contained other articles on the book.

... ...... very high tension indeed, and
your dangerous act may by-pass the natural and artificial
resistances, and produce a glad and warm light.

Apologies for the cumbrous allegory—especially if the
physics are incorrect.

There are now two ways of evaluating this book. Because it has broken through the normal channels, just to
look at it for its academic value, its consistency and so on,
and just to gauge its likely usefulness, is not enough. What
effect has it had, even at the time of writing? It received
welcoming reviews from Jack Lucas in the *Daily Herald*,
and from Christopher Driver in the *Guardian*. It was received with cold disapproval by the *Daily Mail*, which
asked the obvious question, 'Ought this man to be a
Bishop?', and this was the only outside comment quoted
by the *Church Times*, for whom it was 'the national press'.
Here Bishop Wand's comments were rather saner, if
shallow; but the editor obviously disapproved of this
'charitable review'. The best review, I think many would
agree, was that by F. W. Dillistone, *Sunday Times*,
24 March.[1]

Comment in the *Observer* elicited from leading churchmen was varied, and (this confessedly) not always fully in-
formed; but this was only representative of the wider public

[1] A favourable summary of the Bishop's argument, with a question about the effect of social attitudes on the individual's attitude
to God, morality, etc. (Ed.).

reaction. There was a huge response based only on garbled reports in papers, and hurried interviews on television. The inaccuracy of the impression may be judged from some letters in the *Daily Herald*, 22 March. 'I share the ideas of the Bishop of Woolwich . . . That is why I am not a member of the Church of England.' 'The Bishop would be completely at home in the Unitarian Church.' 'Spiritualists . . . have been giving teaching similar to that of the Bishop for many years.' 'Most Salvation Army officers and soldiers would say "Amen" to the Bishop's views, as quoted, on the redemptive death of Jesus.'

These representatives of varied religious traditions may be right, and I may have long been misunderstanding them. But I think that the initial publicity has given a confused picture. Only if it results in the book being read and thought about will it in this way become a 'good book'. But if this is the result, it may be a very good book indeed.

The book has shorted the usual circuits; but the fuses down at consumer level look as if they will hold. In the book, then, John Robinson writes for those who seek to *live* as Christians, but for whom tradition has provided no usable words to express or to focus their Christianity. He writes for those for whom atheism is the only genuine possibility in the face of the unmeaning and even plain moral inadequacy of much Christian talk of God; whether their atheism be relieved or reluctant. He writes for ordinary Christians who would come to terms with a secular culture, which is the culture of the real world, the world as it is.

He would abolish the supernaturalism that relegates the divine to an easily avoidable, because quite irrelevant, realm that is half-physically, half-symbolically 'out there'. He would discard a theology that (by its devotion to imagery dr...

...

...to be honest to the
... *really* believe? Is your faith
...and today; or is it a mummy that would
...to dust if you stripped off the tattered bandages
that seem to surround it—the protective layer of people
afraid, clergy entrenched, and the good-natured tolerance
of *de mortuis nil nisi bonum*?' [A summary followed.]

The sheer life and light that come from reading the theologians quoted here (and the others to which they in turn
introduce you) have been too long confined to universities
and theological colleges. 'It would not do for the fifth form.
Still less would it go in the parish.' Even if you disagree
with the book, even if everyone found it was largely wrong;
if it does let these ideas break out of the few specialized
circuits they run round in this country, it will be very good.

But when all this is said, to be honest I must confess
that as a 'recasting' of the Faith, I think the book fails. It
fails because it tries to pit only the strongest sectors of Paul
Tillich's new religion against only the weakest sectors of
traditional Christianity. The hymnals, for instance, contain
the immanence of *Saint Patrick's Breastplate* as well as the
absentee transcendence of *Come down, O Love Divine*.
Again, it is possible to distrust the community's *account* of
its prayer, without refusing to trust its practice; and the
practice starts to suggest a better and quite realistic ration-
ale, if you maintain it.

But it is the brave effort to combine so many modern

E

theologians that brings the most serious failure. On p. 86, note 2, Dr Robinson tries to clear up the difficulty that arises when Paul Tillich seems very much in favour of 'religion', and Dietrich Bonhoeffer would discard it. We are told that Bonhoeffer's is a 'narrower sense', and that this sort of religion Tillich would not countenance either.

But this is not true, even for passages quoted from the two in the text of the book. Bonhoeffer is allowed to say on p. 36: 'Christian apologetic has taken the most varying forms of opposition to this (modern) self-assurance. Efforts are made to prove to a world thus come of age that it cannot live without the tutelage of "God". Even though there has been surrender on all secular problems, there still remain the so-called ultimate questions—death, guilt—on which only "God" can furnish an answer. . . . Thus we (clergy and theologians) live to some extent by these ultimate questions of humanity. But what if one day they no longer exist as such, if they too can be answered without "God"?' And there could hardly be a greater contrast with the passages from Tillich quoted later (pp. 79-82): 'We always remain in the power of that from which we are estranged. The fact brings us to the ultimate depth of sin: separated and yet bound, estranged and yet belonging, destroyed and yet preserved, the state which is called despair. . . . Grace strikes us when we are in great pain and restlessness. It strikes us when we walk through the dark valley of a meaningless and empty life . . .' Dr Robinson noted that Bonhoeffer did not find Rudolf Bultmann's 'demythologizing' adequate in the modern situation (p. 36). He could have noted that Bonhoeffer also found it necessary to reject the efforts of Tillich, and I think the latter's post-war theology is similar enough to make the remark relevant: 'Tillich set out to interpret the evolution of the world

...who would have everything religious, and would wait for a man to grow weak so that he might talk to him; and Bonhoeffer who expected 'an entire absence of religion', and if he spoke Christian ideas at all, would want to speak to a man in his strength, at the centre of life—not on the edge of despair, where I guess he would just have cared for him. When Tillich says the word 'God' is too meaningless to keep using, he goes off and talks at length in other terms; Bonhoeffer prefers silence.

In effect, Dr Robinson prefers Tillich. Is he right to? He wants to talk to modern man; he wants to talk truth. Now obviously, Tillich does get through to some, and deserves to, for his sympathies are with the whole of modern man's life. But I venture the guess that Bonhoeffer was right, and that in the main modern man is interested in, if you will, 'penultimate' things, not 'ultimate'; he does not even find language about 'the ground of being' that is 'beyond being' sufficiently clear to be able either to agree or disagree with Tillich. He just does not know what Tillich is saying. Julian Huxley in the *Observer*, 31 March, was right to call this language 'semantic cheating, and so vague as to be effectively meaningless'. A similar impression can be traced in various ways in a symposium, *Religious Experience and Truth*, ed. S. Hook (Oliver and Boyd, 1962). Although Dr Robinson is right to suggest that much linguistic analysis of talk about 'God' has been concerned with peripheral examples, Tillich's translation into abstract categories is no help at all. It is just as vulnerable, some think more so. The linguistic philosopher represents 'the modern man' and, by and large, he can make no sense of Tillich. This means, too, that Tillichian theology is no real defence against a naturalistic humanism (as contributors to the symposium quoted above make clear). The *impression* that Tillich gives is of an atheistic idealist naturalism based in the last century, with frequent purely formal, verbally confusing protests that this is not what he intends. This is the *impression* he gives. He may be on to real, Christian truth of 'God' and 'the universe', but he just has not yet found convincing ways of showing most Christians or most non-Christians that this is so. For the time being, his ontology, his abstract defence of 'transcendence', is too unsure a horse to back, especially in a popular book.

Of course, Tillich has much else to say that is good, true, and useful; and of course we would gratefully pay the same tribute to Dr Robinson's book. But (irrespective of the still debated question of the 'truth' of Tillich's position), it is unlikely for the present that the ontological mysticism that Dr Robinson accepts from Tillich as the 'theological' substance of the book will appeal to more than the few who are only at home with abstract thought. It is not 'childish' to think pictorially; it is a constant feature of the mental life of a certain proportion of people, intelligent or dim, adult or child. A large proportion can think either way (graphically or abstractly). But then (at least for most) to talk of an abstraction 'loving', to talk of 'love' exercised by one who is not 'a being' does not say anything at all. The word 'love' is completely evacuated of meaning. Every attempt to make 'God' 'more than personal' succeeds only in making him (it?) less; impersonal, an object, and so, unable 'to love' or 'to be love'. In one quite frequent sense

of 'myth' (any no
we attemp

⠿⠿⠿ religion' without
⠿⠿⠿ ...ity' without 'religion'. It
⠿⠿ or the latter (rather than Tillich,
⠿⠿, Huxley) that may become meaningful
⠿⠿ man. For the moment, most Christians do want
⠿⠿ retain some sort of myth, pictorial or abstract. The one thing that they are likely to find difficult is holding to either sort while believing it untrue. The reviewer must admit that he does believe the traditional pictorial and dramatic 'myths' of Christendom 'true', while hoping to be able to interpret them as Dietrich Bonhoeffer proposed, in a totally 'secular' way.

And this may be the way the Bishop would really have us go; for he makes it clear that the test for worship—and so, we may deduce, for any other activity of Christians among themselves, including thinking and theologizing—is 'how far it makes us *more sensitive* . . . to the Christ in the hungry, the naked, the homeless and the prisoner' (p. 90). This *is* a secular interpretation, if the words we have omitted are left unsaid.

As a theological statement (even as a theological reconnoitre), the book probably fails. It is not so much that (as the Bishop thought might be) it is 'not radical enough', though that too may be true; it is that it is not radical in the right direction. Yet as a stimulant, as a programme for action, widely accepted, it would be tremendous.

## 17 · RUDOLF BULTMANN

*Emeritus Professor in the University of Marburg*
*from an article in* Die Zeit (*10 May*)[1]

IN view of what is often being hastily said (in Germany at any rate) by those who mistake the real point of the book (even when they have not read it!), it seems to be necessary to present his ideas in rather more detail.

We must speak with a new understanding about God and about the truth of his actions as attested in the Bible and proclaimed in the Church. The mythological language of the old tradition must be demythologized. One may say that for many people, especially for German theologians, the author's intention, and often its achievement in detail, are not new. Nor does he make any such claim, for he continually appeals, with ample quotations, to his precursors, especially Paul Tillich and Dietrich Bonhoeffer, as well as to the Scottish theologian Ronald Gregor Smith and, although not without critical reservations, to my attempt at demythologizing. Yet it seems to me very unjust when German voices, as far as they have come to my knowledge, say rather lightly, 'Nothing new for us!' For the book deserves all respect as evidence of an attempt to wrestle with the problems involved in the situation, and the author is entitled to ask us to consider his ideas conscientiously. And is our situation really so enlightened, and have the relevant problems been so finally solved, that there is no need for them to be constantly thought out afresh?

Now in what, according to Dr Robinson, does the 're-luctant revolution' consist?

[1] Translated by Frank Clarke. Other articles from *Die Zeit*, and fresh critiques in German, are being published by Reich Verlag, Hamburg. Eberhard Bethge introduces the German edition (Chr. Kaiser Verlag, Munich).

...spiritually or meta-
physically out there'). Both these conceptions, however,
have this in common, that they separate God and the world,
and think of God as a 'separate entity', whose relation to
the world does not belong to his own essential being. But
that now is the revolution—a transformation of the image
of God, in which the contrast between world and God,
between the here and the beyond, is overcome. That means
at the same time that man's relation to God is not a specifically religious one in which man turns away from the
world. God must be grasped—as the author likes to say in
Tillich's terminology—as the depth and ground of all being
(that is how it must probably be formulated, though it is
sometimes uncertain precisely how Dr Robinson understands 'being').

Does that mean that the idea of transcendence, which is
indeed essential to the idea of God, is abandoned? By no
means! Just as Dr Robinson is against supranaturalism,
so he is against naturalism—shall we say Huxley's? But the
transcendent must be understood afresh beyond supranaturalism and naturalism, namely as the Beyond in our
midst, as Dr Robinson likes to formulate it after Bonhoeffer. God must be discerned as the Unlimited in the
limited. This experience is not specifically religious, however positively it can be expressed in religious language. It
can be had in the consciousness of what claims one as an
unconditional obligation, in the consciousness of 'the

ultimate concern' that moves him, of something to which he can give himself without 'reservation'—and, I would add, of the most sinister and alarming thing that may terrify him.

Of course, Dr Robinson is not so naïve as to suppose that a man could be brought by intellectual argument to a belief in the depth and ground of his being. For the existence of God as the ultimate reality there can in the nature of things be no argument. But a man can be called to consider what it is to which he feels himself to be under unconditional obligation; he can be asked what is the ultimate concern which motivates him, consciously or unconsciously.

This can be illustrated from two sides:

1. It is obvious that this existential knowledge of the depth and ground of all being may be contained, and as it were concealed, in all the traditional conceptions of God. Those who cling to them can be quite content to go on doing so, provided they do not imagine that in the conceptions as such they already have an existential relationship to God.

2. It is just as obvious that the existential relationship to the depth and ground of all being may be alive even in those who reject all conceptions of God—and therefore in atheists. They may in certain circumstances be regarded as better Christians than those who call themselves Christians. Thus Dr Robinson, varying a well-known passage from Paul (I Cor. 9.20, 21), can venture to say: 'I am prepared to be an agnostic with the agnostic, even an atheist with the atheists.' The relationship to God is not identical with religion, whether it is the Christian religion or any form of religiosity.

But, one will ask—and Dr Robinson has been asked—does that mean that 'God' is only a metaphor? Is the Christian image of God out of date in the sense that we must no long~~~

Rob~~~

~~~line of
~~~erstanding Jesus
~~~an for Others', the deepest
~~~ed as love, that is as God himself. I
~~~u, that Dr Robinson could have carried out his
~~~ention more convincingly if he had considered the Christian belief's assertion of the paradoxical identity of a historical event with the eschatological event. But in his book the eschatological theme, which is so decisive for the New Testament, plays no part; and consequently he does not see in the Church an eschatological phenomenon, with Christ present and speaking to it.

But I entirely agree that the Church with its worship must not be a separate sphere of religious matters partitioned off from the world, a place reserved for what is sacred. Rather is the 'common', everyday life in its depth, the dwelling-place of what is sacred. It is certainly legitimate that in the everyday world we use worship and prayer for 'withdrawal' or 'disengagement' from everyday things, but this is right only if a dialectical relationship exists between 'engagement' and 'withdrawal'. Prayer, and participation in the organized religious life of the Church, must not be a flight from 'this world' into the 'other world', but must be brought into an organic relationship to daily life; and in such a function they have their positive meaning. The whole life of a Christian is lived in such a dialectic, as it is at the same time a life of unconditional dependence on God as well as a life in freedom; it is a life at a distance from God which must not be misunderstood as merely the distance from 'another world'. 'Ultimacy' and 'intimacy' form a unity. This seems to me to characterize very suitably the paradox of Christian existence.[1]

[1] Since *Honest to God*, p. 25, referred to a letter which Dr Bultmann wrote to the Sheffield Industrial Mission about the Gospel (*kerygma* in Greek), part of the letter is reprinted here from *Prism* (June, translated by Michael Jackson).

'By nature men live by their own will and want to achieve their security by their own power. That is what the NT calls sin. For the basic sin is not the breaking of moral commandments (this follows from the basic sin), but man's self-will and his intention of trying to live by his own wisdom and power. Need for acceptance also belongs to the life of man, and by nature man tries to satisfy this need for acceptance through his own power.

'The grace of God is grace for the sinner. The *kerygma* tells the natural man (which we all are) that he can only find his security if he lets go his self-security and that he can only find acceptance if he lets it be given by God in the knowledge that without God he is nothing. The grace of God releases him from all feverish searching for security and from all resentments and from the complexes which grow out of an unsatisfied need for acceptance.

'Since the *kerygma* demands the surrender of all human self-will and of all self-security, the *kerygma* of the grace of God seems to the natural man to be primarily a stern demand, an "offence", a stumbling block. For to abandon himself to the grace of God means in fact that man must be ready to trust in the grace of God amid all the blows of fate, in all suffering. That is why the *kerygma* of the grace of God is at the same time the *kerygma* of the Cross.

'While the *kerygma* demands the surrender of self-will it also demands at the same time *love* of the other, of the "neighbour". For love means to live for the other, at the same time surrendering one's self-will and being ready to sacrifice one's self-security for the other. The surrender of self-will to God occurs in actual life through loving one's neighbour.

'To such surrender to the grace of God and to the neighbour, the *kerygma* promises freedom, power and life. If man gives himself up to the grace of God he is released from all anxiety for himself and his security, and in such freedom he gains a quite new power; for he gains along with it a new *hope*.

'Together with the cross the resurrection is proclaimed. This means that the man who trusts in the grace of God, and who lets go all anxiety about security, is also freed from all fear of death. He knows that he is not the one who has to worry about his future. God takes care of it; God gives him his future and therefore God's grace encounters him even in death. We cannot of course form any clear picture of a life after death. Yet it belongs to the radical surrender to God's grace that we renounce all pictures of a future after

18 · THE

ex...

...nt that
...ave way high

...mounting in terms of pages to
...ook, are concerned in the main with
...od. Dr Robinson, following the contemporary
...can theologian Paul Tillich, begins by describing as the 'supranaturalist' image of God the notion of God as a being in some way spatially situated above the physical universe—'God up there'—or (its historical successor) the idea of God as a special being at the extremities of the universe—God 'out there'. He is, of course, quite well aware that those who utilized or who utilize such images do not (ordinarily, at any rate) take them for literally valid expressions of the nature of God, but employ them only in so far as they are helpful to their apprehending the reality of God at all.

Of course, it would be only too easy for us to urge at this point that we Catholics have never really thought of God that way at all, so that what the Bishop is talking about doesn't really apply to us. One could, we think, say in reply that a little self-scrutiny on this score might well produce surprising results. In any case, Dr Robinson goes on to assert that for the old and, as far as contemporary man is concerned, unhelpful images of a God 'up there' or 'out there', we should do well to substitute the new image

---

death and hand over everything to the grace of God, who gives us what is to come. God is always the God who comes.'

or symbol suggested by Tillich: the image of 'depth'. 'There
is no doubt that this simple substitution can make much
religious language suddenly appear more relevant.'

How, then, do we approach God? 'Our experience of
God is distinctively and characteristically an awareness of
the transcendent, the numinous, the unconditional. Yet,
that is a feature of all our experience—in depth. Statements
about God are acknowledgments of the transcendent, unconditional element in all our relationships and supremely
in our relationships with other persons' (p. 52). 'For the
eternal Thou is met only in, with and under the finite Thou,
whether in the encounter with other persons or in the
response to the natural order' (p. 53). In passing, it could
be noted that this view of the way in which men come to
acknowledge the reality of God has a long and reputable
Christian ancestry, going back at least as far as Augustine,
and represented today in the work of a philosopher such
as the English Benedictine, Dom Illtyd Trethowan. But we
could experience a scruple here. Perhaps we have fused
God and the world into one by our fresh descriptions in
terms of 'depth'? Dr Robinson reassures us: 'The eternal
Thou is not to be equated with the finite Thou, nor God
with man or nature. That is the position of naturalism,
whether pantheistic or humanistic' (pp. 53-4). 'It is perhaps
necessary to rebut rather carefully the suspicion of pantheism, which must doubtless cling to any reconstruction
that questions the existence of God as a separate Being'
(p. 130). This is to reaffirm the Christian idea of God
existing as distinct from the world, though not in separation from it.

It is surprising to notice in the face of all this, in the face
of Dr Robinson's avowal that he is concerned 'in no way
to change the Christian doctrine of God' (p. 44), in the

face of his cl...
worl...

...ɔ⅃ a per-
... a man who has
...n in the Anglican Church
...ʜ plain teaching of Jesus Christ about
...un. One can only wonder whether the person
... wrote this ever read Bishop Robinson's book at all.

A fresh interpretation of traditional teaching about the Incarnation and Divinity of Christ that will make this teaching spring to life with new relevance for men of the jet age is the next task our author sets himself. To many Christian ears this chapter may well sound strange. This will be due in part to the frequent use of such words as 'myth' and 'mythical' to refer to some or other central aspect of the Christian message, in part to a certain obscurity in speaking of the divinity of Christ, in part to a rejection of the usual way of framing discussion about the atoning work of Christ. In reading this chapter one must, then, keep in mind that Dr Robinson's use of the words 'myth' and 'mythical' in no way implies a rejection of the historical worth of what the New Testament and Christian theology have said about the nature and work of Christ. For this usage of the words 'myth' and 'mythical' represents no more than a lively reaction to the endless employment of a certain type of spatial metaphor to describe the Incarnation and final Ascension of Christ.

The problem of worship and prayer is next raised in a chapter that is most poignant and moving. [A summary followed.]

It is in his chapter on the 'New Morality' that Catholics would feel themselves unable to go far with Dr Robinson. He gets off to a good start by affirming that 'there is no suggestion in the Gospels that the Christian ethic is for the religious only'. Here the author brings to the fore in a striking way the utter centrality of love, of concern for the inherent values of the person as the vitally relevant basis of a universal Christian ethic. But this insight is jeopardized by a failure to recognize that the centrality of love, of concern for the values of the person, is ultimately expressed and safeguarded in every situation by commitment to the moral imperatives placed upon men by Christ and conveyed to them through the witness of his Church.

This is not a book for comfortable Christians—cosy and complacent warmers of church pews. It speaks with a sense of urgency and high challenge to contemporary man. It blocks a facile return to prepared positions. It confronts those whose brains are bemused by automatically repeating the catch-phrases of the day. There are things in it with which the Catholic will feel compelled to disagree—sure, too, that he does so with reason. But the book is an important one, a profoundly moving testimony made by a man whose sincerity, humility and great love are beyond question. We are grateful to him for it.


## 19 · H. E. W. TURNER

*Van Mildert Professor of Divinity in the University of Durham and Canon of Durham Cathedral*[1]

THE new SCM paperback of the Bishop of Woolwich is

[1] A paper read to the clergy of Houghton-le-Spring Rural Deanery. Reprinted from *The Bishoprick* (May).

a puzzling boo...
moving...

...oth

...moridge and Wells,
...s published works to date
...tology, *In the End God*, and *Jesus
...g.* In both he takes a somewhat extreme
... based upon Dodd's theory of 'realized' eschatology.
This emphasis upon immanence may have more bearing upon his latest work than might at first sight be thought. The forces which have gone on moulding his thought are Bultmann's attack upon 'mythology', Tillich's existential theology and Bonhoeffer's plea for a worldly holiness and his radical attack upon religious activity as such.

With Bultmann he criticizes the 'up there' myth based upon a three-decker theory of the Universe though he admits that this is freely deployed in the New Testament. This is old stuff by now and it may be doubted whether it seriously misleads people nowadays. The difficulty is chiefly caused by the inadequacy of human language when it is used of God. He echoes Bonhoeffer's criticism of Bultmann that he did not carry his argument far enough, and challenges what he calls the 'out there' myth as well. The exploration of outer space raises for him difficulties of theological language which he finds just as serious as those created by the Copernican Revolution in early astronomy. At times he treats with undue seriousness the remark attributed to the eighteenth-century astronomer Laplace to Napoleon. 'Sire, I have scanned the heavens with my telescope and have not found God'. Put in this way the fallacy is clear enough. Telescopes and sputniks are not appropriate ways of discovering the Divine.

With Tillich (a more formidable ally) he tries to short-circuit the usual ways of trying to prove the existence of God. They are relevant (if at all) to a God 'out there'. 'You must forget everything traditional that you have learned about God, perhaps even the word itself.' That is a tall order and it is up to the Bishop to prove his case up to the hilt. This, as we shall see, he fails to do. God is by definition ultimate reality and one cannot argue whether ultimate reality exists but only what it is like. If we abandon the attempt to think of God as a Person 'out there' and look for him rather in the depths of our being we are not only freed from an awkward and unprofitable apologetic task but also can establish new and fruitful points of contact with the outsider. Whether the analogy of depth psychology is as valuable a point of contact as he thinks is arguable. Christian theology has certainly never spoken of God as a Person in exactly this sense.

In one passage he seems to recognize that depth is as much a metaphor or myth as the other two ways of thinking which he has so far excluded. 'Down there' is no less a turn of speech as 'up there' or 'out there'. We cannot get out of our difficulties of language on precisely these terms. He would, however, argue that to speak of depth is more profound or less misleading than to use the language of extension or exaltation. But are there not fruitful overtones in both methods of speech which he advises us to exclude? It is impossible to establish a preferential tariff in favour of one set of expressions or against the others. The difficulty is a universal one of applying human language to God and it is inescapable over the whole field. He is, however, concerned to set a radical question mark against the whole

supranatura...
crit...

... I think,
... as transcendence,
...ust be expressed in terms of
...xtension or exaltation ('down there' as
...here' or 'up there'). The snag is of course in the
phrase 'whatever is essential', and here Robinson and his readers may not be of a single mind. He admits that on his view the traditional lines of demarcation between theist and atheist have been largely overcome. The rueful comment of Professor Antony Flew that it would be hard now to be an atheist (presumably to know what one was being atheist about) seems amply justified.

The Bishop notes himself the kind of language which would need to be rephrased if the 'out there' myth were abandoned: the idea of the Trinity as a self-subsistent Being (presumably 'out there'), the doctrine of Creation whereby God called into existence a Universe 'over against' himself, the calling 'out' of a people under covenant, the sending by God of his Son 'into' the world and his 'return' in glory to judge the living and the dead. This is a serious enough agenda; even for a transposition of doctrine it is wholly arguable whether all this or 'whatever is essential' in all this can be included in the depth formula. If the problem really lies in the inadequacy of all language applied to the Divine and not merely of some language it is even questionable whether it ought to be attempted.

With Bonhoeffer, the tragic and creative martyr in Nazi Germany, the Bishop places a question mark against much of the religious activity in which the Churches indulge. Over the last few centuries man has come of age and much that was appropriate at an earlier period has long since lost its power to convince. Whether man has become adult morally and spiritually, even if he is becoming mature technologically and scientifically is far from certain. It is not often that people share their difficulties about prayer as honestly and as fully as the Bishop. He clearly found the schematic teaching about prayer which he received at his theological college completely unusable. In the name of Bonhoeffer's 'worldly holiness' he pleads for the concept of prayer as engagement and not simply as withdrawal even for the purposes of re-engagement. There are clearly different patterns of Christian Spirituality and no man has the right to follow another uninvited into the recesses of his soul. The Bishop obviously finds his prayer in engagement and who shall say him nay? And probably coming from quite a different spiritual and theological tradition from the Bishop I should have found the mould of prayer to which he refers equally unhelpful. But I cannot as easily detach myself as the Bishop seems to do from the double rhythm of prayer as withdrawal for re-engagement. If he is protesting against withdrawal without engagement, then his protest is timely and ripe. At one point, however, he goes further and urges that a modern Christian must learn to live towards God as one who can get on very well without him. This may of course merely be Bonhoeffer making a virtue of stern personal necessity, but in the Bishop it is sheer Pelagianism and denotes (to use a favourite catchword of his own) a loss of depth. Patterns of spirituality may certainly vary but the central conviction that man cannot get on without God is not for sale.

There are many charges which can be brought against

be so urgently necessary. This is of course only tentative and is far from being a full-scale blueprint.

God is to be understood as 'the infinite and inexhaustible depth and ground of Being'. He is not strictly a Being at all but the ground of all existence. When we associate personality with the idea of God we are really saying that personality is of ultimate significance in the constitution of the Universe. Theological statements express ultimate concern. This is the real meaning of St John's statement 'God is Love'. Here Robinson finds himself in deep waters. He admits that Feuerbach (a philosophical predecessor of Karl Marx) was right in wanting to translate 'theology' into 'anthropology' (the doctrine of God into the doctrine of man); he claimed to accept the attributes of God but to detach them from their subject. Theological statements thus become assertions about human life. That this is odd advice seems a trite enough observation to make but it will become clear as we proceed that there is no really satisfactory ground for his convictions apart from the Being of God conceived in what the Bishop regards as a wrong and objectionable sense. It is a curious procedure to attack the association of personality with God and yet to insist that the ground of reality honours description as personal. He commends John Macmurray for noting that transcendence is a category which applies to humanity but this tells for, rather than against, the ascription of transcendence to God. This means that we have already a reliable analogue within our own experience. He can commend Bonhoeffer for his insistence on the 'beyond in our midst' and uses of his own accord similar language about the Eucharist. But this balance of transcendence and immanence is precisely what a supranaturalist would maintain. He appears to me to be trying to make the best of both worlds in accepting the

natura...

...de-
... is a reaffirma-
... full weight given to the
...ying to assert. Against the massive
...phasis upon transcendence and virtual re-
... to recognize dovetails in our own experience which points to God, his stress upon immanence expressed in terms of depth may well be justified. But I cannot resist the conclusion that the modern agnostic whom he largely has in mind will soon be asking the Bishop what grounds he has on his own premises for pointing to depths in our experience at all, and above all for his confident assertion that personality is of ultimate concern. I do not think that the notion of depth alone will help him much here. Apart from a proper dovetail into the God Who is, I do not think he could persuade me to take this step.

In his chapter 'The Man for others' he tackles the Incarnation. This is obviously central to the Christian message and therefore crucial for his reinterpretation of it. Like Tillich he believes that 'the Christological dogma saved the Church but with very inadequate conceptual tools'. The last phrase is undeniably true because on any showing here is a fact which is too big for human language and even human thought. The description of our Lord as a 'window into God at work' is a fruitful idea for which we can only be grateful. The paradox that 'Jesus made no claims for Himself in his own right and at the same times makes the most tremendous claims about what God was doing through Him and uniquely through Him' is nearly though not quite true.

Again after Bonhoeffer he describes Jesus as 'the man for others', the One in whom Love has completely taken over, the One Who is utterly open to and united with the ground of His Being. This life for others through participation in the Being of God is 'transcendence'. The solidarity of Christ with ourselves which is one half of the classical Christology is plainly asserted here. He is 'the man for others', 'most entirely man', the 'proper man'. It is evident that the Bishop also wishes to assert the complementary truth of his solidarity with God. He is one with the Father because God is Love. He is utterly open to and united to the Ground of His Being. The source and spring of his whole being is God. His is a life conceived and sustained utterly by the Holy Ghost. This is an admirable statement of an orthodox intention, and seen against a different context could be the starting point for an adequate Christology. But what does it really amount to on Robinson's previously attempted reconstruction of the doctrine of God? How on his premises does the Bishop know all this and to what extent does it really demand the previously rejected supranaturalist frame of reference to make it work? On the Atonement (the acid test of a doctrine of the Incarnation) he rightly rejects many of the older theories on the ground that they imply a view of God as 'the God from the machine' (presumably the idea of a powerful rescue operation for humanity by God in Christ is excluded as well). Here he prefers to speak with Tillich of a radical estrangement from the ground of our being, the origin and aim of our lives, and of the acceptance of the completely unacceptable. So far, so good, and here at least neither Tillich nor his Anglican disciple can be accused of a low estimate of sin and its effects. But it is not simply what Robinson would call supranaturalist prejudice which makes me feel that a vital step has been left

...... of the transforming and liberating experience which Tillich describes. The acceptance of the unacceptable is only rescued from the threat of being a trick by the self upon itself by the restoration of this middle term. This can certainly be done without the crudities which have disfigured the doctrine of the Atonement in the past. It cannot be done at all on Robinson's premises.

With much in the chapter on worldly holiness we can only register agreement. The plea that holiness means engagement and not merely separation is obviously true though much in practice conspires to make us forget it. The conception of the Holy Communion as the assertion of the beyond in our midst, the point at which the common, the communal, becomes the carrier of the unconditional is finely made. Few could dissent from such a statement as the following, 'For Christianity the holy is the depth of the common, just as the secular is not a godless section of life but the world (God's world, for which Christ died) cut off and alienated from its true depth'. What on the Bishop's terms is meant by the phrase 'for which Christ died' is another question. The major problems come however in his discussion of the topics of engagement and disengagement. We should expect to find here a fruitful and continuing dialectic. This is what always happens ideally in prayer and often practically as well. Disengagement in prayer is never complete and this is not necessarily a sign of failure. The relation between the two is somewhat analogous to special times of meeting and of general awareness with two people who really love one another. Both are certainly found in the Lord's Prayer though presumably this would need transposition in the light of the Bishop's views. His criticism of disengagement that this is comparable to finding God in the gaps will hardly serve unless it is held in addition that God is not the Lord of the engaged life as well. Many of us do not find the agonizing incompatibility which the Bishop discovers between what might be called Christ in Church and Christ in chores. No doubt the ideal of us all is to find Christ in the nearest Thou to hand. We should make a pretty poor job of it apart from times of withdrawal and re-engagement. Dr Robinson does well to remind us of the need for engagement. Is his argument best served by the abandonment of the opposite pole?

He turns finally to Ethics. In a chapter entitled 'The New Morality' he says many good things about the Ethics of Jesus and the supreme principle of Love. Against the method of casuistry, for example, it is a veritable breath of fresh air. He argues that in a rapidly changing world the shape of Christian Ethics can best be described as 'situational' or 'existential' for which love alone has a 'moral built-in compass'. The opposite is a supranaturalist legalism for which he has as little use as for any application of supranaturalism. And yet there is still ground for dissent. The New Testament can speak of the 'new commandment' or 'the law of love'. No doubt Protestant ethics of the type of Tillich has a built-in suspicion of legalism (perhaps on good grounds); it may still be permissible to find a place for law within morality. No doubt to say of a thing 'It is wrong' or 'It is a sin' may not be in itself enough. This must not be held to imply that it has no place within ethical language. Naturally many people will turn first to

his treatment of ...
fundam...

...eturning
...*ua vis fac*' (Love
...is room for other ethical
...can I want what I ought?' It seems
...are two levels for moral conduct. There
...jective norms capable of translation into duties and
obligations, the Right (to use the title of a famous treatment of ethics by Sir David Ross). But there is also the
affirmation of this moral scaffolding of life because it is
the law, principle or ground of one's own life, the Good (to
use the other half of the title). This presupposes but does
not negate the other level of moral experience. To use the
rather unhandy terms taken by Robinson from Tillich, the
one is heteronomous (deriving its norm from 'out there'),
the other autonomous (deriving its norm from acceptance
within ourselves). Only when both (and not one only) are
regarded as theonomous (deriving from God) can a reconciliation be found between the two. Once again the Bishop
has given vigorous expression to something like half the
truth.

While there is much in the second half of the book which
can be warmly welcomed, it is as a whole vitiated by a
number of faults. While the Bishop is evidently the sworn
enemy of supranaturalism nothing can excuse the parody
of the views of his opponents. Often enough a hard-bitten
supranaturalist will not recognize himself in Robinson's
statement of his case. He will feel impelled to protest time
and again 'But this is not what I hold or what I mean when

I use supranaturalist language'. Few champions of this point of view really fail to try to provide for divine immanence, though not always on the terms in which Robinson tries to assert it. Many will find it difficult to harmonize the appalling negativism of the first part of the book with the positive attempts at construction in the second. The Bishop's concern for the outsider is plain from start to finish but there are situations in my experience in which it is not the belief but the unbelief of Christians which horrifies the agnostic. Unkind critics in a recent edition of a Sunday newspaper who complained that this was really humanism which failed to take the final plunge were not wholly wide of the mark. But perhaps the most penetrating comment came from Professor Antony Flew that the Bishop was refusing his cake and trying to have it too. Time and again he seems to me to be saying true and important things and to have part of the answer. But I do not find here the full answer to any of my questions and I doubt very much whether others will be able to stop precisely where he stops himself. He has given us not a platform but a slope.

## 20 · JOHN LAWRENCE

*Editorial in the Christian quarterly* Frontier (*Summer 1963*)

A LITTLE book can make a great stir. *Honest to God* has brought to a wide public some ideas which, in one form or another, have long been discussed among theologians, both lay and clerical; and in his chapter on prayer Dr Robinson makes an important contribution to the debate. Whatever one may think of the Bishop's tentative conclusions—and it is only fair to emphasize that his con-

clusions are tentativ
brought to the
   The
:

...ands re-
...oury ringing in
...eves to be the essential
...oeen led to ask some radical
...ıı. 'The most fundamental categories
...y—of God, of the supernatural, and of re-
...elf—must go into the melting.' 'There is a growing
...ıı between the traditional orthodox supernaturalism in
which our Faith has been framed and the categories which
the "lay" world (for want of a better term) finds meaningful
today.'

No question can be too radical, but one must ask whether
the questions are rightly put, as well as whether they are
rightly answered, and still more whether the answers are
not incomplete.

Dr Robinson indicates that he is still in two minds. 'The
line . . . runs right through the middle of myself.' This
makes the book hard to evaluate. Sometimes the author
quotes with apparent approval, or expresses in his own
words, views which, if consistently carried through, would
reduce Christianity to an off-beat variety of humanism. At
other times he speaks as one who believes in the living God.
I have read the book twice, once with my critical faculties
uppermost, and once in search of positive elements. It was
like reading two books. Others have pointed out some of
the astonishing inconsistencies in the book, and it would
be easy to build up a picture of it as a piece of hopelessly
muddled thinking, but that would serve no purpose.

These ideas have a vitality stronger than logic and they cannot be disposed of merely by pointing out, what is true, that there is a great deal of loose thinking in *Honest to God*. Theologians tend to say that none of this book is new, and that, in any case, these matters have all been treated more profoundly by previous writers, from Irenaeus in the second century, right down to the present day. That is true, but the theologians don't get through to most of us, and Dr Robinson does. Therefore, many of the laity hail the Bishop of Woolwich as a liberator. Theology has come to a pretty pass when *Honest to God* is the *only* theological book that has got through to the mass public for many years. It is high time that the theologians began the re-assessment of their role in the world which Dr Vidler and others have been urging on them. Dr Robinson starts from 'the number of people who instinctively seem to feel that it is no longer possible to believe in God in the space age'. The picture of God in heaven above us and hell some-where beneath our feet—the 'three-decker universe'—no longer makes sense and we have nothing adequate to put in its place. Much of our thinking about God 'up there', or, since Galileo, 'out there' has been crudely physical. It is better to think of God in terms of depth rather than height.

Dr Robinson seems to be shocked that 'it is the two most mature theologians of the New Testament, St John and the later Paul, who write most uninhibitedly of this "going up" and "coming down"'. But St John and St Paul also write most freely of God as dwelling within us. There is a real point here, but Dr Robinson has mistaken the nature of the difficulty. Nowadays, too much is made of the literal application of spatial metaphors to God. No human language is adequate; yet metaphors such as shepherd, king,

height, dep~~th~~
of ~~th~~

~~ch~~ildren
provided that they

developed a theology of outer space
justice to the facts as then known and gave a
concrete meaning to the words of the psalmist, 'The heavens declare the glory of God'. The Ptolemaic astronomy received its perfect theological expression in the *Paradiso* of Dante, but when this astronomy was overthrown nothing was done to re-think the theology which went with it. It was as if the Church had evacuated outer space. To the seventeenth-century astronomer outer space seemed cold and lifeless. '*Le silence éternel de ces éspaces infinis m'effraie*,' wrote Pascal. Dr Robinson observes that no place was found ' "out there" for the Devil and his angels, the pit and the lake of fire. This element, therefore, tended to drop out of popular Christianity altogether—much to the detriment of the Gospel.' True, but neither was there place found for heaven. We need theologians to analyse in what sense heaven and hell are states, in what sense these states are to be associated with places and where and of what kind those places may be. The galaxies are wide enough for many heavens and many hells, and there may be, for all we know, other systems that are not subject to our four-dimensional space-time. The relations between this world and outer space has become a necessary subject for theology; otherwise bogus theology will come in through space fiction.

In the minds of Dr Robinson and of some of the writers whom he quotes, the conception of God 'up there' or 'out there' is bound up with the picture of God as 'a being, not being itself', as '*a* Being whose separate existence over and above the sum of things has to be demonstrated'. One sees what he means, but the point is by no means as new as he seems to imply, nor did it become any more urgent after the picture of the 'three-decker universe' was discarded. The medieval philosophy of Western Europe, which thought out the model of the 'three-decker universe' in the greatest detail, also insisted on the radical distinction between God as Being and all other beings. This is what Etienne Gilson in his Gifford Lectures calls 'the theology of Exodus', referring to Exodus 3.14.

This is not the only point where one would like to see Dr Robinson's conceptions brought into relation with other ways of thought. He speaks of 'a depth at the centre of life' and he expounds Bonhoeffer's 'God is the beyond in the midst'. Excellent, but it is not clear why this should exclude transcendence in its classical sense. The Greek Christian tradition in the East, and the Quakers in the West, developed the doctrine of God's indwelling in man in different ways, but both do it in a way that gives the fullest meaning to the phrase 'a depth at the centre of life', and neither saw any contradiction between this and God's transcendence. The Greeks insisted that God is unknowable in His 'essence', and thereby they provided the best possible defence against the view of God as 'an old man in the sky' which Dr Robinson rejects so fervently. But the Greeks did not, therefore, forget the complementary truth that God makes himself known to us and dwells among us as 'the beyond in the midst'. Greek medieval theology needs to be re-expressed in modern terms, and the doctrine of God's

...gy of the Eastern Church (Clarke, 1957).

The most puzzling chapter in *Honest to God* is called 'The End of Theism? : Must Christianity be "Supranaturalist"?' The question marks indicate a doubt, and it is hard to make out how far Dr Robinson associates himself with the passages he quotes from Tillich, Bultmann and Bonhoeffer, and in what sense he understands these sometimes obscure writers.

On the one hand, he thinks Bultmann 'unwarrantably distrustful' of the tradition enshrined in the New Testament, and he quotes with apparent approval Bonhoeffer''s statement that 'you cannot, as Bultmann imagines, separate God and miracles'. On the other hand, he seems to associate himself with Tillich's view of God as the ground of being in such a way as to exclude 'the supranatural' altogether. It is impossible to criticize this without being sure of the sense in which the words are used. What is nature? And what is excluded by the rejection of the 'supranatural'? This part of the argument has a Hindu taste, though I gather that Dr Robinson has not read any Hindu writings.

Dr Robinson denies that he is substituting an immanent for a transcendent God, but he uses the word transcendent in a special sense derived from Tillich. What is transcended? If it is merely stated that human relations point to something beyond themselves, that is interesting but it would not indicate that the ground of our being is transcendent in the sense in which we are accustomed to say that God is transcendent. The weakness of the argument at this point leads to a confused treatment of the incarnation. Modern man cannot believe 'the Christmas story'. Yet 'the love revealed in Jesus is indeed the nature of ultimate reality'. Jesus 'is a window through the surface of things into God'. Is Jesus here the risen Lord or merely the man who was crucified under Pontius Pilate? If he is the risen Lord in what sense is the 'supranatural' rejected, and, if he is not, what reason can there be for supposing that he is 'a window through the surface of things into God'?

This book will be read by many people who would not read any other religious book, and it may start them thinking more deeply about the purpose of life, but it will provide no resting place. It takes you half way up a precipice and leaves you there. You must go up or down with the aid of other guides. Either you will find that because of what you believe already you must believe more, or you will find that because of what you do not believe you cannot believe anything. If one train of thought in *Honest to God* is followed to the end it will lead to a full-blooded trinitarian theology, and if another train of thought is followed it will lead to existential despair.

The book is full of arresting things, and there is something worth thinking about in every chapter, but it seems to be assumed throughout that what 'modern man' can or cannot believe is the test of truth. Yet the problems of 'modern man' are not always so new as they are made out to be. Christianity is not easy for the natural man to accept in any age. Nor is mid-twentieth century man of necessity the type of the future. In the next century man may be astonished at the confidence of some of our current dis-

adulthood of modern man, but he does not face all its limitations. Modern man is profoundly disturbed, and it is not only hydrogen bombs that disturb. Why are authors like Sartre, Samuel Beckett, Ionesco and Pinter so popular? Why did H. G. Wells come to think that mind was 'at the end of its tether'? Modern man is not complacent all through and he may be nearer to repentance and conversion than is commonly supposed.

Dr Robinson quotes Julian Huxley with approval and one would like to see him bring the evolutionary strand of modern thought more explicitly into his picture. *Honest to God* gives a curiously static view of the universe. The doctrine of the creation hardly seems to come into it, and one wonders what has become of the biblical teaching that there is a consummation to which things are moving. This uncertainty flows from the quasi-Hindu elements in Dr Robinson's thought, and it is doubtful whether this way of thinking can be accommodated in any theology that is recognizably Christian. Teilhard de Chardin is needed at this point to complete the thought of the existential writers on whom Dr Robinson leans so heavily. Indeed, I miss Teilhard continually for he is, among other things, the best example of 'holy worldliness' and 'religionless Christianity'.

When he comes to consider the type of spirituality which goes with his theology, Dr Robinson tries to work out some of the implications of Bonhoeffer's 'religionless Christi-

F

anity'. The trouble is that Bonhoeffer's letters from prison are so tantalizingly brief that one can read what one likes into them. For myself, I think that 'religionless Christianity' is an illuminating phrase but that it represents an abstraction, like the square-root of minus two, which one will never meet in flesh and blood. A too literal pursuit of 'religionless Christianity' leads to what is called by a happy misprint on p. 104 'regionless Christianity'. Dr Robinson does not altogether escape this danger, but he does disentangle one strand in 'holy worldliness' which ought to be central to Christian life but which has been greatly neglected. If religion is treated as merely one department of life, prayer becomes an occasional activity and most of life is lived apart from God. Dr Robinson is concerned with prayer-in-action: he helps one to see the meaning of St John's 'doing the truth'. He seems to be concerned with what de Caussade called 'the sacrament of the present moment'. His chapter on prayer is one-sided, but it says some things that needed saying, and it says them in a way that comes home. He found that the traditional teaching on prayer given at his theological college did not help him, because the writers he was told to read saw prayer as a withdrawal at certain times and apparently no more. One wonders what this teaching can have been like. Apparently it left out the 'Jesus prayer' of the Eastern Church by which prayer becomes a continuous activity, waking and sleeping. At any rate Dr Robinson does not seem to know *The Way of a Pilgrim* (reprinted in Fedotov's *Treasury of Russian Spirituality*, Sheed & Ward, 1950). The 'holy worldliness' and lay spirituality for which the Church is seeking will have some strikingly new elements, but it will also draw on Christian experience from the past.

Church, and for the masses of people who no longer attend church, to indulge in complacent self-congratulation or to take refuge in the conventional and familiar. The Church has for some time now been losing its hold on the people of Great Britain. Attendance at services of worship and the number of committed members have decreased noticeably during the years of this century. More than that, people today are not only casually turning from the Church, but openly rejecting its Faith. On radio programmes people of undoubted intellectual powers speak publicly of their rejection of all belief in God, let alone the other articles of the Christian Faith. Our Faith, in the forms in which it is usually expressed, has come increasingly to appear as something no longer intellectually respectable, perhaps not even honest.

In this situation no serious-minded Christian can be other than deeply concerned. Is this growing mood of unbelief just one of those recurring recessions of true religion, which will in time reach a low ebb and then begin to flood back—as has happened often before? Or can we comfort ourselves with the explanation that people are rejecting God only because they want that freedom to do evil which a belief in God restricts? Or are there other, less comfortable, reasons for the rising tide of unbelief? May it not be that the 'image of God' which we within the Church have

¹ Extracts from a review in the *Expository Times* (published by T. and T. Clark, Edinburgh, June).

grown used to and accept without much self-criticism is in fact so inadequate as a thought of God to be offered to non-Christians today, that they may even be put off by it? Is it possible some are rejecting only God as we present him, because we present him so misleadingly for people of our time? Is it that they are, in fact, rejecting not God himself as he really is, but the inadequate thought of him we conventionally present? Do we need for this new and revolutionary day in which we live a new way of speaking of the God in whom we believe?

It is this urgent and uncomfortable question that the Bishop has dared to ask and seeks to answer. It is a question which needs a frank and radical answer. The Bishop's answer is offered out of a passionate concern, and an illness that kept him in bed for three months provided the leisure for it to be written. Passionate concern dominates the book. It is as though something inside him 'boiled over' and had to be dealt with without delay. Had he laid it aside to be revised and then re-written, and published say in 1965, no doubt some ambiguities might have been clarified and some inconsistencies removed, perhaps some sharp expressions softened a little. But the sense of urgency could brook no such delay, and so what we have is not the balanced presentation of a conciliator, but the uncompromising call of the prophet, characterized by an almost brutal frankness rather than polite discretion. [A summary followed.]

There is much in the book which is provokingly unconventional; there is also much which is deeply moving. Many readers will have found in it not only new thoughts of God, but a new awareness of God, a new insight into the significance of Christ, and into the purpose of God in human life and the possibility of its attainment through the gift of God in Christ. Sometimes we wonder if the new emphasis

for which he ask̶
as well as t̶
we ̶

̶w
̶ ̶ ̶ ̶ his three
̶y mean that their
̶ ̶n the less logical British
̶ ̶ut however we meet this sharp
̶ ̶nought and heart, we should accept it
̶ ̶s meant to be—not a final definitive solution of
̶ ̶sing problems, but suggestions which the author himself describes as 'tentative and exploratory'. There may well be modifications to be made in some of these suggestions, but that does not mean that they should be taken less than very seriously. Though what he says may sometimes seem startlingly radical and extreme, he himself adds a warning note: 'I am fairly sure that, in retrospect, it will be seen to have erred in not being nearly radical enough.' But the Bishop has written not merely for the sake of being radical and causing consternation, but with the purpose of discovering a way of effectively presenting the essential truth of the Christian gospel to this modern world in imminent danger of totally ignoring it—to its own deep and abiding hurt. The book is fundamentally not an essay in unorthodox theology, but a venture in evangelism.

## 22 · HERBERT McCABE, O.P.[1]

DR ROBINSON has written an important book about

[1] Reprinted from the Roman Catholic review *Blackfriars* (July/August).

God, Christ, the nature of religion and morality. He does not claim to be a professional theologian; it is not, as he says, his academic field, but the book will nevertheless be of great interest to theologians as well as to the general reader, and it deserves a more discriminating reception than it has so far received in the press. Those of us in particular who are grateful to the Bishop for his work in his own field of New Testament scholarship will want to pay him the compliment of treating his book seriously and critically.

The book suffers a good deal from the author's lack of acquaintance with the history of theology. Thus he can open Chapter Two with the astonishing statement: 'Traditional Christian theology has been based upon the proofs for the existence of God.' This is, of course, flatly untrue. Traditional theology has always been based on faith in the Word of God. Whether and how God may be known apart from such revelation is itself a question within theology. To satisfy oneself that this is so one needs only to read the first three questions of such a classic of traditional theology as the *Summa Theologica*. In fact we might well complain that the area of theology connected with such proofs has been unduly neglected in recent years by conventional theologians—one good effect of the Bishop's book may be to remind us that this is after all an important topic. He exemplifies some of the mistakes that may be made when it is neglected.

Dr Robinson does not seem to realize that some of the positions he puts forward as revolutionary discoveries, especially suited to twentieth century man who has 'come of age', are in fact commonplaces of traditional thought. This is especially true of his first chapters dealing with the idea of God. He distinguishes three stages in the development of this idea. First, he says, God was thought of as

literally and physic...
taken to b...
'me...

...does
...what he means
...becomes clear from
...a God who is metaphysically
...a part of reality' (p. 30), 'the highest
...41), related to the world as the sun is to the
...n (p. 45), a 'particular thing' (p. 49) and dwelling in
'another world' (p. 68). The traditional theology which he supposes himself to be supplanting is, however, committed to the proposition that God cannot be any of these things. A very great deal of work has been done, and vastly more books have been written, on the problem of how to speak of the existence of a God who is not a part of reality, who is neither a particular thing nor yet an 'abstraction', who is not any kind of thing at all and who cannot be defined or described. The book contributes nothing towards the solution of these ancient problems but it does considerable service in reminding people that the problems exist.

If I ask the question 'How many are there in the room?' you will be unable to answer, for you will not yet know whether I mean how many people, or how many hair-styles, or how many physical objects, or what. We can in fact only count things when we have placed them within some common class or under some common description. It is for this reason, according to traditional theology, that we cannot count God and the world and make two—two *what*? When the Bishop of Woolwich says that God is not 'metaphysically out there' he may be merely rediscovering this important truth: God is not 'out there' in the sense of beginning where the world stops, as the second mile begins where the first stops, or the second in any series begins where the first stops. He would have very great difficulty in discovering a traditional theologian who thought that God is 'out there' in this sense. It would indeed ordinarily be recognized as a criticism of a theological position that it implied such a view of God. On the other hand we do commonly speak of God as though he were 'out there' in this way, as though he were a particular thing. Whereas the traditional theologian is happy to retain such language while trying to map the limits of its logical field of force, the Bishop seems sometimes to wish to abolish it. If he does this he must either replace it by something else or accept the accusation of agnosticism or even atheism.

One of his proposals is to replace our ordinary phrases about God 'in heaven' with phrases about the ultimate reality. There are, as he sees it, two advantages in this: first, it does away with the idea of a God 'who could or could not be there' (p. 29) which he thinks is entailed by the traditional proofs for the existence of God, and secondly it draws attention to the fact that God is within us. There seems to be some muddle in the first of these considerations. 'They (traditional theologians) argue from something which everyone admits exists (the world) to a Being beyond it who could or could not be there. The purpose of the argument is to show that he must be there, that his being is necessary; but the presupposition behind it is that there is an entity or being "out there" whose existence is problematic and has to be demonstrated' (p. 29). Now of course if a presupposition of the argument were really that 'there is a being' the argument would simply be begging the

question. Mor
is p

_g them
_ and 'But you
_ that we can demonstrate
_ence of something has no tendency
_ its existence is necessary. We do not think that
_ Van Allen Belt exists necessarily. Nor, on the other
hand, does the fact that God's existence 'needs' to be
demonstrated—that people can be found who deny it—
imply that his existence is contingent. It merely shows that
people can be wrong about it but can be put right rationally.

Dr Robinson, however, supposing that any attempt to
demonstrate the existence of a God to someone who did
not find it obvious would be to prove the existence of a
contingent being, one that 'might conceivably not have been
there', proposes to change the question. 'We must start the
other way round. God is, by definition, ultimate reality.
And one cannot argue whether ultimate reality exists. One
can only ask what ultimate reality is like—whether for instance . . . (it) is to be described in personal or impersonal
terms.' This is, of course, simply the latest version of the
ontological argument. The existence of God is to be proved
from the meaning of the word 'God'. It is a long time now
since this fallacy has been exposed: we no longer think
that while there may be doubt about the existence of things
called 'Flying saucers' there can be no doubt about the
existence of things called 'Existent flying saucers'. Without
question if a thing is the ultimate reality, it is real, but we
may still ask whether anything is the ultimate reality.

The Bishop, it is true, does not put great weight on this argument. What he seems really to want to say is that if we look into the depths of ourselves, there we shall find God. No Christian would want to deny this but it is demonstrably possible for atheists to do so. The fact is that the innermost depths of our being are not open to our immediate inspection. That there is anything which, in the Bishop's phrase, 'lies at the heart of things and governs their working' is itself in need of demonstration. It is exactly this that the traditional proofs set out, whether successfully or not, to provide. Twenty-six pages later the Bishop himself comes round to seeing this point: 'The question of God is the question *whether this depth of being is a reality or an illusion*, not whether a Being exists beyond the bright blue sky, or anywhere else' (p. 55, his italics, not mine). Those traditional theologians who believe that the existence of God can be proved have never been concerned with theological space exploration but simply with this matter of reality or illusion.

The Bishop is well aware that some of his assertions might lead to an accusation of pantheism—he is careful to insist that he believes that God is love, not that love is God (e.g. p. 53). But of course it is not the Bishop we are primarily interested in but his theology, and if his statements do imply pantheism, this state of affairs is not made untrue simply by the fact that the Bishop does not wish to be a pantheist. He is however struggling, without the aid of a traditional theological discipline, to say something important which, to him at least, is new, and it would be unfair to scrutinize minutely the logic of every phrase he uses. Instead it will be of interest to see how he deals with the difference between his position and the pantheist one. His argument is I think extremely interesting. 'It is perhaps

necessary to rebut ra...
ism, which m...
questio...
T...

...ll

...ve. For

... reality to its

...inistic one, allowing

...of moral evil. But the Biblical

.... We are not like rays to the sun or

...e: we are united to the source, sustainer

... of our life in a relationship whose only analogy is

...at of *I* to *Thou*—except that the freedom in which we are held is one of utter dependence . . . It is this freedom built into the structure of our being which gives us (within the relationship of dependence) the independence, the "distance" as it were, to be ourselves' (pp. 130-1). The argument seems to be that we are distinguishable from the ground of our being because we are not wholly determined by it, we are free in relation to it. For a pantheist this would not be so; there would be no distance between God and creatures, no free play of one over against the other, for they would be related simply as whole and part.

There seem to me to be two serious objections to this solution. In the first place, what are we to say of creatures which are not free? Are they simply to be identified with God? If it is our freedom which gives us our distance or distinction from God, then clearly freedom is something which belittles us. The unfree creatures are the rays of the divine sun, the leaves of the divine tree; they simply *are* God whereas we are less than he. This theology which should issue in the call to find divinity by abdicating our freedom and personality, by losing ourselves in the instinctive life of nature can hardly be congenial to the Bishop. In the second place, to speak of man as independent of God through his freedom is to make God 'metaphysically out there' in a particularly emphatic way. To say that I can be independent of God is really to say that God and I inhabit side by side a common world, and it is precisely this that the Bishop so rightly wishes to deny. Moreover it is not enlightening to add a parenthesis about 'utter dependence': either our freedom serves to make us distinct from God in which case it simply cannot be reconciled with 'utter dependence' upon him, or it does not, in which case some other ground must be found for our distinction from him, some other way of avoiding pantheism. For traditional theology we are indeed free and utterly dependent on God, but our freedom does not make us free from God, it makes us free from other creatures, it means that our actions are our own in a special way, that our world is therefore a moral world. For the tradition, freedom is the foundation of morality, it cannot also do the work of distinguishing us from God, this must depend on a prior metaphysical analysis. For the tradition, we are free because in a deep sense we are our own, but we are creatures because, in the absolutely final sense, we are not our own—the word *Sein* means, as Kafka says, both to be and to belong to him.

The issue between pantheists and traditional theists comes down to this: Can we make statements which, however much they may derive their meaning and verification from the world, are statements about God and not about the world? For traditional theology, although we can only say 'God is good' because of something we know about the world and not because of some extra information we have about God, nevertheless the statement is not about the

world. It is no...
not. Th...

...it is pos-
...ween falsity and
...at all assertions apparently
...slated without loss into assertions
...bout God but about personal relationships,
... pantheist. If on the other hand 'Love' is used as a
name of God, the assertion says nothing significant. The
same kind of ambiguity attaches to the similar statement
on p. 49: 'theological statements are not a description of
"the highest Being" but an analysis of the depths of personal relationships'. Well, all right; but what *sort* of analysis? The Bishop seems sometimes to leave the impression
that one has to opt *either* for the creator and redeemer of
the world *or* for the reality which underlies the depths of
human love.

The discussion of revelation and of Christ is bedevilled
by the Bishop's curious theology of the supernatural. Frequently he uses Tillich's word 'supranatural' but it is clear
that, for him, the two are interchangeable. He says, giving
an account of what he believes to be traditional Christology: 'As the God-man, he united in his person the supernatural and the natural: and the problem of Christology
so stated is how Jesus can be fully God and fully man,
and yet genuinely one person' (pp. 64-5). It is obvious
from such a passage that the author must have been systematically misled in his reading of traditional theologians:
where they have spoken of the supernatural, he must have
supposed them to mean the divine. (It is true that there are

writers who speak of God as 'entitatively supernatural'
and it may be these who have misled the Bishop.) At least
for the scholastic tradition, it is a mystery and a great
wonder that a man should unite in his person the supernatural and the natural, but it would be more than that, it
would be impossible, to find the supernatural which was
*not* united with the natural. God is not supernatural; the
supernatural is a special relationship of the natural to God.
The supernatural life of man is his sharing in the divine
life. God does not share in the divine life supernaturally,
he *is* the divine life. Tillich is quoted as saying: 'To call
God transcendent in this sense does not mean that one
must establish a "superworld" of divine objects. It does
mean that, within itself, the finite world points beyond itself.
In other words it is self-transcendent' (p. 56). This is a
fairly exact account of what traditional theology means by
the supernatural, not another 'superworld' but the transcendent character of this world, a transcendence which does
not belong to this world of itself but is the response to the
personal call of God's love.

Traditional theology never has seen either the revelation
of God's word in scripture or in Christ as a journey from
'another world', as a 'supernatural order which invades or
"perforates" this one' (p. 24). It is just untrue to say as the
Bishop does (p. 66) that 'However guardedly it may be
stated, the traditional view leaves the impression that God
took a space-trip and arrived on this earth in the form of
a man. Jesus was not really one of us; but through the
miracle of the Virgin Birth he contrived to be born so as
to appear one of us. Really he came from outside.' If such
an 'impression' is left it is not by a guarded expression of
traditional Christianity but, perhaps, by the preaching of
someone whose theological training has been insufficiently

traditional. Eve...
say that ...
...

...orld
...deeply to
...ity which has been
...has been for centuries, the
...hristian theology but hitherto no
...suggested that because of it we should
...speak of the Word 'coming down from heaven', of
the descent of the Holy Spirit' or of Christ 'ascending into
heaven and sitting at the right hand of God the Father'. To
reject such forms of speech surely shows as much theological naïveté as to take them literally. If indeed it were
not for his conviction that he is remodelling Christian ideas,
what the Bishop has to say about God and Christ could be
thoroughly acceptable to any traditional theologian. It
might, again, be thought that someone who can present
traditional Christianity as something new, fresh and revolutionary is doing a great and much needed service to the
Church, but in fact the air of iconoclasm which the author
evokes has merely led to his being interpreted in a non-
christian sense. He has been hailed as an ally for the quaint
evolution-worship of Julian Huxley, he has been widely
regarded as substituting humanism for religion, and for this
he cannot but blame himself. To make Christianity sound
fresh by setting it out in ambiguous language is bound to
have this kind of result.

Most of what he has to say about Christ is an attack
on the heresy that Jesus was not truly man—a very widespread tendency amongst Christians and one which the
Bishop deals with excellently. It is, however, unfortunate

that he should identify this well-known error with Christian tradition: 'Even when it is Christian in content, the whole schema of a supernatural Being coming down from heaven to "save" mankind from sin, in the way that a man might put his finger into a glass of water to rescue a struggling insect, is frankly incredible to man "come of age", who no longer believes in such a *deus ex machina*' (p. 78). It is also, of course, incredible to any Christian; the orthodox belief is that the Word was made flesh, not that he simply rescued flesh from some calamity. Dr Robinson's own version of kenotic christology seems to me excellent. Criticizing the conventional kenotic theory he says: 'The underlying assumption is that it is his omnipotence, his omniscience, and all that makes him "superhuman", that must be shed in order for him to become truly man. On the contrary, it is as he empties himself not of his Godhead but of himself, of any desire to focus attention on himself, of any craving to be "on an equality with God", that he reveals God' (p. 75).

Whereas the central criticism that must be made of his view of God and of Christ is that he does not realize how orthodox and traditional he is, and hence lays himself open to misinterpretation, the same cannot be said, it seems to me, of his views on the Church and on morals. His goal is the entirely acceptable one of Christianity without religion, but he differs radically from traditional Christian thought in supposing that this aim is to be achieved by human reorganization rather than by the second coming of Christ. Religion, he quite rightly observes, depends upon a distinction of sacred and secular. Certain things, places, actions or people are 'sacred', set apart from the common life; this is the necessary condition for cult and religion. Undoubtedly the consequence of the incarnation is the abolition of a real

distinction

...ntly is a

...ill be no temple in

...mighty and the Lamb are its

...onal thought we are in an intermediate

..., while the new world is founded in Christ's

..isen body, we are not yet visibly and gloriously members of that world. The last things are not wholly to come as they were in the Old Testament, nor yet wholly realized as at the last day; hope is still an essential aspect of our divine life. Now it does not seem that the Bishop maintains this difficult tension between realization and hope. He speaks sometimes as though the divine plan were completely realized now in a world which needs no transfiguration (e.g. p. 82). Religious rites which point beyond the present world seem too hastily to be dismissed as escapist. There is almost no discussion of the sacramental life by which we can participate in the world to come. It is not stressed that the eucharist is an eschatological meal, the sacrament seems to find its entire meaning in the present era. There is of course always a dangerous tendency in the Church to think of Christ as the founder of *a* religion, and to think of Christianity in purely religious terms, as a matter of cult and correctly performed liturgy. The Bishop has some excellent things to say about stripping the eucharist of its 'churchiness and religiosity' so that it appears for what it is as 'the place at which the common and communal point through to the beyond in their midst, to the transcendent in, with and under them' (p. 86). Again, this has been said as vehemently by more traditional theologians but it can bear almost any amount of repeating.

It is in the chapter called 'The New Morality' that the Bishop parts company most decisively—as he himself points out—with Roman Catholic thought. The chapter is an account of *situationsethik*, a theory of morals according to which it is not possible to describe a human action which would be in every circumstance morally wrong. The Catholic tradition has been that while the vast majority of moral decisions are to be determined by the situation or circumstances of the particular case, there are certain actions which are wrong 'in themselves' and cannot be justified by consequences, motives or any other circumstances. Thus the Catholic will maintain that there could not be conceivable circumstances in which it would be right for a man to commit murder—and of course that 'murder' can be defined without reference to moral evaluation. The Bishop contrasts this with what he finds a truer account of Christian ethics: 'It is a radical ethic of the situation, with nothing prescribed—except love' (p. 116). The Catholic traditionalist would, of course, maintain that he too holds that nothing is prescribed except love; but for him the analysis of this prescribed love involves certain absolute limits to conduct. There are certain kinds of behaviour which are absolutely ruled out for a lover. 'If you love me, keep my commandments.' In this matter what the Bishop has to say will not seem particularly revolutionary outside the Roman Catholic Church. In England, at least, most moral philosophers would agree with him and it does not seem that the Anglican Communion is in any way committed to a rejection of his view.

It is curious that one so insistent on the unimportance of religion should treat moral demands as on exactly the same foot...

...the
...the sabbath
...whole of morality. 'The
... insistence . . . that compassion
...des all law, is his shocking approbation
...s action in placing human need (even his own)
above all regulations however sacrosanct' (pp. 116-7). The
reader is likely to object that this approbation so far from
being particularly shocking is already implicit in the Old
Testament story, but the most interesting thing about this
quotation is that the Bishop clearly regards a rule about
'eating the bread of the Presence, which it is not lawful for
him to eat' as a 'classic illustration' of moral law: he
seems indeed to regard such rules as more 'sacrosanct' than
laws about adultery, murder, lying and so on, since his
argument appears to be that if the 'sacrosanct regulations'
can be set aside surely 'all law' can be. The traditionalist
would say that, of course, Canon Law and the rules of
religion are made for man, and of course they must be set
aside if they conflict with the demands of human compassion, but this is precisely because they are *not* the moral
law. We have a divinely revealed moral law just because
our compassion cannot reach deeply enough into the mystery of the individual person's needs and destiny. The
divine law is rooted not in our fallible situational judgment
but in the compassion of God. As the Bishop says, quoting
Joseph Fletcher, '. . . persons matter, and the deepest
welfare of these particular persons in this particular situation matters, more than anything else in the world'. This is,

of course, true; the question between us is merely how we
are to know and compass the deepest welfare of persons. Is
it in the end a matter of human contrivance or of the
Mystery, the divine plan for human destiny?

This has been, I am afraid, an unfavourable review of a
book which I and thousands of others have found intensely
interesting to read. I have stressed what seem to me to be
the book's weaknesses simply because so many whose
opinions I respect seem to have received it with uncritical
enthusiasm. I cannot but feel that some of this enthusiasm
is generated by the imprecision and ambiguity of the book's
positions. The Bishop of Woolwich, I suspect, is made uneasy by some of the opinions attributed to him by his
readers. Nevertheless even if it were a bad book, which it
certainly is not, the very extent of its popularity should
make it compulsory reading for anyone who wishes to
understand the religious climate of the day. And those who
read it merely for this reason, even those who come from
it with as many criticisms as I have, will find something
much more important—that in spite of all disagreements
their understanding of Christ and his mission will have
become deeper and more personal.

## 23 · THEODORE O. WEDEL

*Canon Theologian of the Cathedral of St John the Divine,
New York, and President of the House of Deputies,
Protestant Episcopal Church, USA*[1]

A VERITABLE avalanche of news stories from across the
Atlantic is arriving on editorial desks of the religious press

[1] Reprinted from *The Episcopalian* (August).

...at Britain,
...expect journals repre-
...ve churches, the so-called funda-
... to damn the volume heartily and to echo
...tions of heresy. 'So this is Anglicanism! We always
suspected that Episcopalians, despite the piety of their
Prayer Book, had surrendered the true biblical faith.' This
reviewer hopes that Episcopalians, as well as our brethren
of other communions, will not join in a chorus of indiscriminate criticism. The Bishop of Woolwich is not committing a crime in revealing to a wider public what has been
going on for a generation and longer in the world of advanced theological learning. He is attempting to prepare the
laity of the churches for readjustments in some of their
naïve, adolescent, often outdated, and even idolatrous conceptions of the Christian faith.

It is the business of our theologians to reinterpret the
faith to each age of cultural change. *Honest to God* is simply
a bold and, as some theologians may say, premature opening of a Pandora's box of theological novelties under debate
among doctors of the schools behind the scenes. The Church
has lived through many readjustments of its understanding
of the biblical revelation. The Copernican revolution in
astronomy and the emergence of the Darwinian theory of
evolution are only two instances. Modern nuclear science
and, even more importantly, the radical secularization of
our culture present a new challenge for readjustment.

If, to be sure, *Honest to God* is intended as a primer of

contemporary theology for lay consumption, it is, in my view, not wholly successful. It cries aloud, on many a page, for corrective footnotes which would protect the Bishop from being misunderstood. But the Bishop has not tried to write a definitive textbook, not even a primer. He is sharing with his fellow Christians questions which have disturbed his clerical ease, as well as some of his tentative answers. We ought to let him have his say, and to enter into dialogue with him. As a stimulus toward a programme for action, *Honest to God*, with all its faults, could turn out to be a tremendously important event of our time. Any reader should resist the temptation to render a hasty verdict on the book's opening chapters. The total impression of the volume will be very different from what the reader might be led to believe if he lingers only over the book's opening argument.

This argument is, one must grant, a bit startling and, to use the Bishop's own word, 'radical'. The Bishop's theological guide in these early chapters is the American theologian Paul Tillich. Large numbers even of the laity in America are familiar with both Tillich's name and his writings, especially his matchless volume of sermons, *The Shaking of the Foundations*. Basic to Tillich's theology is his symbol for God as 'ground of being'—which he sets over against the concept of God as 'a Being'. Those not familiar with the whole body of Tillich's writings may at once be in trouble; indeed, even many of Tillich's friends and admirers among theologians are not wholly at ease here either, a fact not mentioned by Bishop Robinson. Something of what the opposition to the concept of God as a Being is driving at ought to be plain. The Bishop has an easy time in demolishing trust in a deity, localized in space, either 'up there' or 'out there'. We can all follow him so far. Disturbance arises, however, when the opposition seems to be

directed against ...
person of ...
sim...

...d
...ith such
...ready to hand.
...the volume seizes upon
...misses what, in my view, is the
...t radicalism of the later chapters.

...questions are raised when we substitute the sym-
... ground of being' for our familiar anthropomorphic and
personal symbols of God. How can we pray to a 'ground of
being?' Are we being robbed of a personal God? The Archbishop of Canterbury voiced such a concern in his quoted
comment that the book 'appears to reject the conception of
a personal God as expressed in the Bible and the Creed'. To
defend Tillich and the Bishop fully against a charge of
heresy would take far more space than is available to me
here. A few suggestions must suffice. The Bishop is at pains
later in the volume to assure the reader that God for him
is still a personal God. He might, indeed, have cited Tillich
himself to the same end. 'Certainly,' to quote Tillich, 'in the
I-Thou relationship of man and his God, God becomes a
being, a person, a Thou for us . . . an insight that is important for the meaning of prayer and meditation' (*The
Theology of Paul Tillich*, Macmillan). Bishop Robinson's
and Tillich's attack on popular theism has as its real target
the idolatry lurking behind much of today's popular religion. How easy it is to worship a god created in our own
image—a friendly 'Man Upstairs' or a celestial Daddy!
This is the sort of god we can call on as our omnipotent
servant; whom we can ignore if he be merely a Someone

alongside of us: or whom we can prove, in good logic, to be non-existent; or who can be relegated to a special area called 'religion'.

Furthermore, our popular, dangerously unitarian concept of God needs the correction of the doctrine of the Trinity. *Honest to God* alludes to this help to our understanding, but it might have more fully amplified this particular point. Would any of us identify the Holy Spirit, for example, as merely a Spirit 'out there' somewhere? Does not the Holy Spirit manifest himself precisely in the depth or ground of the fellowship life of the Christian Church as profoundly personal, yet not a Being merely alongside of us? This God is closer than hands or feet. Here the fully biblical phrase, 'God is love', can be of help and *Honest to God* makes good use of it. Love, like the concept 'ground', is not exactly equivalent to a person. The first half of Bishop Robinson's book, a bold attack on the easy idolatry of 'religion in general', is disturbing, yes, and not always too clear, but it is neither irrelevant nor ultimately un-biblical.

As already noted, it is in the later chapters of the book that the full impact of the non-theistic understanding of God receives authentication in terms of our experience. Dietrich Bonhoeffer, a martyr under Hitler, is here the Bishop's theological mainstay. Bonhoeffer has become a stimulus for a theology of readjustment, especially in his *Letters and Papers from Prison* by his twin slogans 'man come of age' and 'religionless Christianity'. If Tillich's theology can disturb today's laymen, the Bonhoeffer theological novelties can, in their turn, disturb the clergy, since they rob the ministry of its monopoly rights. The very word 'religion' is currently being subjected to devastating scrutiny, and we are being invited to embrace a worldly Christianity without religion. This all seems again startling and radical.

... God has
... realm. And, as the
... on prayer points out, nowhere
... more meaning than precisely in that same
... day world. We have to act and to make decisions in
that world 'as if God did not exist', but the decisions are
nevertheless *before* God. 'The "matter" of prayer is supplied
by the world'—by the engagement pad and the telephone.
'God,' to quote Bonhoeffer, 'is the beyond in the midst of
life.' Prayer is dialogue with a transcendent Thou. And this
Thou meets us first in our neighbour *in the world*. Only as
we become sensitive 'to the Christ in the hungry, the naked,
the homeless', are we living truly before God.

It is in the chapter on prayer that the Bishop's honesty is
most daringly exhibited. It will also probably be the chapter
which will receive the most criticism. This reviewer, however, joins hundreds of the Bishop's clerical brethren in welcoming it as a long needed emancipation proclamation from
the tyranny of manuals of piety which have imprisoned
prayer in mystical, claustrophobic closets.

As a teacher by vocation, I was tempted to interrupt the
author's argument here and there with this request: 'Take
pity on the theologically unlearned, please, since you are
not writing for experts. Those who undergo surgery, even
theological surgery, have the right to a preliminary anaes-
thetic. You do favour them with comfortable words towards
the end of your book, but there might be more. In a new
theological climate we are not going to get rid of anthropo-

morphic symbols for God, nor of the spatial "myths" of
heaven and hell. Even your beloved Paul Tillich, after de-
throning such symbolic language when it is literally absolu-
tized, uses it freely in his sermons and fills it with often
unforgettable meaning for day-to-day life.'

Bishop Robinson may, however, have been wise in expos-
ing his own questionings, and the theological questionings
of our time, without too much defence for, or softening of,
them. We are simply in the midst of a theological Copernican revolution. We had best adjust ourselves to it. *Honest
to God* invites sequels and dialogue. Let us welcome the
return of prophesying in the Church. St Paul was not afraid
to encourage prophesying even by obviously inexpert laymen. That even a bishop has dared to exercise his layman's
right to prophesy should be cause for rejoicing.

... question of God, man must already have
... idea of God, for every question has its direction, and
it is impossible to seek anything without having some
understanding of what is sought, however vague and mini-
mal that understanding may be. The next step toward
grappling with our problem is simply a phenomenological
exploration of the question of God itself. What is the structure of this question? How should it properly be formulated? What is already implicit in the question? What conditions would have to be fulfilled for it to receive an
affirmative answer?

We must remember that our question is the *religious*
question of God, and that it has an *existential* structure.
That is to say, it is not a theoretical or speculative question,
raised by the intellect alone, but a practical question posed
by the whole being of man who has to exist in the world
and decide about his existence. Perhaps the question of God
can be raised in a purely theoretical way, but this would
not be a question of any interest to theology, and perhaps
it would not even be a meaningful question. We could think,
for instance, of the question of God as a *cosmological*
question, in which 'God' would stand for an explanatory
hypothesis, put forward to account either for the world as

[1] Part of an Inaugural Lecture delivered on 24 October 1962.

a whole or for certain events in the world. For a long time men did try to account for many happenings in terms of supernatural agencies. With the rise of science, however, we have learned to look for our explanations in terms of factors immanent in the natural process itself. The famous remark of Laplace to Napoleon, 'I have no need of that hypothesis', simply expresses our modern attitude to the world as a self-regulating entity. Science, of course, stops short of the ultimate question of why there is a world at all, but this is simply an acknowledgment that for the finite human intellect which is within the world, such a question is unanswerable. The religious question of God, as existentially structured, is different from any theoretical question about an explanatory hypothesis. We are not looking for some invisible, intangible entity, to the existence of which we might infer. Perhaps we are not looking for an entity at all, or for anything that could be conceived as a possible object among others.

These remarks at once suggest that we must be highly suspicious of the traditional formulation of the question of God—a formulation which runs, 'Does God exist?' For this question already contains implicitly the idea of God as a possible existent entity. The question is parallel to such a question as, 'Does there exist another planet beyond Pluto?' This is not at all like the religious, existentially structured question of God. This latter question would need to be formulated in some such way as: 'Can we regard Being as gracious?' It is a question about the character of grace, so that human life can be lived in the strength of a power from beyond man himself, and ceases to be the tragic contradiction which it would be in the absence of grace.

'God' is the religious word for Being, understood as gracious. The words 'God' and 'Being' are not synonyms,

...... belong ... or 'entities', as they may ...... confusion—of which one can say that they either exist or do not exist. In Heidegger's language, Being stands to entities as the wholly other, the *transcendens*, the non-entity which is nevertheless 'more beingful' (*seinender*) than any possible entity. But if God is equated with Being as gracious, then the question is not whether some entity or other exists, but whether Being has such a character as would fulfil man's quest for grace.

Can we see more clearly what conditions must be fulfilled if Being can be recognized as God? The question of God arises from man's estrangement from himself, and his inability to bring into unity the polarities of finitude and freedom which constitute his being. These two poles must remain in perpetual and frustrating conflict if there is no relation between the Being out of which man has emerged as a finite centre of existence, and the values and ideals towards which in his freedom he aspires as the end of his being. If Being has the character of grace and can be identified with God, the condition to be satisfied is that the Being out of which man arises coincides with the end of his freedom, thus bringing into unity the polarities of his existence and healing his estrangement. Among modern theologians, this idea comes out most clearly in Tillich, who has two typical ways of talking about God, as 'ground of being' and as 'ultimate concern'. But precisely the same structure is discernible in the more traditional ideas of God.

For instance, Oliver Quick writes: 'God is the *alpha* and *omega* of all things, the source from which they proceed, the end towards which they move, the unity in which they cohere.' The language here is cosmological rather than existential, but this description of God has precisely the same structure as the one at which we arrived by an existential and ontological route.

This must suffice for the phenomenological description of the question of God. The question has been clarified and we see its meaning and its requirements. But the matter cannot be left here—otherwise I might be accused of showing that theology is a possible study of the possible, rather than that it is possible as a study of the most concrete reality. But what kind of evidence can we now seek, to bring content into the formal structures of the analysis?

It is clear that I have already cut myself off from the rationalistic natural theology by which so many theologians of the past sought to ground their subject and establish the reality of its matter. Apart from the fact that their arguments have been largely discredited by modern criticism, I have tried to show that their speculative approach was a mistaken one and that their leading question about the existence of God involved a logical defect in its formulation. In any case, all those who tried to prove the existence of God already believed in him, and must have had a more primordial source for their conviction than their own arguments. Where then are we to look?

At the risk of lapsing into theological incomprehensibility, I must now boldly introduce the word 'revelation'. Yet this is not a word that need frighten us. Clearly, nothing whatever can be known unless in some way it reveals or manifests itself. The character of Being can be known only if Being reveals itself. Of course, something more than this

... word 'revelation' is simply to remain true to the phenomenological analysis of belief in God, for such belief testifies that God makes himself known to us rather than that we attain to the knowledge of him. The Bible never suggests that man has to strain his mind to figure out a shadowy Something behind the phenomena. There is indeed recognition of man's innate quest for God, but God himself meets and satisfies the quest. Man does not search out God, but rather the reverse is true. One of the greatest of the Psalms begins: 'O Lord, thou hast searched me and known me!' and goes on to describe the ubiquity and inevitability of the encounter with God.

What kind of language is this? Of what kind is this knowledge of God where that which is known towers above us, as it were, and it is as if we ourselves were known and brought into subjection? Perhaps we glimpse an answer to these questions if we consider three possible ways in which we may be related to that which stands over against us. The first case is our everyday relation to things, as objects of which we make use or have knowledge. They are at our disposal, and even by knowing them we acquire a certain mastery over them. The second case is our relation to other persons. This 'I-thou' relation, as Buber taught us to call it, is of a different order, for the other person is not my object and is not at my disposal. The relation is one between subjects. It is a mutual relation, founded on the same kind of being—personality—on both sides. Now it is also possible to envisage a third kind of relation in which we stand over against Being itself. In this kind of relation, we do not have the other term of the relation at our disposal, nor do we stand to it in a relation of equality, but rather we are grasped by it and brought into subjection to it, but in such a way that something of its character is disclosed to us.

Correspondingly there are three modes of thinking. We think of things in objective terms, the commonest type of thinking. We think of our friends differently, as those with whom all kinds of relations are possible that are impossible with things. And it is possible to think too of Being which, though it towers above us and subjects us, does not annihilate us but rather communicates itself and gives itself in the experience of grace. To talk of revelation does not mean an abrogation of thinking, but only that all our thinking is not the same pattern. Tillich talks of the ecstatic reason which still does not cease to be reason. Heidegger speaks more soberly of the thinking that is submissive to Being. Whatever expression we may prefer, it is this kind of thinking that makes theology possible, as the task of sifting and explicating and interpreting God's encounter with man, as it is recollected in tranquillity.

If someone is still asking, 'What does all this prove?' then the answer must be in line with what has already been said—it proves precisely nothing. Perhaps what we take to be the encounter with God is an illusion; perhaps it is all explicable in terms of a naturalistic psychology; perhaps all our talk of sin and grace and existence and Being is only mystification. These are possibilities that cannot be entirely excluded even when the experience of grace has begun to produce its fruits of wholeness and serenity in place of estrangement and anxiety. The impossibility of demonstration in these matters is simply a consequence of

what we have lear

that he is f

w

...ng has
...ued that leads
...seif to his confrontation
... of the concepts of contemporary
...eology, that way has been shown to
...onerent pattern, an intelligible structure, and an
...ner logic. When challenged to produce the credentials of his subject, the theologian cannot in the nature of the case offer a proof, but he can describe this area of experience in which his discourse about God is meaningful, he can ask his questioner whether he recognizes his own existence in the Christian doctrine of man as finite, responsible and sinful; whether he finds hidden in himself the question of God. He can show that faith is not just an arbitrary matter, and he can make clear what is the alternative to faith. Beyond this, perhaps, he cannot go, but is not this sufficient? For it brings us to the point where we see that this discourse about God has to do with the most radical matter in life, the point where, exercising our freedom in finitude, we decide to take either the risk of faith or the risk of unfaith.

G

# CONCERNING THEISM

## DAVID JENKINS

*Fellow and Chaplain of the Queen's College, Oxford*

I ASSUME that the '*Honest to God* debate' is sufficiently shown to be an urgently necessary one by the response which the original book has evoked. The evidence of my own contacts and those of many of my friends is sufficient to convince me that the approach of the book has encouraged many people to feel able to look again, with a very real possibility of discovery, at questions concerning God, the meaning and context of life, and the practice and possibility of religion. Persons who have felt encouraged and set free by the example of the book to renew their quest into these matters include both some who have hitherto 'written off' all talk of God and all practice of religion and some who have succeeded in clinging with more or less difficulty and desperation to a 'Faith' and the practices of a Faith which they have not dared to investigate deeply because they have more than half suspected that under investigation the 'Faith' will collapse. Thus the book constitutes an occasion of liberation and advance, whatever occasions of stumbling it may also be in danger of offering.

This being so, merely negative criticism would be a disaster and a faithless and disobedient throwing away of the opportunities opened up. But genuinely to further this discussion, full and careful use must be made of the resources at our disposal. At some stage in the continuing search for, and witness to, the truth about God and the

world, a careful and
made which w^ill
Christia^n
le^

_g
_e is an
, both Western
_n the insights of the
_asters of the spiritual life,
_ry sharply and then very profitably
_s poverty of much current 'theism'. The
_t of the scandal is peculiarly well shown by the
_t that not only does the theism against which the Bishop
protests seem to very many people to be recognizably the
theism of the Christian Church (and the only possible
theism—hence the need and justification for atheism) but
also the Bishop actually seems to be trapped in this belief
himself. His attempt to be honest to God is so dishonest to
the God of, for example, Athanasius or the fourth century
Cappadocian writers or of Thomas Aquinas, let alone
Augustine or, again, to the God of the author of the *Cloud
of Unknowing* or, say, to the God who is worshipped in
and through the shape of the Orthodox Liturgy, that it is
clearly high time that we were confronted by an explosive
reminder of the need to 'get our theism right'. It must,
however, not be taken for granted that we can do this by
forgetting all the traditional language because we super-
ficially focus attention on its imagery and ignore its insights. Certainly the Bishop is in no position to be our
guide here, as he is plainly ignorant of, or indifferent to,
what has been said and what has been meant by what has
been said. But this, in so far as it is true, must be taken not
as a satisfactory criticism or refutation of what the Bishop

has said, but as a challenge to those who are more familiar
with those insights to bring them to bear on the situation
which the Bishop indicates and exemplifies.

As I have neither time nor space here and now to take
up my own challenge I wish, as a contribution to the continuing debate and as a prelude to the type of enterprise I
have asked for, to try to show that it is extremely unlikely
that the way forward will lead to a restatement of Christian
belief which is in any way 'the end of theism' or the giving
up of the notion of God as personal. It may be that I am
committed to arguing in this way not by the points to which
I shall later draw attention but entirely by my own personal predilections. For while I very greatly sympathize
with and believe that I share in the Bishop's bewilderment,
agnosticism and protests, I would not, I think, spontaneously
or even on consideration, state the position from which I
face and attack these bewilderments as he does. When he
says (and again I find myself in agreement) that often in
debates between Christians and Humanists his 'sympathies
are on the humanist's side' he goes on to say: 'This is not
in the least because my faith or commitment is in doubt'
(p. 8). The difficulty I find with this statement is that, for
me, 'faith' implies 'faith in', and 'commitment' implies
'commitment to'. I do not think this is just a question of
language—or, alternatively, if it is, it is a point to be
followed up because, in one sense, the whole discussion is
about language—about how we should talk and have
grounds for talking about 'ultimate realities'. I feel a similar disquiet when he says (p. 27): 'I have never really
doubted the fundamental truth of the Christian faith—
though I have constantly found myself questioning its expression.' I am unable to be at all clear what it is that the
Bishop has never really doubted. I do not think one could

be altogether blamed f̶
the Bishop has ̶
own 'atti̶
su̶

...e

...nnot be

...ar what is the

...y not only unfair but also
...one the less it may serve to bring
...t whatever the difficulties about objective
...n talk about God there are also very grave ones
...subjective language. The only way I can describe my
own attitude to, and in, the doubtings and difficulties to
which the Bishop so rightly and with such evident sincerity
directs our attention seems to be this. Even in moments of
complete intellectual—and still worse, moral—bafflement,
or when I feel wholehearted assent to a 'Humanist' case
apparently over against a 'Christian' one, I am still unable
to doubt my faith *in God* and if I could in any way direct
or control my commitment I would wish it to be commitment *to God*. Indeed I think I would go so far as to say
that I do not really care about the truth, fundamental or
otherwise, of the 'Christian faith'. I am only concerned with
whatever the Christian faith is in so far as it helps on the
question of God, his being, his nature and the possibility
of relationship to him. I am, it is true, thus far only describing my attitude, and it may quite plausibly be argued
that this attitude is (*a*) subjectively immature and (*b*) objectively wrong. But the fact that it is possible to attack it
on, say, Freudian or existentialist grounds under (*a*) is not
the same thing as proving (*b*)—unless one holds that the
only possible theory of knowledge (as a whole, not merely

knowledge of God) is the extreme existentialist position or that Freudian insights define and exhaust reality. I may perhaps, therefore, be allowed to maintain for the purposes of the argument that my attitude has built into it an objective reference to God, although I should add that 'God' operates not so much as the name of an object but much more like a proper name. (I understand faith in or commitment to persons or causes. I do not understand, or perhaps rather do not accept, the notion of faith in or commitment to an object. That certainly is idolatry—or insanity.)

If I try to maintain such a position, including that my attitude is a 'proper' attitude (i.e. is related to truth, to the way things really are), I clearly lay myself open to plain and straightforward contradiction powerfully urged. 'You say that you are unable to doubt your commitment to a *personal God*. That may be your psychological state but it is a regrettable one (or at least a delusion if that is not necessarily regrettable). There is no God.' I have in fact demonstrated just what Tillich says (quoted by Robinson, p. 57): 'The first step to atheism is always a theology which drags God down to the level of doubtful things.' This may be so, but I very much fear that there is a real sense in which the existence of God *is* doubtful (i.e. capable of being doubted), that atheism will always seem a real existential possibility, and that this remains so even if you attempt to restate the doctrine of God in terms of 'ultimate concern' and the like. In this connection a remark of the Bishop's is very instructive (p. 29): 'God is, by definition, ultimate reality. And one cannot argue whether ultimate reality *exists*.' We have, I think, detected some very determinedly anti-traditional-metaphysic thinkers trying to get away with a concealed and possibly inverted version of the

traditional ontological
that the *idea* of G
*must* exist.
to be

ding to
argue whether
ask whether preten-
ly' are wanted at all and,
any case for bringing the word
g distance of the argument. Moreover
.eality' or 'ultimate concern' of Robinson and
(in the quotations Robinson uses) is no more an
vious, self-evident or demonstrably necessary feature of
the world or of our experiences in the world than God is.

Thus Robinson continues the passage I have just referred
to (p. 29): '. . . one cannot argue whether ultimate reality
*exists*. One can only ask what ultimate reality is like. . . .'
It is quite clear that the answer he wishes to maintain as
the true answer to *that* question is by no means self-evident,
and if it is not self-evident it is, of course, doubtful and
deniable (like the God of the theism he is wondering
whether to repudiate). For example, on p. 49 he writes:
'To believe in God as love means to believe that in pure
personal relationship we encounter, not merely what ought
to be, but what is, the deepest, veriest truth about the
structure of reality. This, in face of all the evidence, is a
tremendous act of faith. But it is not the feat of persuading
oneself of the existence of a super-Being beyond this world
endowed with personal qualities. Belief in God is the trust,
the well-nigh incredible trust, that to give ourselves to the
uttermost in love is not to be confounded but to be "accepted", that Love is the ground of our being, to which

ultimately we "come home".' 'In face of all the evidence', 'the well-nigh incredible trust' and so on make it quite clear that talk about the existence of ultimate reality not being arguable is irrelevant bluff. 'Ultimate reality' is a trivial and meaningless phrase until you begin to characterize 'it', and the character the Bishop (and Tillich) want to give 'it' is something over and above 'it' where 'it' is just plain matter of fact reality (the 'stuff' that is 'all the evidence'). They say, in fact, that 'it' is to be described in 'personal categories', and that 'Love is the ground of our being'. Since *all* human conduct is manifestly not loving, and it is very doubtful in what sense any of the processes of the physical universe could ordinarily be so described, it begins to appear that 'ultimate reality' is logically very much like a phrase describing an 'object' which is 'other than' the objects we actually encounter, even if it is thought of as 'underlying' rather than 'being above' the phenomenal world.

The fact that this 'Ground' is 'something' which is other than the stuff of our ordinary life and existence even if it is in that ordinary stuff that 'it' is encountered is made clear enough at numerous points, despite repeated statements which try to equate the two. Compare for example the quotation above where 'Love' suddenly gets a capital letter and we are said to be 'accepted' and 'come home', even if only in inverted commas (i.e. it is at least *as if* we were in a personal relationship with the Other—why not then a (carefully guarded) conception of a personal God?) Further, we are warned that 'the eternal *Thou* is not to be equated with the finite *Thou*, nor God with man or nature' (p. 53), just after we have been told (correctly on the basis of the first epistle of John) that the statement that 'God is love' is not reversible, i.e. God is the subject and love is the

predicate. But all th...
logic we ar...
we d...

...n what
...aintain.
...ism are not even clari-
...their procedure. Indeed, a good
... seems in danger of being less clear and,
...ssibly more dishonest than some more tradi-
...i statements. Take, for example, the extended quote
from Tillich on p. 81, where the talk is of grace. Grace is
carefully referred to as 'it' but 'it' behaves in a very personal way (and, indeed, since the 'happenings' involved are
said not to be at our command it looks very much as if
grace 'comes in from outside'—at any rate from outside us).
The situation referred to is 'as though a voice were saying
"You are accepted"'. Now 'seeming to be addressed' and
still more 'accepting the fact that we are accepted' sounds
like descriptions of a personal relationship with a being
who is at least personal and we may perhaps believe that
this *is* what is being pointed to, as later on the term 'Ground'
gets a capital 'G' which suggests that perhaps it is being
treated as very like a proper name. Again statements like
'we all know that we are bound eternally and inescapably
to the Ground of our being' (cited on p. 80) are just not
true save where 'we all' means 'all we who believe in an
eternal personal God who will not let us go'. If, for example, 'we all' meant 'I and my friends' then there would
be some who would hold that any 'I' is simply a temporary
and temporal collocation of matter who could only be
spoken of as 'bound eternally and inescapably to the

Ground of our being', in so far as it is true that matter or energy cannot be created or destroyed. (A very doubtful proposition, I believe.)

I should maintain, therefore, that the traditional theistic talk about a personal God is no more (although admittedly no less) *logically* difficult than is the talk about 'ultimate reality' and 'ultimate concern' which is urged upon us. For *as used* the term 'ultimate reality' no more refers to some self-evident existence than does the name 'God'. One can refuse or be unable to believe in God and one can refuse or be unable to believe that 'ultimate reality' has the character asserted.

Further, *if* ultimate reality does have the character asserted of 'it', then it looks very much as if it remains true that there exists a personal God who is other than and more than the stuff and phenomena of our life, however true it must be that he is to be encountered only in and through this stuff.

Hence the task to which the Bishop of Woolwich's book and the response to it summon us is that of re-deepening our theism by drawing much more fully on the rich and deep truths of the Christian tradition, always with a full consciousness of the difficulties and demands which modern insights make upon us (although by no means all these demands are in essence new; I suspect that the only thing which has always counted decisively against the difficulty of believing in God is that as a matter of fact he exists and makes himself known).

In connection with this task I would like to add two brief postscripts. First, it is by no means self-evident that images of depth are richer or more satisfactory than images of height—and that especially in the area of personal relationships and personal development. Here is a matter for

urgent discussion between
How far does 'depth'
escape from reali̲
to the womb'
of inte̲
ot̲                                                          ̲o,
                                                         ̲emand
                                               ̲ence wherein
                                     ̲ves? Ought we to
                            ̲ing 'deeper into our-
                      ̲e concern) is to reach out
                ̲eyond ourselves to a fulfilment
          ̲rsons? It might perhaps be true that
        ̲ranscendence is the problem of the fulfil-
     ̲an personality in a fullness of personality that
   ̲es all personal possibilities in a Transcendent which
̲ho) is fully personal. To this end the best symbolism
might be the challenge of height symbolism. Perhaps it may
turn out that the doctrine of the Trinity (the transcendent
'personalness' of God which is more than 'persons' and yet
the perfection of unified personality) is not all that irrelevant psychologically, metaphysically or theologically.

And secondly, if the conviction that ultimate reality is
love does require us to continue to believe in a personal
God (or does depend for its truth on the existence of a
personal God—whichever way we happen to or always have
to come to the truth), then it may very well turn out that
the material which the Bishop brings to bear in his fourth
chapter on the question of Christology is again to be used
to re-enliven rather than replace the traditional understanding of the person of Jesus.

For example, on p. 74 Robinson writes: 'It is in Jesus,
and Jesus alone, that there is nothing of self to be seen, but
solely the ultimate, unconditional love of God. It is as he

emptied himself utterly of himself that he became the carrier of "the name which is above every name", the revealer of the Father's glory—for that name and that glory is simply Love.' But Love is the ultimate reality of the Universe who is God. If one were wanting to relate this directly to the traditional way of stating Christian doctrine (based on the Greek language of the third and fourth Christian centuries) one could point out that 'ultimate reality' could legitimately be tied up with the Greek word *hypostasis* ('that which stands under', 'what in each individual case is really there'). One would want to make this tie up because *hypostasis* is the traditional word for the 'persons' of the Trinity and for the 'person' of Jesus Christ. But since this ultimate reality is rightly thought of as personal (i.e. *is* —really—Love) and since Jesus is 'solely the ultimate, unconditional love of God', is it not legitimate to say that the *hypostasis* who is Jesus (i.e. the *reality* of the person who is called 'Jesus') is, as the Creed says, 'of one substance with the Father' (i.e. a real expression of the reality which/ who is God)? For Jesus is the perfect, particular, personal expression of the underlying personal reality of the Universe. Further, as the Bishop indicates in his talk of 'emptied himself utterly of himself', we are now in a position to have a much richer understanding of the traditional doctrine of the divine self-emptying in Jesus. For if love is 'existence for others' then to be 'really Love' (an 'hypostasis' who is 'of one substance' with the Father) is identical with existing wholly for others and emptying oneself of one's own self-existence to that end, so that the human personal existence of Jesus *is* the divine existence in the terms of our limited and creaturely existence.

This is not just theological word-play or logic-chopping, but is closely related to this matter of a 'tremendous act of

faith' or 'the well-nigh
(on p. 49) sp
troubl

... as the
...cern is really
...gs as they hit me and
...ely related to ultimate reality,
... decision whether you decide that it is
...ation which is ultimate or Love or what
... But acts of faith and trust are not to be commended for being 'tremendous' or 'well-nigh incredible'. To
be anything other than irresponsible escapism they must
have grounds. And one very powerful ground for deciding
that ultimate reality is Love is belief in God and one of
the most powerful grounds for believing in God is Jesus,
especially Jesus as both the climax of a long tradition of
belief in God and the source of such a tradition. Hence
'who Jesus really is' is directly linked with 'what is the
nature of ultimate reality'.

Of course there are very great difficulties in all this. In
particular I am personally convinced that the Bishop's
strictures about traditional Christology in practice being
alarmingly and misleadingly monophysite (i.e. treating
Jesus as God absorbing and in effect removing human
nature) are far more generally true than his strictures on the
practice of theism (which are true enough). But I wished
simply to give a brief indication in the area of Christology
of my general thesis which is that the way forward to do
justice to the insights and challenges perceived and conveyed by such as Tillich, Bonhoeffer and, in their steps,
the Bishop of Woolwich, lies in taking very seriously, far

more seriously than is current practice over an alarmingly large area of the Church, the insights and assertions of the continuing Christian tradition. For our primary concern is surely not that 'they', whoever they are, should agree with 'us', whoever 'we' are, but that 'we' and 'they' should together be taken beyond our present partial insights and errors nearer to the wholeness of understanding which is truth.

To this end total surrender to what are alleged to be the 'necessary' ways for modern thinking is likely to be as stultifying and misleading as is abject and unreflective clinging to older statements and ways of thinking treated as mere formulae. But in so far as they represent an understanding of God and ultimate reality which our fathers wrested from their own encounters with life and with God we surely neglect them at our peril. I believe that the Bishop is wholly right to seek to shock the Church into really awakening to the fact that the way we look at the world we live in must be radically different from the views acceptable to those who lived before us. But if there is any sense in talking about God at all we can scarcely suppose that we shall know what we may *truthfully* say if we neglect what others have, under the pressure of their ultimate concerns, learnt to say of the God who was ultimate reality to them.[1]

[1] In *Learning for Living*, a journal of Christian education (SCM Press, September 1s 6d), Mr Jenkins contributes a more positive and popular article on 'Where is God?' Other articles discuss the problems involved for teachers in schools.

...nis fresh and lively book
...of interest in theological matters
...n reached in this country for many years.
...uch attention is focused unexpectedly upon a
...cular piece of work, it is inevitably expected to bear
more weight than it was intended to carry. To say, therefore, that the book raises more questions than it answers is
not necessarily to criticize it. After all, it says as much itself
and it is to its credit that it has raised so many questions so
sharply in minds where they had evidently been lying dor-
mant. Yet these are questions which require answers. The
comments I want to make will certainly not provide those
answers—they will often raise even more questions—but I
hope they will serve to carry the discussion a little further
in the direction of some of the answers.

First, it is clear that the idea of God as the ground of
being, as distinct from the God 'up there' or 'out there',
represents a real break-through in Dr Robinson's mind, as
it does in the mind of Tillich and his many followers, but
it is worth enquiring what kind of break-through this is.
The reaction of most naturalistic unbelievers to the notion
of 'the ground of being' appears to be just as negative as it
is to that of the God 'up there' or 'out there'. The leap of
faith it involves is just as great, as indeed Dr Robinson
himself recognizes at one point, even though it may be in

a different direction. The significance of this notion appears, therefore, to be much greater for the believer seeking better understanding of his faith, or for the half-believer who is in danger of losing faith because of confusion of mind, than it is for the obstinate unbeliever. This may be true of any philosophical formulation of Christian truth but it is, perhaps, of some help to be clear that the chief difficulty men have with God is with the fact of his existence as a reality other than themselves rather than with the way in which that fact is expressed.

Secondly, I wonder whether *Honest to God* does justice to the Biblical idea of God and to the ideas of many of the great theologians of the Church who have recalled us to the Bible. It is true that the Biblical and the traditional views of God and his action in relation to men and the world are expressed in terms of an understanding of the physical world and man's place in it which is no longer tenable. But is not the striking thing about the Bible the independence which it shows in relation to the world-views which it has to use? Its concern is to make clear the Lordship of God over the world and men, and his freedom in his revelation. No reformer of images could be more radical than the Old Testament about the 'image' men have of God. God is the nameless One, whom no man has seen, upon whose face man cannot look and live. He is not the One who simply is; he is the One 'who will be', revealed only in his free action. He is not a God whom we can 'project' by the use of our own imagination. To say that the men of the Bible 'literally' believed in a God who dwelt in a place 'above the bright blue sky' is surely to be guilty of anachronism. They thought in very concrete terms but did not have our conception of a literal statement and their understanding of God was so dynamic that it is unjust to

charge them with a ...
their belief w...
verse ...

...ection
...ole clearer if
...elation between God,
...e vision of the light of the
... which we have in the face of Jesus
..., it is surely correct to say that the New
...nt, against the background of the Old, has *no* image of God except as he is seen in Jesus Christ. It is only here that, as Paul reminded the Corinthians, the veil is removed and that men are able to use great boldness of speech in relation to God. The history of theology can be read as a series of attempts to recover the authentic Biblical Lordship of God as revealed in Christ when men are in danger of naturalizing or falsely supernaturalizing him. It is misleading to start upon this task of recovery with the assumption that it is something peculiar to our own age.

This is not to deny that there are peculiar elements in the situation of our age which may prompt us to more radical re-casting than has ever before been previously attempted. Our awareness of the character of other religions and the scope of modern science and scientific method, and our knowledge of the mysterious immensities of space and time within which our little planet is set—all should make us realize that many of the old issues of theology may need to be looked at in a different perspective. This may well prompt us to a new agnosticism on many levels where Christians in the past have been dogmatic about God, but it is not necessarily one which will have a great deal in common with what passes for agnosticism in these days. Faith in the 'God above God' may well make us reserved and cautious in attempting fresh formulations about God and his ways with men, but it will also make us more radical than we are often accustomed to be about much modern 'secular' thought as well as about the churches and traditional Christianity. We may need to learn to become as radical as the Bible is about the depth of the estrangement between man and God and about the fact that the initiative in revelation comes from God's side rather than ours. From this point of view, we may have to say that while Karl Barth does not answer all our questions, he may yet point more clearly to the places where their answer is to be found than some of the theologians quoted so frequently in *Honest to God*.

Thirdly, much more work clearly still needs to be done about 'religion' and 'man's coming of age'. We can argue that if 'religion' is understood in the sense in which it is apparently used by both Barth and Bonhoeffer, as man's search for God on man's own terms, as his effort to make some kind of adjustment to the 'ground of being' on a level less radical than that of the self-forgetful commitment of faith, it clearly can become faith's greatest enemy, the last bastion of human pride to hold out against God. The experience of the Jews in relation to Jesus, and of the churches throughout the ages, demonstrates that this is the most persistent and far-reaching temptation which confronts men. To call attention to this is always an urgently necessary part of the prophetic ministry within the Church. Yet if attacks on 'religion' are not to confuse us as much as they prompt us to radical self-criticism, these further things need to be said.

First, the word 'religion' is used most commonly to de-

scribe the whole sph<br>
ground of his <br>
'religi

ıcligion'

ınadequate, is

ρeople suppose.

whether it is fair to think of
...ore limited sense in purely negative
write off the whole vast history of man's
..., in all its variety, quite as easily as that? And does
not a response to God's self-revelation inevitably produce
that love of God and 'love of the brethren' which finds its
natural expression in religious forms, so that the children
of the most 'religionless Christians' are bound to have to
come to terms again with a religious heritage? The relation
between faith and religion must surely always be thought
of as a complicated and many-sided one, and over-simpli-
fication is likely to lead to serious misunderstanding.

A similar danger of confusion arises when we come to
our third set of questions, those which are related to man's
coming of age. It is hard to know what Bonhoeffer meant
when he spoke of this. Did he mean man's sense of his
ability to master himself without outside resource and to
control his own destiny, an ability which has developed
since, perhaps, the Renaissance and has found its most
obvious expression in the natural sciences and technology?
Certainly, as I should have recognized more clearly in my
treatment of these matters in *Beyond Religion*, the plain
sense of much of what he says suggests as much. If this is
so, Bonhoeffer is calling attention to an important aspect of
the truth, but it cannot be overlooked that an equally strik-

ing development in the modern world has been a great intensification of self-awareness, 'the passionate subjectivity of modern man', which has led to a preoccupation with religion in Bonhoeffer's own narrow sense at least as pronounced as that of many ancient men. It is this, incidentally, which has led to the obsessive sense of guilt on the part of many modern men which often takes neurotic forms. And, as Mr H. A. Williams in his lecture in *Objections to Christian Belief* might have realized, it may be this characteristic weakness of modern men, rather than any fault in the traditional presentation of the Gospel which reaches them, that makes them unable to bear the impact of the strong, direct and surely much more adult moral challenge with which the old preachers were able to confront their hearers.

An alternative explanation of man's 'coming of age', which fits in very well with the characteristic emphasis of Bonhoeffer's thought as a whole—although, as I say, not quite so well with what he actually says in the *Letters and Papers from Prison*—is that man has come of age in Jesus Christ. He has entered into his heritage of freedom as the child of God through Christ and, as the fourth chapter of Ephesians makes clear, the gifts and graces of the Spirit have now been poured over mankind so that together we can grow to full-grown manhood in God's image. Men can now live without 'the religious presupposition' in Bonhoeffer's phrase: without the burden of guilt and without 'the feeling of absolute dependence', but with the freedom and responsibility of men who have found their true natures. The great power over themselves and their environment which modern men possess may be a *consequence* of this maturity, but it is not itself its *cause*. This power has not been achieved by a combination of purely 'secular'

historical forces. a~
efforts of i~
a~

...address
..., rather than the
...y of us are still 'religious'
... part of the time). But it is an
...misunderstood if we fail to see that it is
...it of Christ that we discover maturity.

It is only when this is seen that the answer can be given to our fourth and last question: how do these thinkers in their various ways differ from ordinary humanism? They differ because of their recognition that maturity is *not* something which men automatically possess. It is something given from a source other than themselves, something which they have to accept and which cannot be accepted without the out-going act of commitment called faith. They recognize that everything depends on the grace of God. The 'man come of age' who does not need 'the religious presupposition' must see this with greater clarity than any other if his very maturity is not to work all the more speedily to his own destruction. The secularity which Dr Robinson rightly admires (like D. L. Munby in his book *The Idea of a Secular Society* and many others) is not the product of the natural vitality of distinctively modern man in his particular situation—that tends to produce arrogant positivism. It is the consequence of a humble acceptance on man's part of his creaturely status. It is not an accident that the spread of science, and of what later came to be called democratic ideas, was related to the spread of early Calvinism.

It is true that the values of modern scientific and democratic society can become so firmly embedded in our
consciousness that they may seem to shine by their own
light and to need no external sanction. But it is also true,
as experience in our own century has spectacularly demonstrated, that when men hold to them in pride, rather than
humble gratitude, they become distorted and corrupt and
lead to disaster. This is why we still need Baptism, the
Lord's Supper and the Christian community. These also
can become either demonic or insignificant when left to
themselves. But we cannot achieve true maturity without
the reality which they signify. If we think otherwise and
begin to give ourselves airs as the founding members of a
new race of 'religionless Christians' we shall quickly find
ourselves losing our mature manhood and becoming again
children tossed to and fro by every wind of false teaching.
We shall need to have the 'religious presupposition' established again, to be convicted of sin and led to righteousness
and, like the old Israel, to learn again, the hard way, that
we owe everything to God in Christ and that we find our
life only as we lose it.

...out Dr Robinson's book is first and
...e is an atheist. He devotes a good deal of his
...o attacking the notion of a being 'out there'. He
quotes Bonhoeffer as saying that 'Man has learned to cope
with all questions of importance without recourse to God as
a working hypothesis . . .' But not only this: he is prepared to translate theological statements into non-theologi-
cal. He says that what we mean when we speak of God is
'that which concerns us ultimately'; that to speak of God
is to speak of the deepest things we experience. 'Belief in
God is a matter of "what you take seriously without any
reservation"', and to assert that God is love is to assert the
supremacy of personal relationships. All theological statements can consequently be translated into statements about
human concern.

Dr Robinson explicitly contrasts his view with what he
calls 'supranaturalism' and with what he calls 'religion'. Yet,
even although he is prepared to assert with Feuerbach that
'the true atheist is not the man who denies God, the subject;
it is the man for whom the attributes of divinity, such as
love, wisdom and justice are nothing', he is unwilling to
abandon the word 'God' and a great many kindred theo-

[1] Reprinted from *Encounter* (September) with abbreviations (see
Preface).

logical words.[1] Yet I think that we might well be puzzled by this strong desire for a theological vocabulary; for the only reason given for preserving the name 'God' is that 'our being has depths which naturalism whether evolutionary, mechanistic, dialectical or humanistic, cannot or will not recognize'. But this is to say that all atheists to date have described 'our being' inadequately. And that our accounts of human nature are all inadequate, most atheists would concede. But what, according to the Bishop, is at issue *is* how to describe *our* nature and not anything else. So the Bishop is fundamentally at one with Hume and Feuerbach, and at odds with Aquinas, Luther, and Billy Graham.

The second half of *Honest to God* reveals that the Bishop is a very conservative atheist. He wants an atheist Christology, he wishes to retain and to revise the notion of worship, and his moral attitudes are in fact intensely conservative. Sex outside marriage turns out to be just as wrong in the eyes of the Bishop, who says we must ask what the demands of love are, as it ever was for any Bishop who asked what ecclesiastical authority said. Indeed the combination of radical intellectual doubt with conservative moralism is intensely reminiscent of *Robert Elsmere* and of the agonies of Victorian clergymen. Only Dr Robinson scarcely appears in agony; he has a cheerful, even brisk, style. And he recognizes much less clearly than some of his episcopal critics the implications for traditional Christianity of what he is saying.

[1] Dr Robinson writes sometimes as if he is concerned with whether and what God is and sometimes as if it is merely a matter of finding conveniently different images to suit different audiences. So he can say that he does not wish to disturb those who find it possible still to think of God in traditional ways. This makes it possible for the Archbishop of Canterbury to present Dr Robinson as a mildly erroneous and over-enthusiastic champion of some aspects of orthodoxy at the expense of others. But in fact if Dr

But Dr R...
book

...

...our sort of
...than merely quote
..., Dietrich Bonhoeffer, and
...ents his views as the outcome of a
...Protestant theology defined by those names.
...that two questions press on us: is Protestant theology,
and not merely Dr Robinson, essentially atheistic now? And
what light does such theology throw upon our social life?

Modern Protestant theology is rooted in catastrophe. The
liberal idealism which easily confused a secular faith in un-
interrupted progress with belief in the actions of a divine
providence could not survive the trenches of World War I.
Tillich was an army chaplain, as Bultmann was to be later
on. Bonhoeffer was to be executed by the Nazis. The problem of evil had to be more than an academic exercise.
Moreover the matter of traditional Protestant preaching
with its moralizing and its promise of pietistic consolations
could scarcely survive. Two questions pressed in: how can
we think of God after the Somme, after Auschwitz? And
how can we preach to contemporary man?

The first answer to these questions was Barth's commen-
tary on *Romans*, where St Paul's Greek is conjured into a
blend of Luther, Calvin, Dostoievsky, and Kierkegaard.
(Not so misleading either, for each of them had digested
large quantities of St Paul.) Barth's message is that any

---

Robinson's argument is right, the traditional views of God are not
merely outmoded; they are simply false. And in other passages Dr
Robinson recognizes this.

attempt to justify belief in God, or any attempt to comprehend God's ways by translating revelation into terms other than its own, is bound to fail. God is infinitely distant from man and totally other. In revelation he condescends to us: we can only accept or reject, we cannot argue. Evil cannot be explained; but we can be redeemed and saved from its power. At first sight Barth's starting-point in theology is at the opposite pole from that of Dr Robinson. And certainly as Barthian theology has developed systematically it has remained a keystone of orthodoxy, by now a major influence among Roman Catholics as well as among Protestants. But Barthian theology nonetheless contains the materials for its own self-transformation. For if the Word of God cannot be identified with *any* frail human attempt to comprehend it, the way is open for sympathy with those who reject human theologies which have attempted to substitute for the Divine Word (and perhaps Barthian theology among them).

*Bultmann's* theology has three quite separate elements to it. There is first of all his historical scepticism about the New Testament events. Closely connected with this is his belief that the New Testament message is presented in terms of a pre-scientific cosmology and that consequently the gospel must be 'de-mythologized' before it can be preached to scientific man. And there is, thirdly, his view of what the de-mythologized message in fact is. The pre-scientific cosmology is one of a three-tiered universe to which belong notions of a descent into hell, an ascent into heaven, a coming again from the heavens, of angelic and demonic hierarchies and indeed of miraculous powers. This mythology conceals rather than conveys the message that man is a prey to an inauthentic existence, that Jesus summons him to a decision, by which he can face up to his being as

that of one who i...
tically. W...
a...

... ... pointing
... faith to be makes
... of the occurrence of any
... first century and, indeed, of the
... supernatural being. Christianity is secularized
... into an atheistic philosophy. Bultmann's own
... of some elements of traditional Christian theism
appears to have no rational jurisdiction within the framework of his own thought.

*Tillich's* contrast with Bultmann is at first sight sharp.
Tillich sees himself as the heir of 'the Protestant principle'
that no finite being must be confused with the divine. In so
far as secularization has been an insistence that nothing in
nature must be identified with God, secularization is a
genuine ally of Protestant Christianity. God is not *a* being,
who just happens to exist, an additional individual: in deny-
ing the existence of God the atheists are in the right. It is true
that in his *Systematic Theology* Tillich slips into ascribing
to God predicates which we would normally take to imply
that God was *a* being. God creates and God reveals himself,
for example. But he believes that in doing this he is able
to rely on his own doctrine of God. This is two-sided. In
the first volume of the *Systematic Theology* there is a good
deal of traditional metaphysical play with being and not-
being. But the rules of play are all governed by an initial
criterion whose implications are far more drastic than Tillich realizes: theological statements are statements about
what ultimately concerns us, and we learn the nature of

what ultimately concerns us by 'an analysis of the concept "ultimate concern" . . .' If the object of theological discourse is our own ultimate concern, what of God? It turns out that 'God' just is the name for that concern. We get the transition from ontological assertion to ultimate human concern very clearly stated in a sermon [quoted on p. 261 below].

Clearly, however, the conversion of the unbeliever is only so easy for Tillich because belief in God has been evacuated of all its traditional content. It consists now in moral seriousness and nothing more. Even if we were to concede Tillich a verbal triumph over the atheist, the substance of atheism has been conceded. Just as Bultmann's view of the New Testament points towards scepticism, so does Tillich's analysis of the doctrine of God. It seems that Dr Robinson is not alone as a theological atheist.

But what of Dietrich Bonhoeffer? Those who have written of him have usually dwelt on the posthumously collected *Letters and Papers from Prison* at the expense of his earlier books, and more expressly at the expense of *Sanctorum Communio* and *Akt und Sein*.[1] What Bonhoeffer tried to explain was the specific character of a Christian way of life in a Christian community. In *Akt und Sein* he even tries to solve theological problems by showing the role of the concepts in question in the life of the church. And the life of the Christian community in *Sanctorum Communio* is specified in terms of sociological categories borrowed from Ferdinand Tönnies, the familiar categories of *Gemeinschaft* and *Gesellschaft*. But Bonhoeffer wishes to show not what Christian societies share with other societies, but precisely what distinguishes Christian from other shared ways of life. He rejects the answer which both some religious apologists

[1] Now available in English translations (Collins).

and secular s...
enti...

...ot in any
...or on divine power
...ssness, lived totally for others.
...nclusion in his notes in prison that

... transcendence consists not in tasks beyond our scope
and power, but in the nearest Thou at hand. God in human
form, not, as in other religions, in animal form—the mon-
strous, chaotic, remote and terrifying—nor yet in abstract
form—the absolute, metaphysical infinite, etc.—nor yet in
the Greek divine-human of autonomous man, but man
exising for others, and hence the Crucified. . . .

So the distinction between secular atheistic man and Christian man is that the latter acknowledges his powerlessness
in his concern for others. But what would it be like to do
this in the world of today, of the welfare state and of the
under-developed countries, facing the patterns of world
revolution? One gets from Bonhoeffer's writings no clear
picture of what type of action he would actually be recommending now in 1963, but one gets the clearest picture of
what Bonhoeffer means if one sees it in the context out of
which he wrote. For in Nazi Germany, and in the Europe
of the 'thirties, the Christian role was at best one of suffering witness. The Nazi regress to gods of race made relevant
a Christian regress to a witness of the catacombs and of the
martyrs. There was available then a simple form in which
to relive Christ's passion. Bonhoeffer lived it. And in all
situations where nothing else remains for Christians this
remains.

But what has this Christianity to say not of powerlessness, but of the handling of power? Nothing; and hence the oddity of trying to reissue Bonhoeffer's message in our world. Consider Bonhoeffer's cry from prison:

> Man's religiosity makes him look in his distress to the power of God in the world; he uses God as a *Deus ex machina*. The Bible however directs him to the powerlessness and suffering of God; only a suffering God can help.

Imagine it directed to a church which is providing chaplains for the West German armed forces, as Bonhoeffer's church is, or to a church which chose the right moment to get out of gilt-edged and into equities, as Dr Robinson's did. Only a suffering God can help?

Bonhoeffer's Christianity is, then, intelligible only in one sort of context. Outside that context it lacks precisely any specific differentia from the way of life of sensitive generous liberals. It does not issue in atheism as the conclusion of an argument (as Bultmann's theology does), and it does not present atheism in theological language (as Tillich's theology does), but it fails in the task for which it was designed and in our sort of society it becomes a form of practical atheism, for it clothes ordinary liberal forms of life with the romantic unreality of a catacombic vocabulary.

We can see the harsh dilemma of a would-be contemporary theology. The theologians begin from orthodoxy, but the orthodoxy which has learnt from Kierkegaard and Barth becomes too easily a closed circle, in which believer speaks only to believer, in which all human content is concealed. Turning aside from this arid in-group theology, the most perceptive theologians wish to translate what they have to say to an atheistic world. But they are doomed to one of two failures. Either they succeed in their translation:

in which case w~~...~~
transform~~...~~
i~~...~~

~~...~~ it is the
~~...~~ .clusions. We can
~~...~~ e is not just that of an
~~...~~ stifies to the existence of a whole
~~...~~ which have retained a theistic vocabu-
~~...~~ acquired an atheistic substance. Yet how can these
~~...~~ continue to coexist? To answer this question we must look
at the social context of this type of theology.

Dr Robinson writes as if the secularization of the modern
world were an accomplished and a recognized fact. If he
were correct we should expect a corresponding sense of
triumph in secularist writers. In fact we find too often the
same uneasiness that we discover in the theologians.

England is perhaps an untypical country. We have neither
the ecclesiastical political parties of Europe nor the majority church-going of the United States. But we experience
many of the same pressures, and therefore find analogous
religious phenomena. The number of Easter communicants
in the Church of England has risen very slowly but fairly
steadily for a decade and a half. Over half the marriages in
England take place in Anglican churches. Over half the
children eligible for Anglican baptism are so baptized. Between the 10 per cent or so of clear and convinced Christians
at one end of the scale and the 10 per cent or so of convinced sceptics at the other, there is the vast mass of the
population, mostly superstitious to some degree, using the
churches and especially the Church of England to celebrate
birth, marriage, and death, and to a lesser degree Christmas.

This use or misuse of the churches is rooted in a set of vague, half-formulated and inconsistent beliefs.

In 1944-45 *Mass-Observation* carried out a survey in a London borough on the topic of religious belief which was published under the title of *Puzzled People*. In 1960 they quota-sampled the same borough. The inconsistency of both self-styled believers and self-styled unbelievers is perhaps the most striking single fact. In both 1945 and 1960 over 40 per cent of those attending Anglican services said that they did not believe in a life after death, while at least a quarter of those classed as doubters, agnostics, and atheists said that they prayed, and over 20 per cent of them said that Christ was more than a man. Tom Harrison's account of these people's beliefs in *Britain Revisited* is consistent with the answers that industrial workers gave to Dr Ferdynand Zweig on religious questions, and in *The British Worker* Dr Zweig concludes that 80 per cent of workers have some sort of 'vague belief'. But it would be sadly mistaken to suppose that this state of affairs is confined to working-class adults and children. The survey of contemporary attitudes among the readers of *New Society* (May 1963) showed a majority both for the belief that Christian morality is moribund and for the belief that this is a sad thing. But the majority also believe—what the authoritative exponents of Christianity deny—that divorce should be made easier. So we find among some of the best-educated by our conventional standards a paradoxical wish to hold on to a morality which conflicts with their own morality on matters of central importance. Behind this paradox one senses a belief that Christian theology is false and a wish that it were not, which at other social levels appears as the kind of half-belief which I have described.

The sources of this lack of consistency are several. The

folk-belief⁓

⁓ per
⁓ᴜ there is another
⁓ aᴅult church-going.

⁓ that children in this country are in-
⁓ᴀᴛᴇᴅ in Christianity as a result of the 1944 Education
Act. What they *are* indoctrinated in is confusion. This confusion is rooted in the fact that on the one hand religious
instruction is compulsory, and yet on the other it is clear
that schools do not take it seriously in the way they do basic
literacy or subjects such as history or chemistry. Since
teachers usually do not even attempt to give any criteria for
accepting or rejecting belief, many children naturally remain in a half-light between acceptance and rejection. Secularized? Not at all. The secondary modern school-children
of whom Harold Loukes wrote in *Teenage Religion* would
suggest, for example, that the question of whether God did
or did not make the world could not be answered because
nobody else can have been there to see. If they do believe
in God, it is often the God 'up there' (literally, physically
'up') whom Dr Robinson thinks has been incredible for a
long time.

Christianity provided pre-industrial England with a common frame of reference, with a sense of over-all meaning
and with a pattern which gave form to life. Revolutionary
protest from the Levellers to the Chartists could express
itself within this pattern just as much as the conservatism
of the squirearchy. But industrial society has never been
able to accommodate a religious interpretation of its own

H

activities. The founders of atheist humanism hoped for and predicted secularization not merely in the sense of abandonment of religious belief and practice, but in the sense of a transformation of human goals and hopes from other-worldly into this-worldly. The present was to be judged and transcended, not by looking to the justice of heaven but by looking to that of the future. The hope of glory was to be, and in some important measure was, replaced by the hope of Utopia.

But we have neither glory nor Utopia to hope for. The hope that a secular Utopian tradition, whether Liberal or Marxist, sought to provide was never realized. The routines of working-class life, the competitive ladders of the middle classes, absorb us into immediacy. We are dominated by a present to which the idea of a radically different future is alien. What conventional politics promises us is always a brighter version of what we have now. This is why political talk about ends and aims is always doomed to become rhetoric. In this situation the substance of religious belief is no longer with us, but in our ordinary secular vocabulary we have no language to express common needs, hopes, and fears that go beyond the immediacies of technique and social structure.

What we do have is a religious language, which survives even though we do not know what to say in it. Since it is the only language we have for certain purposes it is not surprising that it cannot be finally discarded. But since we have no answers to give to the questions we ask in it, it remains continually in need of re-interpretation, re-interpretation that is always bound to fail. We should therefore expect to find continual attempts to use religious language to mask an atheistic vacuum, and sooner or later someone was bound to try to preserve the religious language and the

.... of theological discourse. Hence
Dr Robinson's book needs not only to be understood as a
symptom of our condition, but to be sympathized with as a
desperate attempt that cannot succeed.

Because all this is so, it is highly important that the
theologians should not be left alone with their discussions,
to carry them on as *they* please. For the significance of
their discussions extends far beyond theology. The public
response to *Honest to God* helped to make this clear. But
in the next phase when the issues are less immediately news-
worthy, the danger is that God will once more be treated as
an in-group totem. Once there were organized secularist
groups (the Rationalist Press Association, the Ethical Union,
and the like) which could have assisted in ensuring that the
discussion continued in the public forum. But all these
groups essentially became nonconformist churches and
share in the general decline of nonconformity. So one gets
the pathos of humanist groups in universities which are
imitations of the Student Christian Movement. At the moment one cannot dispense with this kind of group, if only
because it provides a counterweight to the Christians. But
the danger is that atheism is then treated as if it too is the
private creed of yet another minority religious group,
whereas atheism is in fact expressed in most of our social
life.

The difficulty lies in the combination of atheism in the
practice of the life of the vast majority, with the profession

of either superstition or theism by that same majority. The creed of the English is that there is no God and that it is wise to pray to him from time to time.

# COMMENT

## BY JOHN A. T. ROBINSON

I AM grateful to Alasdair MacIntyre for his astringent and percipient article on my book. I would fully agree with him (despite his suggestion to the contrary) that we live today in a mixed society, religiously as well as economically. Secularization, like socialization, is not complete, and perhaps it never will be. But it is important to be clear how we understand what is going on. Let me press the parallel I have suggested. Socialization I take to be a development of our age which is occurring at a different pace and in different forms all over the world— almost without respect of political colour: it is a neutral fact pressed upon us by living tighter and tighter together in one world. Secularization is similarly, as I see it, a neutral fact, pressed upon us, in different forms and at various speeds, by taking seriously the presuppositions of modern science: it does not of itself imply a particular attitude towards God. Socialization is indeed anti-capitalist in that it rejects, for example, as incompatible with our world the capitalist definition of free- dom as the right to do what you like with your own. But it is not necessarily Socialist, as though the process admitted of only one political expression. Similarly, secularization repre- sents a revolt against certain thought-patterns of the pre- scientific world-view. But the rejection of these thought- patterns does not in itself require an atheistic view of the world (though it may make untenable certain forms of tradi- tional 'theism'). To greet every sign of secularization as evi- dence of growing godlessness is as wrong-headed and re- actionary as to see each advance in the welfare state as a mask of creeping Socialism.

... there is no God

... .om time to time.' I would

... the English is that there *is* a God

... this out, whatever it may mean, with striking

...unimity), that it *is* wise to pray to him from time to time, but that, in terms of *that* God, they are practical atheists. The decisive thing is that what they identify as 'God' is to all intents and purposes an '*x*'. As Werner Pelz has said,[1] 'We must realize that when we use the word "God" we are talking about something which no longer connects with anything in most people's life, except with whatever happens to be left over when all the vital connections have been made'. God is a Being in whose existence they believe (or disbelieve) over and above (rather than in and through) what for them makes up 'life'. The crediting or discrediting of this Being is almost totally irrelevant to the question of the *reality* of God in any sense in which the Christian is interested. Perhaps, as part of his protest against the current trivialization of God, a Christian has to be prepared to be called an atheist. Atheism after all is no new charge against Christians, and in the second century they survived it with equanimity.

But I believe that in terms of the real issues this is a misconception and that Mr MacIntyre has stated the matter wrongly. He accuses the theology represented by my book of using 'religious language to mask an atheistic vacuum'. I would find that a more apt description of such a book as Julian Huxley's *Religion without Revelation*. I am not wedded to the religious language, but I am deeply concerned for the reality of God.

Obviously the whole relevance of the label 'atheism' turns on the meaning of the word 'God'. If God is equated with a supernatural Being whose existence over and above the world

[1] *Prism*, April 1963, p. 23.

has to be demonstrated, I am not prepared to spend time contending the charge. Not that I would presume to *deny* such a Being (he is not capable of disproof). Rather, I would see this as one particular 'projection' or representation of the reality 'God' which has hitherto helped most people to make him real but which increasingly I believe conspires to make him unreal. MacIntyre, like others, detects an ambivalence in my attitude to 'the traditional views of God'. Are they, he asks, 'merely outmoded' or 'simply false'? I would say, 'Neither'. They represent a way of expressing the truth of God (in the idiom of the supranaturalist world-view) which is entirely valid for those for whom this makes him a reality. My concern is for those for whom this reduces him to irrelevance or incredibility. But I am equally concerned that they shall be able to enter into and make their own the rich heritage of a tradition, in the Bible and the Church, which is expressed in the categories of a pre-secular age.

The question of God is not, I am convinced, to be identified with the validity or invalidity of this particular projection. It is concerned with whether one can speak of *ultimate* reality at all and with what character this reality has. Is there any sense in which one can meaningfully talk of anything unconditional or absolute? The true atheist, such as Marghanita Laski, would answer 'No'. And this, I would agree with her, is the real dividing line between those who can speak of 'God' and those who cannot.

The question of God is the question whether, for instance, Jesus' relationship to the reality he could only address as 'Abba! Father!' is veridical or not. Is the constitution of the universe such that it justifies the trust, 'Father, into thy hands I commend my spirit'? Is reality ultimately gracious, or is it in the last analysis impersonal or neutral? Can love, the *agape* of the Cross, be the last word about it? The man who believes in God, as defined in Christ, believes that in the unconditional constraint of love he encounters something that speaks to him not simply of his own deepest self,[1] nor of what he would like

_____

[1] It is not true, as MacIntyre says, that 'what, according to the Bishop, is at issue is how to describe *our* nature and not anything else'. What is at issue is the reality (to use Professor John Macquarrie's term) of 'Being as gracious', though *we*, of course, can only speak of that Being as we are grounded in it.

...the reality we call 'God' and that my book is concerned for its restoration rather than abolition is confirmed by the reaction of those to whom it has 'spoken'. It has been welcomed not by the atheists nor by the religious but by those who say that it has given God back to them and made him real in a post-religious age. The genuine atheists have rejected it, as have the traditionalists from the other side.

I decline to accept as Mr MacIntyre states it 'the harsh dilemma of a would-be contemporary theology', of either addressing an 'in-group' or accepting the atheism of its hearers. I believe the response to my book has shown that a third alternative is very much of a live option.

# IX

## THE DEBATE CONTINUES

### JOHN A.T. ROBINSON

WHAT follows is not intended as a 'sequel' to *Honest to God*; nor is it a 'Reply to my Critics'. The issues raised by the debate, theoretical and practical, are too big to be taken up so soon or within the scope of an essay, and the atmosphere at some points is still too emotionally charged.[1] Nor do I wish to give the impression that it is I who am in possession of the answers. To believe in the Holy Spirit is to believe that out of the corporate life of the Church, if it is really prepared to be open and expose itself at the deepest level to the truth and power by which it lives, there will come the insight and the wisdom which none of us individually can command.

All I have attempted to do here is to bring the first round of the debate to a constructive close. I have tried to look back on some of the factors that have made it what it is, to clear up a few of the misunderstandings, and to mark out afresh the areas in which, as it seems to me, the discussion could with profit move forward.

---

[1] E.g. on ethics, where discussion on 'the new morality' has got mixed with so much mud that a moratorium is in place. The phrase has simply become an indiscriminate target of abuse and is taken to cover every form of invitation to sexual laxity. It would be difficult to deduce from subsequent comment that in my chapter it represented a sustained plea for chastity of pure personal relationship as the ground of all moral judgements! It is interesting that this chapter in *Honest to God* provoked practically no controversy, until it was linked (in a Church newspaper) with the Profumo affair.

... ̄ the ..., is partly a mystery. ... predicted and arranged. But in retro- ... there will be seen to be both particular occasions and more fundamental causes. One is still far too near the centre of the explosion to assess these in perspective. But it may help to begin these reflections on what has come out of the debate by looking at some of the things which have blown it up to its present dimensions. For it is the sheer scale which has conditioned much of its character. People have been drawn into it who would normally never be affected, and its very proportions have occasioned enthusiasms and anxieties that have clouded judgment.

There is first of all the general issue of publicity and the way in which the book was presented to the public, and secondly the implications of the fact that it was written by a bishop.

1. It is only fair to all concerned to insist in the first instance that the publicity-explosion was neither sought nor expected. If there had been a desire to exploit the market, (a) I should not have given the manuscript to a religious publisher, (b) there would have been a special publicity-campaign to launch it, and (c) I should have written a very different book. As it was, the SCM Press was caught completely unprepared for the sales—though it recovered with impressive efficiency—and much of the subsequent misunderstanding has arisen from the fact that I was *not* writing for the popular audience that has since devoured it. Indeed,

I have the utmost sympathy with those who have struggled with its technical terms and for whom this book, which was constantly seeking to push out beyond the presuppositions of the accepted categories, formed their *introduction* to theology. I should dearly love to be able to write the book for which so many have asked, setting out what I have to say 'in simple language that ordinary people can understand'. It might also help to correct the assumption that what one believes in is *limited* to the themes touched on in a book of 140 pages! Indeed, my slight treatment of many topics was governed by the fact that I had already written on them extensively[1] and was presupposing a public which, if it had not read these books, could easily do so.

Discussion of the publicity that followed has revolved around two themes: (a) the effect produced by my article in the *Observer* the Sunday prior to publication and (b) the doubtful wisdom of publishing the book at all as a paperback.

(a) The initiative for the first came entirely from the staff of the *Observer* and presented (at short notice) what I still believe was a real opportunity outside the normal channels of the Church to engage at a serious level as a Christian in the intellectual debate of our day. Whether I used the opportunity aright must be left to others to judge. To condense into readable form ideas which were bound to be unfamiliar was a calculated hazard. It meant sacrificing qualifications and risking oversimplification. At least it was

---

[1] E.g. on the doctrine of the Church in *The Body* (1952) and *On Being the Church in the World* (1960); on public worship in *Liturgy Coming to Life* (1960; 2nd ed. with a new preface, 1963); on the Last Things in *In the End, God . . .* (1950), *Jesus and His Coming* (1957) and *Christ Comes in* (1960); and on the Resurrection in my article 'Resurrection in the N.T.' in *The Interpreter's Dictionary of the Bible* (1962).

described

... attention
...eller, from which I
...ended the emphasis to fall. It
...ver, upon a quotation from Monica Fur-
..., with which I proposed to end. This, however, was
cut from the article, and the cut left me without a title. The
one suggested to me—'Our image of God must go'—struck
me as negative and arrogant. I resisted it, but under pressure of time and with nothing convincing to propose in its
place, I eventually concurred. Journalistically it was a good
title, as events were to show. But as well as leaving a de-
structive impression, it also had the effect of shifting the
centre of gravity of the subsequent debate.

It centred attention on the question of our *image* of God
—and this was perpetuated by the title of the Archbishop's
subsequent pamphlet, *Image Old and New*. It suggested too
that my chief intention was to *replace* one mental picture
by another. I should like to repeat what I have said several
times since: that there is no question of one image (for
instance, of height) being wrong and another (for instance,
of depth) being right. Both, as many have since pointed
out, have a long and honourable history in Christian
thought and neither excludes the other. I was simply suggesting a mental transposition, which had helped me, for
those who found the other language had the effect, for

[1] In his presidential address to the Convocation of Canterbury
on 7 May 1963.
[2] Reproduced below, pp. 246-7.

them, of making God unreal and remote. I was *also*, indeed, posing the need for a more radical revolution in our day, namely, the detaching of the Christian doctrine of God from any necessary dependence on a 'supranaturalistic' world-view. To this I shall return in greater detail.[1] But my point here is that this is only incidentally connected with the question of *images*. These are concerned with how *any* formulation of doctrine (whether in a supranaturalistic idiom or any other) can most effectively be made vivid. It happens that Tillich draws on the traditional imagery of depth to give body to his attempt at a formulation of Christian doctrine 'beyond naturalism and supranaturalism'. But if this does not help (and it is certainly not exclusive of images of height), there is no need to embrace it; and his sermons in particular show him using the whole gamut of Biblical imagery. The question of images is as old as the hills: the question of a replacement for the supranaturalistic world-view is a modern one. I regret that the two issues have become confused. I trust that the book makes clearer what I meant. Normally one expects the summarizing article to be reviewed in the light of the book, the trailer to be judged by the film, and not *vice versa*.

There is no doubt, however, that the newspaper article acted as a tin-opener. Whether it was desirable that the lid should have been taken off is another question; and this leads into the wider discussion of how such potentially explosive ideas should properly be presented to the public at large.

(*b*) 'Normally in this country', as Gerald Downing expressed it,[2] 'theological currents pass through many transformer stations before they reach "lay" homes.' New theological ideas are put out in academic monographs, books

---

[1] Pp. 256-63 below.          [2] P. 126 above.

...that

...distorted almost beyond
... meanwhile the laity suffer from chronic
inanition.

The first question is not whether this process is desirable but whether it is any longer possible. Obviously to a large extent it is, and it is going on all the time. But it is also being by-passed at all kinds of points by the techniques of mass communication, and in particular by the paperback and the television. The cry for 'hard covers only' is a lost cause, whether in theology or economics or sex. And such is the speed of modern communications that the flash is virtually instantaneous all over the world. There is no time for the slowly-maturing growth of ideas—for one to plant, another to water, another to reap, and for yet others to process and to market. The element of distortion and distension is equally powerful—though I doubt in fact whether its effects are as great as those produced by the old process over a hundred years.

But the fact remains that theologians and churchmen have to learn to live with this situation like everyone else —that is, if they wish their ideas to have public circulation. Sometimes indeed one almost wonders if they do. 'Not in front of the people' seems to be the unwritten rule of decent debate, and the fact that things are taken up by the secular press (and inevitably distorted—though hardly more so than by the religious press) seems to be resented rather than welcomed. I can understand this. But I believe it is an inevitable part of the apostolic mission of the Church in the twentieth century, and one has to be prepared to accept the risks and carry the burden.

But what of the effect? Gerald Downing's analogy again strikes me as putting the matter well. Speaking of the transformer stations he goes on,

> In many places, such stations have never been built, or if built, they have fallen into disrepair. And there are many Luddites who applaud this state of affairs, for currents are very dangerous things, and people should be insulated from them, if not by design, then at least by accident. If you try to by-pass the transformer stations, you may get a very exciting short-circuit: there is a bright flash, and then all goes dead. On the other hand, you may find many of the lay homes and the local churches have all along been wired to stand very high tension indeed, and your dangerous act may by-pass the natural and artificial resistances, and produce a glad and warm light.

Should the laity be 'exposed'? This is simply part of the contemporary 'crisis of the laity' within the life of the Church. I believe that in the long run we have got to learn to 'trust the people'; and there has been ample evidence in my mail that the people are capable of being trusted and thinking for themselves far more than many of the clergy are prepared to allow. The academics are in many cases speaking more directly to the laity than their own parish priests. In 'the educated society' or 'the fraternal society' (to use two current designations of our world) the assumption that the laity will take their theology in penny packets from the pulpit is fast breaking down. Not unexpectedly, the breakdown has also revealed unpreparedness and insecurities on all sides. But the opportunities have also been expanded enormously. For lay men and women are beginning on a large scale to think for themselves. Some,

...ular crisis has exposed the state of our transformer stations. I said in my book that I saw it, among other things, as 'an attempt at communication, at mediation between a realm of discourse in which anything I have to say is very familiar and unoriginal and another, popular world, both within and without the Church, in which it is totally unfamiliar and almost heretical'. One reckoned on the gulf, but one reckoned also on organs of communication that would 'get the message', translate it and pass it on. And of course there have been many such attempts at interpretation—in sermons, reviews and discussion groups beyond number. For all this I am humbly grateful.

But, having said this, I am bound to say that it is the secular 'transformer stations' which have been most help. It was a secular newspaper that saw the significance and asked for a preview. It has been the television companies and the BBC who have been most understanding—and I would like to pay a tribute to their religious advisers and departments who are doing a courageous work of communication, often in the face of obloquy from the Church. While I have been besieged with requests for interviews, it is noteworthy that not a single person from the Church press, national or local, has asked to see me. No one has come and said quite simply, 'Now tell us what you are really trying to say, so that we can be sure we have got inside it—whether we agree with it or not'. There has been extraordinarily little sign of that elementary charity of interpretation (such as one might expect in Christian journalism) which credits a man with believing the best until proved otherwise. It is those who have protested most loudly about the 'irresponsibility' of loosing new and difficult ideas on the unprepared public who have been least responsible in their onerous task of constructive interpretation. Indeed, one Church newspaper had even to be congratulated by the secular press for announcing (to its credit) that it would not print letters from those who had not read the book! But enough said.

2. Closely connected with this task of responsible communication is the propriety of these things being said by a bishop. Part of the problem here is precisely the press 'image' of a bishop—so that things get blown up and reported which would be otherwise quite unnewsworthy. But this in itself is not of any theological significance, and is in any case only a matter of degree. The utterances and activities of canons and deans (though not on the whole the leaders of the non-established churches) have almost the same capacity to hit the headlines. It is simply a phenomenon of our society to be lived with, played down, and taken into responsible account.

More important is the question raised in Church circles about the right of a bishop to indulge in such dangerous and uncertain exercises. For it belongs to his office to be a guardian and defender of the Faith and to 'banish and drive away all erroneous and strange doctrine contrary to God's Word'. Of course, if a bishop were conscientiously unable to teach what the Church teaches then he must of all men be honest enough to resign his office. But the issue here is rather, as I see it, the function of a bishop in a missionary situation.

We have long been used to the role of the missionary

...... be ignored with any realism,
....... of all in the presentation of Christian truth. And I
cannot believe that a man is discharged from this ministry
by consecration as a bishop. On the contrary, it is an essential part of the apostolic office which he is solemnly charged
to perpetuate.

But it is also a very dangerous part. For any creative
task of apologetic involves venturing out along a knife-edge
on which it is easy to slip. It will be a serious day for the
Church if a bishop cannot continue to be an exploratory
theologian, asking questions to which he does not necessarily know the answers, *trusting* the faith he is commis-
sioned to defend. Naturally, he carries an extra responsibility for divining it aright. But it is a corporate task in
which the whole Church is involved: his is not a quite
different responsibility.

## The Contemporary Ferment

I have so far simply been looking at some of the factors
which *occasioned* the eruption. But it cannot be *explained*
without seeing it as part of a much deeper and more widespread ferment.

My own writing was done shut up in my room and was
in the first instance an attempt to come to terms with convictions that had been gathering in my mind over a number
of years. Obviously they were not disconnected with various
streams in current theology, but for the most part these had

not broken surface. I had a feeling that convictions that had formed for me might also be shared by a growing number of my contemporaries, and it was for this reason that I was anxious to try them out rather than wait—perhaps for years —until I had the leisure to write a more polished and considered book.

Little did I realize two things. First, that during this same time a number of other things were bubbling up, independently of each other, which could all be recognized subsequently as belonging to the same ferment. There was *Soundings*,[1] which came out just in time for me to include a few references to it; and then in 1963, from entirely separate directions, such very different books as Werner Pelz's *God is No More*; John Taylor's *The Primal Vision: Christian Presence amid African Religion*; Sir Richard Acland's *We Teach Them Wrong: Religion and the Young*; and from Austin, Texas, Paul van Buren's *The Secular Meaning of the Gospel*.[2] There have also been a number of articles, particularly in *Prism* and the *Guardian*, whose weekly column on 'The Churches' contains some of the most astringent religious writing in Britain today, which have helped to prepare one for what the editor of the former described as the 'almost audible gasp of relief' 'when these things are at last being said openly'.

This phrase must have been quoted back at me many times in the correspondence I have received and points to the second factor in the situation. The book appears to have touched a nerve, which no one could quite have predicted. And this accounts for a number of features in the reaction. At least no one seems to have thought it was

[1] Ed., A. R. Vidler (1962).
[2] This list will perhaps serve to show how misleading it is to talk of a 'Cambridge' movement or to dismiss the whole thing as the vapours of a Combination Room mentality.

...... to recognize and respond—or even to hear—what the book was saying. The perversity of some of the things that have been read into or out of it cannot, I believe, be explained simply on rational grounds, nor can the alarming failure of communication attested by many of the comments be attributed wholly (I hope) to the obscurity of my style. For others have appeared to understand instinctively what I was getting at: it spoke to their condition and immediately made sense, even when they had had much less theological training.

But the apprehensions disclosed have not been wholly subjective. For the book has undoubtedly played its part in bringing to a head a crisis in confidence, which will be shown, I believe, to go very deep for our generation. I can put it best, perhaps, in terms of an analogy—though all analogies are dangerous, especially in a field which is not one's own.

### A Currency Crisis

The situation could be described by saying that we live in the midst—or at any rate at the beginning—of a currency crisis. It is one that affects all the traditionally accepted means of exchange among Christians and between Christians and the world in which they live: doctrinal formulations, moral codes, liturgical forms, and the rest. These are, as it were, the paper money with which the business of communication is regularly conducted. They are backed in the last resort by certain commitments, certain 'promises to pay', of which they are the token and expression.

Thus, all credal statements, all doctrines, are explications, definitions in the intellectual field, of the commitment contained in the words 'I believe in'. They describe not truths in themselves out of the context of any personal response, but a relationship-in-trust to the various aspects of the truth as it is in Jesus. They say, in greater detail or in less: 'This, when you spell it out, is what is involved in *loving* God with all your *mind*'. Similarly, moral rules, patterns of worship, forms of Church order, and the whole Christian style of life, are in the final analysis definitions, declensions of the Christian's commitment-in-love to God and neighbour with all his heart and soul and strength.

To stress this existential, experiential element behind all the Christian's affirmations is not in the least to say that they are purely subjective, in the sense that they represent merely his way of looking at things, his resolve to think or live in a certain manner. The 'promise to pay' is a two-way process. They are expressions of trust in a Reality which is trust-worthy; and the clauses of the Creed, the doctrines and forms of the Church, *describe this Reality, not just the individual's inner state*. But they *are* subjective in the sense in which Kierkegaard said that 'Truth is subjectivity'. For truth beyond the level of mere information cannot, he insisted, be apprehended in a purely objective, 'spectator' relationship, but only as a man is prepared to stand, as subject, in an I-Thou relationship of engagement, trust and commitment. It is in this sense that Tillich can say that 'all theological statements are existential':[1] they have all in the last resort to be referred back to this relationship, and their cash value tested by it.

[1] *Systematic Theology*, vol i (1953), p. 299.

work,
...er and the rest, on
... is an area of exchange within
...ymbols are accepted and valid. And, of course,
there is. But in our generation people are increasingly
beginning to question whether in fact they *mean anything*
or stand for anything real. They ask for their backing, for
their cash value.

Within the sterling area, so to speak, the currency holds
its own. For those for whom it means business and buys
goods there is nothing whatever the matter with it, even
though its purchasing power may not be as great as it was
in the 'ages of faith', before, as it were, we went off the
gold-standard. But the trouble is that the area of convert-
ibility is becoming dangerously restricted: it is increasingly confined to the circle of a religious in-group. The
uneasy suspicion is growing that churchmen may find themselves holding wads of paper money whose exchange value
is virtually nil.

There is nothing more unsettling than a currency crisis.
It exposes hidden insecurities, it produces panic reactions.
And particularly it affects those living on inherited capital
or fixed incomes, with nothing new coming in. It is under-
standable that they should resent anything that appears to
weaken confidence still further—even though it may simply
be drawing attention to what is happening. And since we
all have a far greater stake in the old than we care to admit,
no one can treat such a crisis lightly or irresponsibly.

It demands endless sympathy, patience and technical skill, to ensure that in the process of revaluation as few as possible get hurt.

Nevertheless, there are two ways of reacting to such a situation. One is to stress the value of the old money at all costs, to strengthen its purchasing power by internal reforms, and to try to extend its area of exchange. The other is to admit that it probably has a limited life and to set about seeing how it can be replaced, while there is time, by other currency, with as little real loss as may be managed.

Both courses may be necessary in the short run if there is not to be a collapse of confidence. And if those carrying responsibility for economic policy in such situations are apt, without loss of integrity, to speak with two voices at once, it is not surprising if responsible theologians and church leaders are to be found doing so too. But what those whom David Edwards describes as 'Christian radicals' are saying is essentially that we should not *fear* the crisis. Indeed, we may actually welcome it, as an opportunity for the Church to test on the pulses of experience and commitment what the old paper money is really worth. It is this that accounts for the sense of exhilaration, almost of abandon, that marks some statements of it.

Here, for instance, is Monica Furlong in the *Guardian* of 11 January 1963—from which I proposed to quote some of the more positive sentences to close my *Observer* article:

> The best thing about being a Christian at the moment is that organized religion has collapsed. I know, of course, that the Vatican Council meets, that in churches and chapels up and down the land people still meet to worship God, that the splendid farce of established religion still continues, and that the Mothers' Union continues unabashed.
>
> I am deeply involved in formal religion myself, owe it an

*Chacun à son gout*, of course, but I cannot imagine a more enjoyable time to be a Christian, except possibly in the first few centuries of the Church. For while the great holocaust is sweeping away much that is beautiful and all that is safe and comfortable and unquestioned, it is relieving us of the mounds of Christian bric-à-brac as well, and the liberation is unspeakable. Stripped of our nonsense we may almost be like the early Christians painting their primitive symbols on the walls of the catacombs—the fish, the grapes, the loaves of bread, the cross, the monogram of Christ—confident that in having done so they had described the necessities of life. . . .

What seems clear is that within all the denominations there is a new mutation of Christian (as yet only faintly discernible from the inert mass) who is willing and eager to question every item of his faith, who is bored to death with the old clichés, the old humbug and the great herd of sacred cows, and who believes that to disable either his mind or his senses is to dishonour Christ.

That, no doubt, is gorgeously irresponsible; and I would not identify myself with it anything like ninety per cent of the time. But I believe that with all due soberness and watchfulness we must welcome the judgment that is beginning at the house of God and read in the signs of the times the coming of the Christ for *our* age.

The task with which we are confronted is a double one. First, we must be prepared to ask with rigorous honesty what is the real cash value of the statements we make and the forms we use. We must be ready to be stripped down,

in the way of which Monica Furlong speaks and of which
Bonhoeffer spoke, and ask how much of the baggage which
the Christian Church now carries around with it is really
necessary, how the doctrines, the liturgies, the systems of
morality, the structures and strategies of our church life, are
really related to our basic commitment to the grace of our
Lord Jesus Christ and the love of God and the fellowship
of the Holy Spirit. A currency crisis, if it forces us back
on our real assets, can be a salutary shock.

But the second task is that of finding a new currency,
that will be convertible in the modern world. And the most
distinctive fact about this world is that it is a *secular* world.

## The Significance of the Secular

Our whole assessment of the contemporary situation is
bound up with our judgement about the meaning of secularization. A book published about the same time as mine,
*The Christian Mind* by Harry Blamires, takes, in an admittedly extreme form, the position widely assumed in Church
circles that secularization represents the great defection
from Christianity in our day and that there is a simple
antithesis between 'Christian thinking' and 'secular thinking'. In similar vein, Bishop Trevor Huddleston wrote at
the same time in a newspaper article,[1] 'Secularism, of
course, is as old as recorded history', and identified the
Christian war against it with that against 'the world, the
flesh and the Devil'.

With all respect, I believe this is a serious misreading of
the situation. I believe that secularization as we know it is
essentially a modern phenomenon. Where it is godless it
certainly provides plentiful evidence of what St Paul spoke
of as 'the mind of the flesh',[2] which is the nearest Biblical

[1] The *Sunday Telegraph*, 31 March 1963.  [2] Rom. 8. 7.

equivalent of

... to it as a God-given fact, as the
world-view within which Christ has to be made flesh for
modern man.

This will not be easy for the Church, because secularization stands among other things[1] for a revolt against three
ways of viewing the world, and probably four, which have
been intimately bound up in the past with the presentation
of the Christian gospel.

### Secularization and Metaphysics

The fourth (to take it first) is the whole possibility of
*metaphysics* as a meaningful enterprise. Whether, or in
what sense, the Gospel can be given expression without
recourse to metaphysical statements I do not know. That
is why I have left the issue open. So much depends on what
one means by metaphysics, and I am not a linguistic philosopher. Professor Paul van Buren, whose book *The Secular
Meaning of the Gospel* I mentioned earlier, clearly believes
that the Christian who takes his secularity seriously can and

---

[1] For a sage Christian assessment of secularization see D. L.
Munby, *The Idea of a Secular Society* (1963); also a special number
of *Student World*, First Quarter 1963, entitled 'Secularization';
M. A. C. Warren, CMS Newsletter, May 1963, 'Our Secular God';
and Gibson Winter, *The New Creation as Metropolis* (1963), ch. II
('The Servant Church in a Secularized World'). Cf., earlier, E. R.
Wickham, *Church and People in an Industrial City* (1957), pp.
225-38.

must abjure metaphysics, though he quotes Professor Ian Ramsey,[1] on whose position he builds, as defending the term.

Van Buren's book I regard as one of the most exciting and disturbing I have read. It is a sustained attempt to answer the question, 'How may a Christian who is himself a secular man understand the Gospel in a secular way?'[2] A brilliantly original thesis and something of a theological *tour de force*, it seeks to do justice to an orthodox Christology based on Barth and Bonhoeffer at the same time as taking the philosophical critique of Wittgenstein and the linguistic analysts with equal seriousness.[3] I believe it is a major contribution and may already bear out my conviction that in retrospect *Honest to God* 'will be seen to have erred in not being nearly radical enough'. Certainly, if my book has revealed the gap in communication between the radicals and conservative churchmen, this will do so even more— though it has the merit of being safely academic.

But I must confine myself here to the question which his whole thesis raises about the relation between the Christian's commitment as a secular man and the possibility of metaphysics.

The book could be said to be written round the statement of John 14.9, that he who has seen Jesus has seen the Father

[1] *Freedom and Immortality* (1960), p. 152; cited *op. cit.*, p. 88.
[2] *Op. cit.*, p. xiv.
[3] It shows, incidentally, how facile it is to see current theological radicalism, as some have, simply as a new version of liberal modernism. In fact, it cuts right across the theological lines, and, like practically every living movement in the Church today, across the ecclesiastical—including that between Rome and the rest. I cannot share the dismay which some have voiced about the damage done to ecumenical relations. It has led to much creative ferment and cross-conversation. And if it prevents a premature closing of the ecclesiastical ranks at the cost of maintaining or widening the gulf between the Church and the world, it may even be salutary.

in the

.......... the Church, which he seems to
deny.[4]

On the other side, the words are interpreted to mean
that the request 'Show us the Father' is a pointless one and
that all questions about 'God' must come to rest in Jesus.
Any statement about 'the beyond' or 'ultimate reality' is
without possibility of verification, in the sense that nothing
could count for or against it. Statements of Christian
theology describe not 'how things are' in the world[5] but
'how things are for, and what has happened to, a man
who sees a certain piece of history in a certain way'.[6]
They characterize the particular perspective on life of a
man who acknowledges 'Jesus as Lord'. They are not about
'God' (which is a strictly meaningless term), but about the
way of life which accepts as decisive the Easter experience
of liberation in Christ. In other words, the reality they
describe is the reality of a man's own conviction. The
affirmation that 'nothing can separate us from the love of
God in Christ' tells us nothing about 'things', but a great
deal about 'us': the doctrine of Providence is 'an assertion
of the strength of the grasp that the Christian's perspective

---

[1] *Op. cit.*, pp. 146-8.          [2] *Op. cit.*, pp. 198f. Italics mine.
[3] I would rather support the plea for its revitalization made by
Howard Root in the opening essay of *Soundings*.
[4] *Op. cit.*, pp. 190-2.     [5] *Op. cit.*, p. 5.     [6] *Op. cit.*, p. 171.

has on him'.[1] Similarly, to call a hope 'eschatological' is to say nothing about the final state of man or the world: it is 'to say that one would die rather than abandon it'.[2]

Van Buren is not saying that the Christian's 'perspective' is purely subjective, still less that it is arbitrary: on the contrary, he is constrained to it by the love with which *Christ* has set him free. There is a classical objectivity about his whole exposition of Christian doctrine which makes it profoundly impressive.

Nevertheless, I am not convinced that to be honest as a Christian and as a secular man one must, or indeed can, be shut up to such a complete refusal to speak of 'God' or of how things ultimately 'are'. Of course, the Christian lives by faith and not by sight: his *Te Deum* ends always with the words, 'O Lord, in thee have I trusted: let me never be confounded'. But the affirmation of the New Testament that he who has seen Jesus has seen the Father is *not* a statement that the whole quest for the Father is futile, but that men have no need to look *further* for the Father. For in Jesus they *have* a revelation of ultimate Reality: 'No one has ever seen God; but God's only Son, he who is nearest to the Father's heart, he has made him known.'[3]

What I believe is true is, as van Buren says, that we live 'in an age in which statements about "How things are" are expected to have some sort of relationship to men's experience of each other and of things'.[4] In other words, theology is not making affirmations about metaphysical realities *per se*, but always describes an experienced relationship or engagement to the truth. It is in this sense that I would agree with Tillich's dictum, quoted earlier, that 'all theological statements are existential'. They are not objec-

[1] *Op. cit.*, p. 178.               [2] *Op. cit.*, pp. 154f.
[3] John 1. 18.                    [4] *Op. cit.*, p. 195.

tive propositions

............y.

ɪne fundamental affirmation which the Christian is making when he says that God is personal is that at its deepest level the reality in which his life is rooted cannot be described exhaustively in terms of impersonal, mathematical regularities but only in the last resort in terms of an utterly gracious and unconditional love, which he can trust as implicitly as at another level he can trust the regularities which science describes. Theological statements are affirmations about the constraint of this love—both as grace and demand—in which the Christian finds himself held. They are descriptions, analyses of the relationship in which he is encountered by reality at this level.

In the past Christians have tended to make many statements which have appeared to characterize a Person in himself rather than a personal relationship. But what lies outside or beyond this relationship we can never say. And if pressed we must be modest and moderate our metaphysical claims. Hitherto we have not been pressed. But the process of secularization, with its distrust of any proposition going beyond the empirical evidence, is forcing the Church to strip down its statements and be rigorously honest about what it can claim. In this I believe we have nothing ultimately to lose: indeed, there is a natural reticence in the Biblical tradition about 'naming' God or making any pronouncements about him as he is in himself. God is known through his effects. And what theology analyses and describes is the existential relationship in which those effects are known. It is no more speaking of something outside human experience than are comparable analyses of mother-love as an essential constituent of the child's existence as a person. Theology is concerned with the fact that in this relationship of mother-love, as in every other relationship or commitment of life, there are also elements of 'the beyond', claims of the unconditional, which bespeak a depth of reality in which all human love and indeed everything else is grounded. This is the reality which the Christian revelation interprets and defines in terms of the love and grace and fellowship of the Trinity.

The doctrine of the Trinity is not, as it has often been represented, a model of the divine life as it is in itself. It is a formula or definition describing the distinctively Christian encounter with God. Hence all the features in the Trinitarian formula are in the last analysis representations of elements in the existential relationship. For example, the witness of the New Testament and of Christian experience is that it is *in* the Spirit (the medium of the New Being) that we come to the Son and *through* the Son that we come to the Father. Hence, on the 'map' the truth cannot be represented simply by three equidistant points, but only by some way of putting it that includes a progression (the classical doctrine of the 'procession' of the Persons). Nor can the experience be depicted adequately by three relationships to separate 'persons' in the modern sense, each of whom does different things—as, for instance, in the popular theology of the Catechism: 'I believe in God the Father, who hath *made* me, and all the world, . . . in God the Son, who hath *redeemed* me, and all mankind, . . . and in

God the Holy ~~Ch~~

~~described~~ otherwise (the doctrine of a purely 'economic' Trinity). And so one could go through all the various 'heresies', seen as false or inadequate transcripts of the existential relationship.

Positively, one can say that for the Christian the deepest awareness of ultimate reality, of what for him is most truly and finally real, can only be described *at one and the same time* in terms of the love of God *and* of the grace of our Lord Jesus Christ *and* of the fellowship of the Holy Spirit. All these are equally true and equally deep insights into and understandings of reality, and yet they all palpably express and define *one* reality, not competing realities. None is before or after, in the sense that one is a deeper truth than the others—so that one is 'divine', and the others merely human. In contrast, the unitarian would say that for him only one mode of experience is ultimate: Jesus is not a window through into ultimate reality (he is a man and no more), just as the fellowship of the Spirit is nothing more, nothing deeper, than human fellowship. But the trinitarian Christian insists that he cannot from his experience deny that in *each* of these he meets the unconditional. Something that holds these three together is for him the only satisfactory model of final truth and reality. The deepest of all mysteries cannot be expressed in terms which deny ultimacy to any of these.

The doctrine of the Trinity is about God. But except on the 'supranaturalist projection' (to which I shall be coming in the next section), it is not the description of *a* Being—so that we have to visualize a sort of Divine triangle or Divine society 'existing' somewhere 'out there' or 'up there'. It is a description of Being, as it is known 'in Christ'. It is the final Christian definition of reality, the 'Christian name' (as Karl Barth puts it) of God. The doctrine is to the experienced reality what the map is to the earth or a model for the scientist. Inevitably, it will desiccate and distort. But it is better to have a map than no map, and to have a true map than a false. Hence the importance of Trinitarian doctrine. But it is equally important to be able to see the map for what it is. It is a transcript. Its truths are truths about the relational experience and are 'readings' from it: they are not statements about metaphysical entities beyond our ken.

The three other ways of thinking about the world against which secularization marks a revolt are ones that I have already touched on in my book, and I return to them now to try to set out more clearly what I meant.

## Secularization and the Supranatural

Secularism rejects a *supranaturalistic* world-view. This does not mean that it rejects God: that would be to beg the whole question at issue. What it does reject is *a picture of the world in which the* reality *of* God *is represented by the* existence *of* gods *or of* a God *in some other order or realm of being 'above' or 'beyond' the world in which we live*. 'The supernatural' is used so loosely in ordinary speech as equivalent to 'the divine' that I have preferred to retain Tillich's term 'supranatural' to characterize this particular description or 'projection' (in the map-maker's sense) of

partly because my post-bag confirms what the surveys suggest, that many popular religious ideas are still incredibly more naive than bishops and clergy often suppose. But, more importantly, because the Biblical and medieval picture of the world, which determines almost all popular theology, liturgy, hymnody and art, *was* supranaturalist in a sense in which our conception of the universe is not and cannot be. I have never said that intelligent people believed or believe that God is *literally* 'up there' or 'out there'. Nor did I say that they believed that he was *only* 'up there' or 'out there' (and not immanent as well). In fact I specifically denied it.[1] I am indeed grateful to all those who have kindly supplied me with quotations from Augustine and the mystics and the entire range of classical Christian theology, eastern and western, which it was implied that I had ignored. They have helped to provide a valuable corrective. But, of course, I did not intend to suggest that the language which Tillich, for instance, uses about depth or the ground of being was anything radically new. He is well aware that he stands in the classical Platonist tradition of Christian ontology. I drew on him because he speaks, I believe, to post-Freudian man and to thousands today to whom, say, the Cappadocian Fathers would not. But I drew on him also because he seems

---

[1] *Honest to God*, p. 44.

I

to me to have clarified one vital difference between our age and previous ages in the way in which we can talk about God.

Perhaps I can express this best by taking an example from another department of Christian theology. A hundred years ago the Church was forced to clarify whether it accepted the Adam story as history or as myth.[1] Until then there had been many theologians (St Paul probably among them) who, if pressed, would not have thought the truth of the story depended upon Adam being an actual historical individual. But the point is that they were not pressed. There was no compelling need to distinguish between the categories of history and myth. But with the Darwinian controversy on evolution it became a vital necessity. It was imperative for Christian apologetic to be clear that Genesis was *not* a rival account of primitive anthropology. If the distinction had not been made it would have been virtually impossible to continue commending the Biblical faith to modern scientific man. This was not a compromise or a watering down of the faith to what Jones could swallow (though it seemed so to many at the time). It meant accepting with humility the fact that there had been a shift in thinking about the world which turned what previously was an entirely valid way of putting things into an occasion of stumbling and error. In fact, what was forced upon the Church with reluctance has since proved a source of liberation: the meaning and relevance of the story has been greatly enriched.

In the same way, Christian theology has been used to making different sorts of statements about the being of God, which until now it has not been forced to distinguish.

[1] For a closer definition of the meaning of 'myth', see below pp. 263-8.

... three-decker universe, at any rate in dualistic terms of a natural realm (inhabited by man and nature) and of a supra-natural order (inhabited by God and spirits). There is nothing particularly Christian about this world-view: indeed it is much older than Christianity. Nor is there any particular reason to weep at its demise. Christian theology could quite happily be expressed through it. But it did not depend on it. Now, however, it is necessary to *show* that it does not depend upon it. Otherwise there is danger that it may be discredited with it.

It is here, I believe, that Tillich has rendered a service to our generation. He has sought to demonstrate that the Biblical faith in the reality of God can be stated in all its majesty and mystery, both of transcendence and immanence, without dependence on the supranaturalist scheme. Hitherto it has not mattered much whether the reality of God has been framed in terms of the *existence* of *a God*; whether John 4.24 has been (mis)translated, with the Authorized Version, God is *a* spirit'; or whether the 'otherness' of God has been expressed in the projection of him as a separate super-Being. These are valid ways of stating the matter, with which there is nothing intrinsically wrong, and from which we can still learn as much as, for instance, we can learn from St Paul on Adam. Indeed, it is precisely that we may be able to go on using this language and preserving this heritage that I believe that we must be prepared to face the transposition required of us. Otherwise it may be lost to us. Nor is it a capitulation to take seriously the secular world-view of our age. It may provide an equal source of release. It is not for nothing that many have said in recent months that they feel God has been 'given back' to them.

Beyond this I do not wish to be committed to Tillich's particular ontology. I am profoundly grateful for what I have learnt from him, but if dogmatic theologians or philosophers cleverer than myself find it unsatisfactory I will not argue with them. I would, however, draw attention to some sentences of John Macquarrie's earlier in this book,[1] which put in the words of a professional philosopher what I was stumbling to say. After questioning the propriety of the traditional question, 'Does God exist?', he goes on:

> 'God' is the religious word for Being, understood as gracious. The words 'God' and 'Being' are not synonyms, for Being may have the character of indifference, and in that case it could not be called 'God'. 'Being' can be equated with 'God' only if Being has the character of grace and is responsive to man's existential predicament. Now Being itself cannot be regarded as an entity, for it is manifestly absurd to say 'Being exists'. . . . But if God is equated with Being as gracious, then the question is not whether some entity or other exists, but whether Being has such a character as would fulfil man's quest for grace.

I would add two further comments. A number of people have suggested that all this involves a (dishonestly) concealed form of the ontological argument[2] which would make

[1] Pp. 188-9 above.
[2] The argument that the very idea of the non-existence of God involves a contradiction.

otherwise you are not. He who knows about depth knows
about God.

These words as they stand give the impression that anyone
who takes seriously the depth and mysteries of life must
believe in God. I accept the criticism expressed in a most
percipient letter which I have received from Dr Donald D.
Evans of McGill University, Montreal: 'Tillich's utterance
occurs within a sermon which may *produce* or *evoke* an
*interpretation* of depth-experience which does bring knowledge of God. But as it stands, the utterance is false. A
depth-experience by itself brings, at best, only an unconscious knowledge of God.' I must agree with him when he
contests my statement that 'the question of God is the
question whether this depth of being is a reality or an illusion'.[2] I would rephrase it thus. The question of God is
whether these experiences of depth (and everything else in
life) are to be interpreted in terms of 'Being as gracious'—
that is, for the Christian, in terms of the grace of our Lord
Jesus Christ and the love of God and the fellowship of the
Holy Spirit.

The other point concerns criticisms which have centred
in the phrase 'the ground of our being'—such as 'How do
you pray to the ground of your being?' I would say at once

---

[1] *Honest to God*, p. 22.          [2] *Honest to God*, p. 55.

that I do not pray to the ground of my being. I pray to God as Father. Prayer, for the Christian, is the opening of oneself to that utterly gracious personal reality which Jesus could only address as 'Abba, Father!'. I have no interest whatever in a God conceived in some vaguely impersonal pantheistic terms. The only God who meets my need as a Christian is 'the God of Abraham, Isaac and Jacob', the God and Father of our Lord Jesus Christ—not 'the God of the philosophers', who, as Brunner once put it, 'simply allows himself to be looked at'. I have been, and I remain, primarily a Biblical theologian and a fairly conservative one at that. I have no desire to 'preach any other gospel', nor do I wish to deny anything in the faith which the Creeds enshrine. My sole concern and contention is for the Scriptural revelation of God as dynamic personal love. And it is precisely because I am contending for this (and not for some non-biblical *philosophia perennis*) that I am so concerned for its meaningfulness in an age which has decisively turned its back on the picture of the world presupposed by the Biblical writers.

The only question at issue is *how* the Biblical doctrine is to be given expression today, in a non-supranaturalistic world-view. For the New Testament writers the conviction of the personal character of God as gracious, holy, self-giving love was expressed unquestioningly in the representation of him as *a* Being, a supreme Person. This was the only available projection, and to say that Jesus is used it is in itself to say no more than he was genuinely a man of the first century. The question is whether the reality of the experience which Jesus knew—and to which Christians have testified ever since—is tied to this projection: for if it is, I fear for its ability to *become* a reality for many in our generation.

it to the great Scriptural categories of the Living God, the Creator, Lord, and Father,[1] and no one who has steeped himself in his sermons[2] could seriously accuse him of preaching any other God than that of the Bible. What he is seeking to show is how these great, and indispensable, Biblical words can describe for modern secular man the reality of unfathomable Love in which he lives and moves and has his being.

## Secularization and the Mythological

Closely associated with the supranaturalist aspect of this world-view is its *mythological* character. For the connection between the 'superworld of divine objects' and this earth was thought of in terms of transactions depicted in the language of mythology.

It is evident that the word 'myth' is still a source of misunderstanding to great numbers of people, and means simply that which is untrue. Had I realized the circles to which my book would penetrate, I should have taken more care to disarm criticism at this point. For to describe some-

---

[1] *Systematic Theology*, vol. i, chs. X and XI.
[2] *The Shaking of the Foundations* (1949), *The New Being* (1955) and *The Eternal Now* (1963).

thing as 'myth' is not in any way to prejudge whether it is true or false. Myth, in itself, merely means a story, a pictorial representation in words. In the context with which we are concerned, it is a way of expressing and making vivid the relationship between 'this world' and 'that world', conceived in terms of the natural and the supranatural. Thus, there are myths of the beginning and end, depicting how God made the world and how he will finally complete his purpose for it. But there are also myths which indicate and describe the action of God *within history*. To say that 'God was in this event' was expressed for the Biblical writers by saying that 'the Lord sent his angel' or 'there appeared to them a multitude of the heavenly host'. To say that 'God was uniquely in this event' came out in the language of mythology as 'God sent his only-begotten Son'. And to express the continuous commerce between heaven and earth there were goings up and comings down of all kinds, theophanies and portents, Michael and his angels at war with the Devil and his angels, and so on. Behind the history and giving spiritual significance to it was this other world of mythological 'events', which provided, as it were, a fourth dimension and supplied its meaning 'in depth'.

Myth is of profound and permanent significance in human thought: most of us will always think and theologize in pictures. The crisis of our age is simply bound up with the necessity of being forced to *distinguish* myth for what it is, so that we may be able to evaluate it aright and use it without dishonesty and inhibition. We saw how a hundred years ago the Church was compelled to do this in relation to the myths of the beginning. It has still not done it adequately (and certainly not communicated it adequately) with regard to the myths of the end—so that to describe the Second Coming or the Last Judgement as myth is still

... Hinduism and other religions there are numerous references to incarnations and virgin births, the difference in Christianity is that the incarnation and virgin birth of Jesus *really happened*: they were historical. There is indeed here a very real difference between Christianity and other faiths, and hitherto this was an adequate enough way of describing it. But we are being forced today to disentangle myth and history much more carefully than to say simply that 'our' myth is historical. Of course, what is recorded in the New Testament is claiming to be history in a way that is never claimed by the Hindu scriptures. But to say that 'the Incarnation' or 'the Virgin Birth' were historical events is to

---

[1] See my book, *In the End, God . . .* (1950), to which, together with chapters XI-XIII of my later book, *On Being the Church in the World* (1960), I would refer the many who have asked for my views on life after death. Here I would simply say that the relationship to God in which the Christian finds the ultimate meaning and significance of his life *could* not have its unconditional character were it dependent upon the fact that the world does not blow itself up or I am not run over by a bus tomorrow. From his present faith the Christian knows that, when the proximate relationships of this life are stripped away, he is left in relationship not to nothing, but to the infinite and eternal love of God, in which even now he is sustained and grounded. Our destiny is to be with him for ever. For some this will be heaven, for some hell—for most a mixture of both. But this does not necessarily mean that God, as almighty Love, is statically content that any of his creatures should live with him for ever and find it hell.

[2] Translated in *Kerygma and Myth*, ed. H. W. Bartsch, vol. i (1953), pp. 1-44.

[3] 25 March 1942.

beg the question. That the man Jesus was born is a statement
of history. That 'God sent his only-begotten Son' (which is
what is meant by calling the birth at Bethlehem 'the Incarnation') is a mythological statement—*not* in the sense
that it is not true, but in the sense that it represents (in the
picture-language of the supranaturalist world-view) the
theological *significance* of the history. The infancy narratives in the Gospels are quite clearly introduced by the
Evangelists to indicate from the beginning the *divine significance* of the life that follows. They do this in the accepted
language of their day, in terms of celestial visitations, signs
and portents. Whether the virgin birth belongs wholly or
only in part to this mythological framework, i.e., whether
it is simply meant to indicate the *meaning* of this event or
whether it *also* describes how as an actual biological fact it
took place, can only be decided on the strength of the
historical evidence; and naturally people will differ as to
how they weigh the evidence, according to the presuppositions they bring to it. What is history and what is myth is
often a delicately balanced decision, and will turn on our
assessment of the documents in general.[1]

There are, of course, enormous issues involved here—
e.g., how much of the Resurrection and Ascension stories
one reads as history and how much as myth. I am deliberately not touching in this essay on questions relating to
the person and work of Christ, as I should like, when time
allows, to follow these up in a separate book. All I would
plead for is the unemotional recognition of the validity of
myth in its own right and of the fact that Christians may
differ in assessing its place in the stories and still equally

[1] That is why I said in my book (p. 35) that Bultmann's contribution to the demythologizing debate should be judged independently
of his estimate of the Gospel tradition as a historian (which is a
good deal more sceptical than my own).

ʋut precisely to enable us to use them. But in a secular age we shall not be able to do this unless we are prepared to 'come clean'—and do not attempt to present the myths as history. For modern scientific man cannot accept the mythological world-view as in any sense a *description* of reality, as a statement of how things actually happened or of what goes on in the universe. It seems to him a phantasmagoria, an entirely unreal world which has *nothing to do* with history. That is why, if the Christmas stories, for instance, are presented simply as history, he dismisses them as 'myths' in the popular sense: they become in fact indistinguishable for him from the similar stories in other religions. By failing to differentiate and assess the mythological positively for what it is, we *cause* him to relegate Biblical narratives to a fairy-story world which has no connection with our history at all. In previous ages it was not

---

[1] It becomes evident in discussion that most people simply equate 'the Resurrection' with 'the empty tomb'. But the empty tomb is to the Resurrection what the shell of the cocoon is to the butterfly. St Paul, whose whole gospel is centred in 'Jesus and the resurrection', never once explicitly mentions the empty tomb (though he refers in detail to the appearances). Belief in the Resurrection is the conviction (on which the whole apostolic Church was grounded) that Jesus is not just a historical memory but a living presence. How the disciples first came to the conviction, how physical or psychological were the appearances, or what precisely happened to the body, are secondary, though important, questions. For my own estimate of the New Testament evidence, see the article, mentioned earlier, 'Resurrection in the N.T.', in *The Interpreter's Dictionary of the Bible*.

necessary to distinguish: now I am convinced it is vital. And the vitality is not simply one of evangelistic expediency; it will also, I believe, be shown to be one of renewal for the Church.

## Secularization and the Religious

The third protest involved in the process of secularization is that against *religion*. Indeed, this is the aspect of it which normally features first in any definition. So it does, for instance, in that given by Charles West in the report of the consultation on 'The Meaning of the Secular' held at the Ecumenical Institute at Bossey in 1959, where secularization is provisionally defined as: 'The withdrawal of areas of thought and life from religious—and finally also from metaphysical—control, and the attempt to understand and live in these areas in the terms which they alone offer'. Clearly, the decline in religion and religious observance has been one of the most obvious features of our times, and it is most marked amongst those exposed most directly to the influences of our modern scientific industrialized society. It is also the feature which most readily persuades churchmen that secularization must be the chief enemy of Christianity in our day.

But, again, before judging, I believe we have to be prepared to make distinctions—distinctions which before were not necessary. Hitherto everything that testified to a religious world-view and brought in God (provided it was recognizably Christian) has been welcomed by the Church as being on the side of the angels. But frequently 'religion' has been invoked precisely against the movement of thought which has led to the secular revolution. For secularism stands for the conviction that the circle of explanation and control in human affairs can and should be closed—that

secular man is to close it as fundamentally superstitious.

Now the effect on the modern Christian of putting it like this is at once to provoke the reaction: 'But that's not what I mean by religion at all. It's a caricature—just as your picture of God "up there" or "out there" is a caricature'. To which my answer, again, is that I am not so easily shifted. Of course, it's a caricature, if by that is meant that no intelligent Christian or deeply religious person of any period has *only* had this understanding of religion. Of course, by itself it's a perversion, and it is possible to quote from every classic of the spiritual life that this is not what the masters or indeed what the ordinary faithful have said or meant. I agree. But what they *have* said has also been part and parcel of a way of looking at the world, and of an organization, which has been committed to—or at any rate has not dissociated itself from—the 'religious interest' in the narrower sense. If this were not so, Christians would not feel so jittery or defensive at this point. They would welcome the exposure of such a limited or perverted view; they would commend what is true in Freud's analysis of religion as a neurosis; they would embrace the secularist critique; they would not be so hasty to react to Bonhoeffer by saying that all he was girding at was 'religiosity' or (if they are Anglicans) an inadequate Lutheran piety.

How precisely Bonhoeffer would have defined 'religion'

in his vision of 'religionless Christianity' we shall never know. What is clear is that he did not mean what the Archbishop of Canterbury refers to under that name when he asks,[1] 'Will not religion still be with us: reverence, awe, dependence, adoration, and penitence?' Bonhoeffer's answer would unquestionably have been 'Yes'. Indeed, this is the point of his question, 'What is the place of worship and prayer in an entire absence of religion?'[2] It is because I did not wish to force any premature definition on him and thereby fail to catch what he might be saying to us that I preferred to let him speak in his own words. And to those who are really prepared to feel the impact of his meaning I can only say, 'Go to his letters again, and particularly those of 30 April, 5 May, 25 May, 8 June, 16 July and 18 July, 1944'.

Bonhoeffer's position is that fundamentally the secularist critique of religion is correct (just as Tillich sees its critique of supranaturalism and Bultmann its critique of mythology as correct). But this does not mean the end of Christianity: in fact, in a real sense it means its vindication. Accepting the fact that modern man has opted for a secular world, Bonhoeffer refuses to deplore this. On the contrary, he agrees that the period of religion is over. Man is growing out of it: he is 'coming of age'.[3] By that he does not mean that he is getting better (a prisoner of the Gestapo had few illusions about human nature), but that for good or for ill he is putting the 'religious' world-view behind him as childish and pre-scientific. Till now man has felt the need for a

[1] *Image Old and New*, p. 7.
[2] *Letters and Papers from Prison* (2nd English edition, 1956), p. 123.
[3] This phrase has been endlessly misunderstood, despite my footnote on p. 104. I should be perfectly prepared to accept in its place the notion that man has reached adolescence.

bring God into his science, his morals, his political speeches. Only in the private world of the individual's psychological need and insecurity—in that last corner of 'the sardine-tin of life'—is room apparently left for the God who has been elbowed out of every other sphere. And so the religious evangelist works on men to coerce them at their weakest point into feeling that they cannot get on without the tutelage of God.

But, claims Bonhoeffer boldly, 'God is teaching us that we must live as men who can get along very well without him', that is, without having to bring him in. We *can* be genuinely secular, or as he put it, worldly, without ceasing to be Christian. For this God, he insists, is the God Jesus shows us, the God who refuses to be a *Deus ex machina*, who allows himself to be edged out of the world on to the Cross. Our God is the God who forsakes us—only to meet with us on the Emmaus road, if we are really prepared to abandon him as a long-stop and find him not at the boundaries of life where human powers fail, but at the centre, in the secular, as 'the "beyond" in our midst'.

Bonhoeffer's insistence, which echoes that of classical Christian spirituality all down the ages, is that Christ must be met at the centre of life—*but at the centre of a life where a religious sector can no longer be presupposed as a special point of entry or contact*. This is the new factor, and why

I believe Bonhoeffer's contribution is probably the most radically original of all those I quoted and could not have made before the middle of the twentieth century. Hitherto the Churches have operated on what he calls 'the religious premise', on the assumption that man is naturally religious, that there is a particular wave-band, as it were, in the spectrum of human experience that is distinctively religious and on which he can be addressed. The evangelist uses this wave-length on which to make his appeal: the parson puts on popular services—on the assumption that it is 'religion' to which men will respond if it is made sufficiently attractive. But this, in my judgement, and in that of parish priests who seem to me most alert to what is happening, is becoming increasingly unrealistic as a presupposition. Men and women are coming to commitment to Christ as the clue to life not because they are specially drawn by 'religion' nor because he meets them as the answer to their 'religious' needs. Indeed, they are not particularly interested in religion, let alone in the Church as a religious club. They look for a Christ who could be Lord of a genuinely secular world, who does not require of them that they become religious first before they can become Christian.

To draw this discussion to a conclusion I should like to quote some words of the Dutch professor Hans Hoekendijk spoken at Strasbourg in 1960: [1]

We will not be able really to get alongside man in our modern world unless we begin to 'dereligionize' Christianity. Christianity is a secular movement, and this is basic for an understanding of it. We have no business to make it a religion again. That would mean a correction of what Christ has done. And we have no business to make a Christian

[1] Quoted at the head of the editorial in the *Student World* number on 'Secularization', *op. cit.*, p. 1.

for us today?'[1] And the answer to his question is 'the secular Christ', in the sense in which John Taylor writes:[2]

> Either we must think of the Christian Mission in terms of bringing the Muslim, the Hindu, the Animist into Christendom, or we must go with Christ as he stands in the midst of Islam, of Hinduism, of the primal world-view, and watch with him, fearfully and wonderingly, as he becomes—dare we say it?—Muslim or Hindu or Animist, as once he became Man, and a Jew. Once, led by the Spirit, the Church made its choice in this matter at the Council of Jerusalem and dared to win the Gentiles by becoming Gentile. Paul and those who followed him did not wait for history to reduce the Graeco-Roman world to chaos and drive its derelicts into the arms of the Church. They claimed that world in its strength and reformulated the Gospel in the terms of its wisdom. So Christ in his Church answered the call of the Greeks; he came where they were and became what they were. From within their own culture he challenged their strength and judged their wisdom. He turned their world upside down, just as he had turned Judaism upside down—just as, indeed, if he enters our Churches today, he turns our Christianity upside down. So he would challenge and judge and revolutionize the African world-view; but he must do it from the inside.

One has only to change the single word 'African' in the last

---

[1] *Op. cit.*, p. 122, but correcting 'what?' to 'who?'. Bonhoeffer wrote *'wer?'*, *Widerstand und Ergebung* (1951), p. 178.
[2] *The Primal Vision* (1963), pp. 113-14.

sentence to 'secular' to make the point for our world. And the corollary is that as Christians *we* are inside this secular world-view. For this is the only standpoint from which the mission, seen in terms of 'Christian presence',[1] can be conducted.

But the necessity which the Gospel lays upon us at this point is not simply in relation to those without. As van Buren well puts it,[2] the position in which we find ourselves is of

> the Christian, himself a secular man, who realizes that the juxtaposition of his faith, expressed in traditional terms, and his ordinary way of thinking, causes a spiritual schizophrenia. . . . To rectify this situation he has the choice of forgetting about the Gospel and abandoning his faith or of finding a secular way in which to understand it. If he cannot forget the claim of the Gospel, then the 'necessity' arises, not from some evangelistic task for the church, but from his desire to be a responsible and self-integrated Christian.

Steven Mackie[3] makes the same observation with regard to Bonhoeffer:

> His point was not, 'Aha! I have now hit on a device which will persuade men of the truth of Christianity', but rather, 'I am beginning to understand the way I myself think and react to Christian preaching. Perhaps it is God's intention that I should react in this way. At any rate, I am beginning to see that it could all make sense.'

It is in this sense that I see *Honest to God* as a piece of missionary theology. Leslie Mitton ends his understanding review in *The Expository Times*[4] with the words: 'The book is fundamentally not an essay in unorthodox theology,

---

[1] The title of the series in which John Taylor's book appears. For an expansion of it, see Ch. 13 and Max Warren's Introduction.
[2] *The Secular Meaning of the Gospel*, pp. 77-8.
[3] *Student World, op. cit.*, p. 10.    [4] Pp. 163-5 above.

that I knew myself to be a man commi̶t̶t̶e̶d̶ ̶to a man committed, without possibility of
return, to modern twentieth-century secular society. It was
written out of the belief that both these convictions must
be taken with equal seriousness and that they *cannot* be
incompatible.

*Appendix 1*

# WHY I WROTE IT

In its first number after changing its name from the *Sunday Pictorial* (7 April), the London *Sunday Mirror* asked Dr Robinson to present the theme of his book.

SOME years ago Mr Gaitskell proposed revising the famous Clause Four of the Labour Party's constitution (on nationalization).

Those who opposed him dubbed it all 'theology'—theoretical statements about things that make no practical difference.

Such is the name that 'theology' has gained. But suddenly that image seems to have changed.

Up till now the Press took notice of clergymen only if they spoke on morals or politics. What they said on God and the Gospel was ignored. Archbishop William Temple constantly complained of this. But now 'God' is news!

My book seems to have touched people at a point where truth really matters to them. And of that I am glad—even if it has meant some pain.

For God is to be found at the point where things really do matter to us.

What drove me to write my book was that this is simply not true for most people.

What matters to them most in life seems to have nothing to do with 'God'; and God has no connection with what really concerns them day by day.

At best he seems to come in only at the edges of life. He is out there somewhere as a sort of long-stop—at death, or to turn to in tragedy (either to pray to or to blame).

So let's start not from a heavenly Being, whose very existence many would doubt. Let's start from what actually is most real to people in everyday life—and find God there.

What is most real to you? What matters most for you? Is it money, and what money can buy?

I doubt it, deep down. For you know that you 'can't take it with you'. And seldom does it bring real happiness.

Is it love? That's a good deal nearer, because it has to do with persons not things.

But what is love? Sex? Sex is a marvellous part of it. But sex by itself can leave people deeply unsatisfied. Remember Marilyn Monroe?

We all need, more than anything else, to love and be loved. That's what the psychologists tell us. But by that they mean we need to be *accepted* as persons, as whole persons, for our own sake.

And this is what true love does. It accepts people, without any strings, simply for what they are. It gives them worth. It 'makes their lives'.

That is precisely what we see Jesus doing in the Gospels, making and re-making men's lives, bringing meaning back to them.

In him we see love at work, in a way that the world has never seen before or since.

And that's why the New Testament sees God at work in him—for God is love. In the Cross that love comes out to the uttermost. 'There's love for you!' says Calvary.

And in the Resurrection we see that not even death was able to destroy its power to transform and heal. Love still came out top.

The Christian is the man who believes in *that* love as the last word for his life.

It is quite simply for him the ultimate reality: it is God.

The universe, like a human being, is not built merely to a mathematical formula. It's only love that gives you the deepest clue to it.

'It's love that makes the world go round.' That's what all Christians have always said. But so often they have *pictured* it in a way that makes it difficult for modern man to see it.

They have spoken as though what makes the world go round were an old man in the sky, a supernatural Person.

Of course, they don't take that literally. It helps only to make God easier to *imagine*. But it can also hinder.

Perhaps a comparison will show what I mean.

The ancient Greeks thought of the earth being upheld on the shoulders of a superman called Atlas. That was their way of saying that it doesn't support itself in space.

We also know that it doesn't. For us it is held in orbit by the sun's gravitational pull.

The ancient myth was saying something true. But such language today would not convey the truth to modern man. It would be much more likely to conceal it.

So with Christian truth. The reality is that in Jesus we see the clue to all life. To say that he was the Son of a supernatural Being sent to earth from heaven may help to bring this home.

I tried simply to be honest about what God means to me —in the second half of the twentieth century.

The hundreds of letters I have received, particularly from the younger generation, inside the Church and out of it, have convinced me that I may have rung a bell for others too.

For that I can only be humbly thankful.

For I want God to be as real for our modern secular, scientific world as he ever was for the 'ages of faith'.

*Appendix 2*

## HONEST TO CHILDREN

### RUTH ROBINSON

Reprinted from *Prism* (April) with some abbreviations and changes. Material from Mrs Robinson's article appeared in the *Sunday Times* (7 April).

A SENSE of wonder and mystery, an aptitude for fancy and fantasy, an apprehension of things almost tangible yet unseen—this we recognize as an unquestionable item in the basic equipment with which a child comes provided. This, for the most part, is what we mean when we say a child is instinctively religious. Too often, however, we are cowards. We pretend to ourselves that we are answering our child's instinctive religious aspirations when in reality we are trading on the equally unquestionable fact that a child will believe anything, however improbable, from anyone he trusts. That he *does* believe what we tell him we regard as proof that the religious framework we present corresponds to his own inner awareness. In this way we hide from ourselves the much more searching fact that all depends, not on the child's readiness to believe *what* he is told, but on his *trust* in the *person* who tells him.

A child is born trusting implicitly in a friendly universe. His universe at first is small but his trust is infinite. From the first he knows his dependence and acknowledges it in no uncertain voice. He takes a loving providence and concern for granted. When his need for love and food is answered he would seem to enjoy a state of bliss and heavenly contentment which is not easily retrieved in later life. The justification for such an unquestioning trust comes to him through his closest personal relationships, and he goes on trusting until or unless bitter experience disillusions him and a loving providence becomes no longer a reality. As Christian parents, we believe he is not mistaken in his trust. But if it is to grow and deepen as his horizons gradually recede, it will depend on how within the universe of his own experience we can communicate and share with him our own trust that we are grounded in a loving purpose. The child will judge love and assess how far he can trust *from experience*, not only by the extent to which he can trust us and how far we trust him, but also by his growing sense of a greater love in which both parents and child are grounded. Such an awareness can only be apprehended by

too great a value on the religious categories in which we dress it up.

Here I should like to suggest an analogy.[1] Father Christmas is an important factor in the lives of most children, but the idea of Father Christmas has different implications in different families. There is first of all what you might call the 'antiseptic' approach. In such a family the whole idea is ruled out as superstitious fantasy, and presents are exchanged without pretence. A friend who was nurtured in such a rarefied atmosphere, although a convinced humanist still, admits to feeling her childhood in this respect was bleak and impoverished. In other families all is staked on the illusion; take it away and life is that much emptier. Father Christmas is himself the reality for the child. Such questions as 'when shall we tell him?' become increasingly pressing. In both instances a very low doctrine of myth is held. That is to say, the myth is in each case considered as pretence, as bogus; it pretends to represent reality whereas reality is known to be something quite different. On the one hand it is rejected as unworthy of an intelligent mind, on the other held on to with desperate intensity because of all that will be lost if it goes. The same too often happens

[1] The purpose of this analogy is *not* to draw a comparison between the myth of Father Christmas and our conception of God, but to illustrate the child's instinctive appreciation of the relation between myth and reality.

with the religious categories in which we define our beliefs.

But the reality represented for the child by Father Christmas consists essentially in the hope, expectancy and mystery of giving and receiving, the mutual sharing of love and gratitude. Where this experienced reality is constant, we can sit lightly to the framework that represents it. The Father Christmas myth is retained as long as it adequately represents the reality, and to discard it involves nothing deeper than a sentimental regret for passing childhood.

The child does not have to have this explained to him: it is his natural frame of reference. Perhaps, as adults, we forget the intense consciousness of what is real to the child in a game he has 'made up'. In much of his play he is 're-presenting' reality, and within the context of the game to refer to it as 'pretence' is an affront to the depths of his conception. None knows better than he that the actual play is made up, though it represents something very real. In childhood he plays at 'mothers and fathers': in adult life he will discard the play and live out for himself the relationship he has begun to apprehend and express through childhood play. He is, in fact, capable of a very high doctrine of myth—that is, he is able to value it not simply for itself, for he can accept it as expendable, but for the reality it embodies upon which he sets an enduring value.

And what of more serious 'myth'? Carols round the Christmas crib, with flying angels, silver star and cotton wool lambs, are an integral part of our family Christmas, and the reading of the Gospel story together on Christmas Eve is the unquestioned focus of our preparation for the festival. The children are not worried to think it may not have happened exactly like that. They accept and value the story in the first instance for the aura which surrounds it, but increasingly, I think, as they get older, because it begins

is our tendency to

him to infer that the myth is, in itself, the reality.

This brings me to the nub of the problem for a Christian parent—how to present Jesus Christ as the Lord of our life. If we begin with a far-off God sending his Son Jesus into our world, we are likely to face our children with two Gods, God and Jesus, who can be prayed to indiscriminately, and we wrestle with such conundrums as Jesus being God. How many of us, thus far pressed, retire from the fray at this point with the promise that 'it all seems difficult now but when you are older you will begin to understand'. Liars! We know it gets harder, not easier.

But what if we don't begin at all with the traditional religious framework which, until we introduce it, is outside the child's experience? Does he not already contain within himself, in his earliest experience of a love he can trust and take for granted, the germ of his own understanding? Perhaps to present Christ to a small child is precisely to let his love *be present* to the child in our love and, for a time, nothing more. As the bounds of his small world widen, experience will teach him, long before his mind can grasp the fact, that all love is not contained in the love his parents have for him. If his own trustfulness is mirrored in theirs he will begin to be aware that they are not after all the source of his trust: they are mediating it from beyond themselves. If by a slow and gradual spiritual growth—*at*

*his own speed*—a child is led to the point where he can
dimly begin to formulate the question 'What is the source
of this love?' or 'Who is it you trust?', is there not then, and
only then, a relevance for him in the category 'God', because there is an element within his own experience to
which a name must be put? And if he is able to frame his
question in terms not of 'Where' but 'Who', are we not
nearer the heart of the matter? For then we can point to
this person Jesus Christ without having *first* to explain how
he fits into the system. Nor do we have to present him as an
alternative to God, or as God dressed up as a man, but
simply as the only way we have of describing what God is
like, because 'God was *in* Christ'. We have no need to look
any further because we have the assurance from Jesus himself: 'Anyone who has seen me has seen the Father'. What
further need then to ask, 'Show us the Father'?

This, too, is the Jesus about whom he has already heard,
who is already a familiar historical figure, who lived and
taught and healed and was killed, a *real person*, just as
William the Conqueror or Florence Nightingale were real
people, but unlike these in that he is the one person through
whom we can see the whole meaning and purpose of life,
and who shows us the hidden source of the trust and love
which the child experiences for himself and sees in his
parents. The miracle stories can then be for him a way of
describing the real power of this love in the lives of those
who felt it, a power which the child can understand because
he already knows *for himself* that love can heal resentment
and irritation, make another person loving, help him to say
he is sorry, cause a grazed knee to feel not so bad after all,
and make what was difficult seem easy. It is real for him
because it corresponds to what he knows for himself in his
own personal relationships.

dren's prayers?' When my first child was born I belonged
fervently to the kneel-by-the-side-of-the-cot-from-the-word-
go school. After 15 years I am more inclined to say
'Don't rush him—let him move at his own speed'. He
needs help in developing his experience of spiritual reality
*before* he needs help in defining or expressing it. This may
sound an easy way out of a daily bedtime chore, but in fact
I find it incessantly more demanding. For what one is committed to is an undertaking consciously to help him to give
worth, express love, say he's sorry, admit his needs, show
concern for others and be grateful, in his *human* relationships. Nor does it end there, for his growing experience of
these realities in himself will depend largely on the extent
to which he is aware of them in our own relationship to
him and to others. His capacity to love, to forgive, to be
sorry, to be concerned, will reflect our own. If in time he
becomes more articulate and begins to sense, through this
shared personal experience with parents who themselves are
trusting, a further commitment to a love beyond them, a
love identified in Jesus Christ, then prayer as we usually
understand it will be a shared way of defining and expressing this commitment. But are we always right in assuming
such a commitment for him before he is aware of it within
himself?

I have sensed in fact a readiness in myself to use prayers

with the children as an easy way out of a more demanding obligation. 'We are sorry for being bad-tempered', we say, 'please forgive us and help us to be more loving tomorrow'; and although we may honestly be identifying ourselves with this prayer it is likely to come over to the child as 'What she really means is she jolly well hopes *I'm* sorry and she hopes *I'll* behave better tomorrow'. So the child is tucked up feeling slightly resentful and we hurry downstairs pretending to ourselves that the situation has been acknowledged and put right. At least the rules have been kept. It is quite a different matter to spend half an hour sitting on the edge of the bed helping a child at odds with himself to understand why he feels and behaves as he does, to share with him the burden of his guilt by admitting and explaining that our own tiredness and absorption have caught him out just when he most needed some reassurance from us, to say sorry for letting him down, to ask what it is that is bothering him, to help him to find out if he doesn't know and to bring to the surface some of his pent-up fears and anxieties. Sometimes on these occasions a prayer is a useful summing-up, sometimes one senses it would be quite out of place and would only re-introduce a feeling of unease. The real praying, one knows, is in the wrestling together with the problem in love and trust, even if no religious language has been used.

I do not offer this approach as the only one possible to an intelligent 20th century Christian parent, or imply that the traditional supernatural approach is one that all of us need necessarily grow out of and discard. For many of my Christian friends, whose spiritual serenity I admire and value, the traditional categories are supremely able to bear and communicate the depth and significance of their faith, and it is in these terms that they most naturally share their

out the stigma of blasphemy, on that Christian the personal is of ultimate significance. And it is in these terms that we feel constrained to share our deepest convictions with our children.

660 / 7

ADVERTISEMENT

# Other books by John A. T. Robinson

## The Body: A Study in Pauline Theology

'A solid piece of biblical exposition. This study is to be welcomed because it comes at a time when the doctrine of the Church is increasingly seen to be the doctrine *par excellence* to which the Spirit of God would seem to be drawing the attention of Christians.'—Dr Coggan, now Archbishop of York, in *The Churchman*.

'A real contribution to the understanding of Pauline thought. The treatment of soteriology and of certain aspects of the Incarnation, as well as of the doctrine of the Church, is excellent'.—*Church Times*.

8s 6d

## Jesus and His Coming

'It would be difficult to exaggerate the importance of Dr Robinson's new book. It is encouraging to find such evident vitality in the Cambridge school of New Testament theology, with its traditional virtues of patient attention to detail, exact understanding of the meaning of words, openness to new light, and a steady maintenance of the connection between theological understanding and the living experiences of faith'.—Bishop Stephen Neill.

9s 6d

## On Being the Church in the World

'A collection of essays and addresses. The most consistently exciting book I have read for a long time. . . . A prophet has arisen indeed'.—Kenneth Slack in *Ecumenical Review*.

'The argument is always thoughtful and temperately expressed. The whole book is very much alive with courage and conviction, and with an awareness of the realities of the world where men and women live'.—*Times Literary Supplement*.

9s 6d

## Twelve New Testament Studies

'He has a lively and brilliant mind, and one of his studies is aptly subtitled by himself "An Essay in Detection" '.—F. F. Bruce in *Christianity Today*.

13s 6d

SCM PRESS LTD